Deep South or in the North where, he emphasized, there is comparable prejudice and discrimination.

The key speeches collected here are an important record of the turbulent civil rights disputes in the early 1960s, with comment on what the Justice department and the Democratic Kennedy-Johnson administrations have done in their efforts to bring about and enforce equal rights for all Americans.

Thomas A. Hopkins has selected and edited Robert Kennedy's speeches according to eight different phases of the civil rights movement. He has contributed an introduction covering the story of civil rights activities during Robert Kennedy's tenure in office. Each section is prefaced with background information bringing the reader up-to-date on the civil rights front, with an appraisal of the import of the speeches. Dr. Hopkins' last section is titled "In Retrospect: An Appraisal," in which he comments on various civil rights actions; the work of the Department of Justice; the effect and import of the Kennedy speeches; and the progress toward civil rights for all made by the Kennedy administration.

RIGHTS FOR AMERICANS is an important history and evaluation of the active civil rights progress as sponsored by Robert F. Kennedy in his role as Attorney General.

THOMAS A. HOPKINS (Ph.D., The Pennsylvania State University) has taught at Penn State and the University of Pittsburgh, and is the Chairman of the Department of Speech at Mount Mercy College in Pittsburgh, Pennsylvania. He has been a longtime observer of the civil rights front and has had a particular interest in the activities of Robert F. Kennedy and the Department of Justice.

RIGHTS FOR AMERICANS:

The Speeches of Robert F. Kennedy

The BOBBS-MERRILL *Company, Inc.*

A Subsidiary of Howard W. Sams & Co., Inc.

Publishers

Indianapolis   Kansas City   New York

RIGHTS FOR AMERICANS:

The Speeches of Robert F. Kennedy

Edited and with commentary

by THOMAS A. HOPKINS

First printing, 1964

Library of Congress catalog card number 64-8711

Manufactured in the United States of America

CONTENTS

ACKNOWLEDGMENTS

I would like to acknowledge with gratitude the assistance of my editor, Geoffrey C. Ryan, during all stages of the preparation of the manuscript.

As early as May 1961, Edwin Guthman, Special Assistant for Public Information, U. S. Department of Justice, supplied me with information pertinent to this study. Since then he allowed the use of the Attorney General's files in this area and has been of inestimable assistance in responding to my many requests.

In February 1962 an article of mine entitled "Attorney General Robert F. Kennedy's Blueprint for Civil Rights Action" was published in *Today's Speech*. It was the editor of that publication, Dr. William S. Tacey of the University of Pittsburgh, who, after learning of my continued study of Mr. Kennedy's speeches in early 1964, urged me to publish them.

I was most fortunate to have the use of the extensive facilities of the Carnegie Library of Pittsburgh in gathering certain pertinent materials.

Of the many newspapers and periodicals used for background none was of such great assistance as *The New York Times*. In particular, I would like to express my debt to the excellent reporting of Anthony Lewis and Claude Sitton of that newspaper.

For help in procuring particular information, I would like to cite the contributions of Miss Eleanor Latsko of the Mount Mercy College Library staff; Jay Carroll Cox, 1961 graduate of the University of Georgia Law School and now an attorney in the Civil Division of the U. S. Department of Justice; and John J. Clarke of the *Scranton Times*.

In every phase of the work my wife, Dorothy, has been indispensable.

PREFACE

From the beginning of his term, January 20, 1961, to the passage of the Civil Rights Act of 1964 (July 2), Attorney General Robert F. Kennedy delivered almost one hundred prepared speeches. Of these, 37 were selected for this book. Those omitted were either not on civil rights or were largely repetitious. A determined attempt was made by the author and the publisher to maintain the integrity of the speeches which were included, thus a minimal amount of repetition was unavoidable.

Civil rights, of course, is only one of the areas for which the United States Department of Justice is responsible. Robert Kennedy, as Attorney General, therefore, dealt with many other national problems. This book, however, will not attempt to discuss any except those related to civil rights.

Each of the speeches in this collection concerns an aspect of civil rights as the topic was approached by the Attorney General; that is, any condition which deprives a citizen of the rights, freedoms and opportunities that he is entitled to as an American.

This book does not purport to be a history of the civil rights struggle of recent years. Rather, it offers the Attorney General's speeches, in the context of their occurrence, as a chapter in that yet unwritten history.

INTRODUCTION

⌈On January 17, 1961 at his last news conference as Attorney General, William P. Rogers—head of the Department of Justice under President Dwight D. Eisenhower—stated that in his opinion civil rights was the chief problem facing the Department. To inherit that challenge in just a few days was Robert Francis Kennedy, the President-elect's thirty-five-year-old brother. To Robert Kennedy, the Rogers statement could not have been news.

At the Democratic National Convention the preceding July, civil rights created far more rancor within the party than any other part of the platform. Yet, a strong civil rights plank was ultimately adopted over the bitter protests of delegates from ten Southern states.

This was a major reason why John F. Kennedy wanted his brother to be his Attorney General. As President he would remain committed to an aggressive attack on the racial issue; yet, special handling would be needed because of the complexity of the problem and because of its potential for dividing the American people. He believed that his brother possessed the qualifications, and literally talked him into accepting the position.⌋

Both realized that the announcement would be severely criticized. They were not wrong. A heavy barrage of criticism came from their political enemies, as expected, but many of their friends were not in favor of the appointment either. For while nepotism is an unholy tradition of American political life, it is one to which politicians are hypersensitive in the face of responsible indignation. Adding somewhat to the "brazenness" of this presidential appointment was the "clean-as-a-hound's tooth" example of the previous occupant of the White House. While Milton S. Eisenhower did perform certain tasks for his brother—especially with respect to inter-American affairs—there was a positive abhorrence of the very suggestion that President Dwight D. Eisenhower would deign to name his brother to an Administrative post.

Yet, when on January 13, 1961, the Senate Judiciary Committee examined Robert Kennedy, the members were accused by columnist James Reston of greeting him like the returning prodigal son. One Committee member, Senator William A. Blakley, Democrat from Texas, was absent, but all fourteen Senators present—Democrat and Republican alike—voted unanimously to approve the appointment for consideration by the Senate as a whole.

During the Committee hearing Senator Everett McKinley Dirksen, a member of the Committee, contended with his usual eloquence that Robert Kennedy was indeed short on general legal experience, but experienced and quite superior in investigation and administration. During the ten years since his graduation from the University of Virginia Law School, the future Attorney General continuously held legal posts in the Federal Government; namely, the Department of Justice, the Hoover Commission, and the United States Senate.*

Of all the appointees whose names were submitted by President Kennedy for approval by the Senate, only Robert F. Kennedy received a dissenting vote. Senator Gordon Allott, Republican of Colorado, voted against his appointment on the grounds of insufficient legal experience. To that charge President Kennedy had a tongue-in-cheek retort: "I see nothing wrong with giving Robert some legal experience as Attorney General before he goes out to practice law."

[The almost unanimous Senate approval of the appointment, in the face of widespread public criticism, was true to an unwritten rule of American politics: both major parties share the belief, notwithstanding personal feelings, that a newly-elected President should have the nominees he chooses for his cabinet.

In the case of Robert Kennedy, his youth† and his limited

---

* Robert F. Kennedy's experience included a year (1951-52) as an attorney in the Criminal Division of the Department of Justice; he served as campaign manager for his brother, John, who was elected to the U. S. Senate in 1952; in 1953 he became the Assistant Counsel for the Senate Permanent Subcommittee on Investigations, and later that year he was made Assistant Counsel for the Hoover Commission; in 1954 he was appointed Chief Counsel to the Minority for the Senate Permanent Subcommittee on Investigation, and from 1955 to 1957 he served as Chief Counsel and Staff Director of that Subcommittee; and from 1957 until 1960 he was Chief Counsel for the Senate Select Committee on Improper Activities in the Labor or Management Field.
† In point of fact, he was less than a year younger than the first Attorney General, Edmund Randolph, who was appointed at the age of 36.

legal experience were facts to which he had to adjust. And these potential handicaps were not overlooked by the leaders of the civil rights groups. They could not help but wonder whether an Attorney General so apparently vulnerable could take the steps they considered necessary for progress in that area.

Nearby Virginia offered an opportunity to find out. Prince Edward County had closed its public school system two years before to avoid desegregation. As a result, the white children were attending "private" schools supported largely by public monies; Negro children had no schools to go to. On April 26, 1961, Attorney General Kennedy —in line with advice he received from Burke Marshall, head of the Civil Rights Division of the Department of Justice—asked the Federal Courts to force the reopening of the public schools in Prince Edward County.

Anthony Lewis of *The New York Times* pointed out two significant aspects of Mr. Kennedy's action: This was the first time that the Federal Government had attempted to enter such a case as a full-fledged plaintiff (rather than as a friend of the court); and secondly, the Government for the first time had alleged that the closing of all public schools in a county could be unconstitutional. Parenthetically, this action also alerted the country that the new Attorney General was not averse to moving boldly into the civil rights maelstrom.

When this step was taken, the Attorney General had been at work for more than a month on a speech he was planning to deliver in Georgia. It was his intention to make public his approach to the civil rights problem, and he wanted to perform the task where he thought it proper to do so: in the Deep South.

The site of the address, the University of Georgia, was the scene of racial riots only a few months before. It will be remembered that two Negroes, Charlayne Hunter and Hamilton Holmes, were suspended from classes in early January, 1961, for "their own safety." Due to a Federal Court order and a courageous faculty, the two students were reinstated shortly thereafter. While the two faced a certain amount of abuse almost daily from fellow students, they were able to continue to attend classes.*

On May 6 Mr. Kennedy delivered his speech. It performed two significant functions: the address contained an appeal by the Attorney

* Both graduated from the University of Georgia in June of 1963. For their story see *An Education in Georgia* by Calvin Trillin.

General for the cooperation of local governments where there existed racial inequities; secondly, Mr. Kennedy told his listeners that when local cooperation was not forthcoming the Federal Government would act.

The speech was not bravado, nor was it misleading in its lack of threats. The Attorney General was simply informing those present—as well as the interested who were not present—that he intended to enforce the law of the land, but only if necessary, a contingency which he hoped would not materialize.

The speech of May 6 stands alone for its historical significance because it was the first such talk delivered by a top Administration official in the Deep South. But the address has special significance, too, because of its presentation at the inception of the Freedom Ride disturbances when only the genuinely interested were deliberately involving themselves in the problem.

The "Freedom Rides" brought Robert Kennedy into the racial crossfire. The President's personal representative, John Seigenthaler, was knocked unconscious by white rioters in Montgomery, Alabama. Federal marshals were sent by the Attorney General to the scene. Mr. Kennedy telephoned Alabama and Mississippi officials to gain protection for the Riders, but he also tried to discourage the Riders from provoking more incidents. In doing so, his request for a "cooling off" period backfired because of the Negro connotation of the expression: To "cool" meant to "back off." Yet when demonstrators were being held in a church by a maddened mob, the Reverend Martin Luther King called the Attorney General and voiced doubts as to whether the Federal officers could protect them. Mr. Kennedy replied reassuringly: "Now, Reverend, you know that without those Federal marshals all of you would be as dead as doornails."

His attitude toward the "Freedom Rides" might be summed up in this fashion: He favored the test case of segregation in interstate facilities, but he decried excessive demonstrations that could not hurry the critical court cases, but could be dangerous for many people.

His preoccupation with order led whites and Negroes in the South to conclude that the Attorney General was hostile to them both. Yet on May 26 in an address for the Voice of America, Robert Kennedy once more proclaimed his thesis: Equality for all. He concluded on the basis of analogy that whereas Irish Catholics had been discriminated against fifty years before, the Negroes, too, in the foreseeable future, could look forward to having a member of their race as President of the United States.

Some progress was made in the fall of 1961. In December the Attorney General could cite school integration in cities such as Atlanta, Dallas, Memphis, Little Rock and New Orleans, and could say with conviction, "We are making progress in this country."

In January 1962 Senator Mike Mansfield, Majority Leader, and Senator Everett Dirksen, Minority Leader, introduced a bill designed to prevent discrimination on the basis of literacy tests against any voter registrant with a sixth grade education. The composition of this bill was influenced greatly by the Attorney General and civil rights experts in the Department of Justice.

At this time more criticism was heard to the effect that President Kennedy was not in favor of additional civil rights legislation. Robert Kennedy answered this charge on NBC's "Today Show" on January 30. The Attorney General said that the President favored meaningful legislation, not bills advocated merely for show, and that the Administration's intent was to improve the position of the Negro by applying laws already on the books, as well as whatever other means it had at its disposal.

In fact, John F. Kennedy—at the outset of his Administration—had asked Senator Joseph S. Clark of Pennsylvania and Representative Emanuel Celler of New York to prepare civil rights bills embodying the commitments of the 1960 Democratic Platform. On May 8, 1961, Clark and Celler introduced six such bills into Congress. But it appears that there was little backing in Congress and less outside; thus the President chose not to press for their passage at that time. While no one can impugn the motives of Senator Clark and Representative Celler in this case, it is well known that introducing legislation is little more than child's play; getting it passed is quite another matter. And with civil rights, passage of a meaningful bill is an historic occasion.

During the "Today Show" of January 30 the Attorney General specified ways in which the Administration was in fact helping the Negro: employing increasing numbers of qualified Negroes on all levels in Federal agencies, including the Department of Justice;

working to increase Negro voter registration; extending job opportunities in industry through Vice President Lyndon B. Johnson's Committee of Equal Employment Opportunity; helping local school districts to desegregate quietly and peacefully; cooperating with some twenty railroads in the desegregation of about two hundred railroad terminals; advocating legislation helpful to the Negro, which would raise minimum wages, expand housing opportunities, and aid education.

The substance of Robert Kennedy's remarks was to be heard many times during the mounting criticism of the next year and a half: The Administration favored legislation when it had a chance of becoming law, but meanwhile there was a complete complement of weapons available and being used to fight the war against racial segregation. And more important, the solution to discrimination is in each individual's behavior, not just in the passage of additional laws.

On May 5, 1962, he told the members of the American Jewish Committee in New York that—in his opinion—the civil rights struggle was "the paramount internal issue in this country." He referred to attempts to eradicate racial and religious prejudice as "a long-term process," and cited the "great effort" being made to deal with the problem. One example of this effort, he went on to say, was the Federal Government's active attack against voting discrimination in more than one hundred counties. And the enormity of the job was pointed up by the fact that just *one* case required the examination of some 36,000 voting records, the testimony of 180 witnesses at the trial, and four lawyers working full time for several months to prepare the case.

A little more than a month later, on June 22, Robert Kennedy, speaking at Morgan State College before the National Newspaper Publishers' Association, stated that the pace was quickening in the civil rights struggle, "the biggest domestic news story of our time." He told of the success in Macon County, Alabama—one of the great number of voting cases tackled by the Department of Justice—where a voting rights injunction permitted the number of Negroes registered to jump from a "handful" to over 2,800. In this speech he reaffirmed the basic approach set down in his "blueprint" speech of May 6, 1961, by stating: "When we cannot get voluntary action we will continue to go to court to enforce the laws. . . ."

School dropouts, as a civil rights related problem, was emphasized by Mr. Kennedy on July 26. During a speech in San Francisco, he told members of the National Insurance Association that this—as well as allied educational problems—was of great significance in the overall civil rights difficulty.

Assistant Attorney General Burke Marshall, head of the Civil Rights Division of the U. S. Department of Justice, was given a great deal of credit for progress made by "Justice" in Mr. Kennedy's speech of August 6. According to the Attorney General, Mr. Marshall and his aides had performed distinguished service by "negotiating, prodding, advising, persuading" on the civil rights front. Said Mr. Kennedy, "We have not filed a single civil rights case without first going to the local authorities."

Another period in the civil rights struggle was entered into when a Negro, James H. Meredith, sought to enroll at the University of Mississippi in September 1962. This brought to a head the Federal-State conflict with Attorney General Kennedy ordering Federal protection for Meredith, while Governor Ross Barnett defiantly opposed the Negro's acceptance by the University. On September 29, speaking at the University of San Francisco Law School, Mr. Kennedy noted that throughout the turmoil there was an "absence of any expression of support from the many distinguished lawyers" of the state of Mississippi: "They have remained silent," he said.

Though James Meredith did matriculate at the University of Mississippi and Governor Ross Barnett did bow to the Federal Government, the rising crescendo of civil rights clashes continued through the fall and winter. There was a slight change of pace when President Kennedy announced on November 20 the Executive Order establishing the President's Committee on Equal Opportunity in Housing.

On January 22, 1963, Robert Kennedy paused to bring the record up to date. All Southern transportation terminals were integrated, except those in Jackson, Mississippi, where an appeal was pending. A very substantial increase had been made in the number of Negroes in Federal jobs at both professional and sub-professional levels. As far as voting progress was concerned, officials in 29 counties in Georgia, Alabama, Mississippi and Louisiana voluntarily made voting records available to "Justice" representatives, and 50 counties in the same states voluntarily abandoned voting discrimination practices; 32 suits and 82 voting record inspections were undertaken by the Department of Justice; and 28 more Southern school districts integrated voluntarily in 1962.

On February 28, 1963, President John F. Kennedy sent a message to Congress requesting specific civil rights legislation. Most of his requests centered on voting: to provide temporary Federal referees and to make a sixth-grade education a minimum requirement for voting. But he also asked Congress to extend the life of the Civil Rights Commission and to provide Federal aid to schools which were desegregating. This message, little of which was new, appealed only to the moderates; the liberals claimed it was insufficient; the Southerners too much. One week later, March 9, the Attorney General took these legislative requests as the text of his speech to the Civil Rights Committee of the New York City Central Labor Council. In asking these men for their help, Robert Kennedy pointedly remarked that discrimination was no less ugly in the North than in the South.

Less than a fortnight later, in Kentucky, at Louisville's Freedom Hall, Robert Kennedy—in a full-scale civil rights address commemorating Kentucky's Centennial of the Emancipation Proclamation—stated: "We are, in short, turning a corner—in a period of great and intense change." But, while stated in the context of progress in civil rights, Mr. Kennedy's words were prophetic in relation to the mounting tension caused by Negro impatience throughout the North and South. In less than two weeks, on April 2, demonstrations would commence in Birmingham, Alabama, which would catalyze the struggle into a new and more violent period, the symbol of which was to be the snarling police dog. Perhaps this influenced the sites of his next two speeches: April 25 in Columbia, South Carolina, and May 17 in Asheville, North Carolina. In Asheville he stated quite simply, "The American Negro is only beginning to raise his voice in protest. His protest is justified, and our responsibility is clear."

On June 3 Chinua Achebe of the Nigerian Broadcasting Company, Lagos—during a U. S. Information Agency interview—put a question to the Attorney General, one which many others were asking throughout the country: "You have laid great stress on moral leadership. There is a certain question here, I think, that the President could do a lot more if he came in personally into this contest. What is your opinion?" To this, Robert Kennedy gave a direct and lengthy reply:

> I think he has come in personally. I am head of the Department of Justice, which encompasses the Civil Rights Division, and, therefore, he is in that extremely personally, the fact that his brother is the one that is involved in all these day-to-day details in connection with this matter. Obviously, I wouldn't be doing anything in this field without his approval and his concurrence. I think that is the first thing.
>
> The major decisions that have had to be made over the period of the last two and one-half years, the decisions on employment within the Government, the decisions on employment of contractors who have business with the Government, the decision on sending marshals into Alabama a year ago, the decision on sending troops, first marshals to Oxford, Mississippi, and then troops to Mississippi, were all made by President Kennedy.
>
> So on major decisions he has spoken out on a number of occasions. He went into Tennessee and he said that he thought these steps should be taken because they were morally right. In his civil rights message in early 1963 he stressed once again that the reason we should take these steps was because they were morally correct steps to take. So I think he has spoken out on it and also acted, if anybody would be interested enough to look at his statements and to examine at all what actually has been done, what has been accomplished over the period of the last two and one-half years.
>
> The stress now is on the problems that we have, and we do have problems. Tremendous things have been accomplished over the past two years.

With June came the enrollment of Vivian Malone and James Hood at the University of Alabama. The night of this event, June 11, President John F. Kennedy told a television audience that he favored legislation to extend the rights of the Negro. The next night, Medgar W. Evers, Mississippi field secretary for the National Association for the Advancement of Colored People, was shot and killed by a sniper. And Negro demonstrations multiplied throughout the country.

On the 19th of June President Kennedy sent a message to Congress requesting comprehensive legislation on behalf of the Negroes. New clauses included the public accommodations feature and a national fair employment practices provision. This bill was what the

Negroes and civil rights advocates were waiting for. The President urged Congress to act promptly.

The "City of Brotherly Love," Philadelphia, Pennsylvania, had been the scene of violent demonstrations prior to the speaking engagement there of the Attorney General on June 21. Speaking in Independence Hall at Ceremonies celebrating the 175th Anniversary of the Ratification of the Constitution of the United States, Robert Kennedy discussed the moral issue in his address. Contrasting legality with morality relative to civil rights he said, "Surely we don't need a new Court decision to tell us that the Negro is entitled to decent housing . . . [and] to insure the Negro equal opportunities in employment. . . . These are moral issues, not legal ones, and their constitutionality is a matter of common sense."

The summer of 1963 witnessed the greatest display of Negro demonstrations in this country to that time, climaxed by the interracial March on Washington, 200,000 strong, on August 28.

A bomb which was detonated at the 16th Street Baptist Church, the largest Negro church in Birmingham, Alabama, on September 15 killed four children during church services and set off a wave of indignation. Unquestionably, this despicable incident created more sympathy for the civil rights movement than any other single act to this time. After a long summer of bloodshed and recrimination, there was virtual unanimity that the killing of these children was a senseless extension of the attempt on the part of the white South to keep the Negro "in his place."

The morning newspapers on October 1 had more disquieting news for "stand-patters," for the United States Commission on Civil Rights issued its annual report. The text was clear: "The Commission recognizes and applauds the sustained efforts of the Department of Justice to assure that the right to vote not be denied on grounds of race." And what made the report more potent was the concurrence of the two Southern members of the Commission—Dr. Robert S. Rankin of Duke University and Robert G. Storey, head of the Southwestern Law Center, Dallas—who had on previous occasion differed about some issues with the rest of the Commission members. The two Southern members agreed with their colleagues that in some states "the evil of arbitrary disfranchisement has not diminished materially," and added "we have concluded sadly, but with firm conviction, that without drastic change in the means used to secure suffrage for many of our citizens, disfranchisement will continue to be handed down from father to son." The Commission was, in essence, sympathetic to the voting sections of the Administration's Civil Rights Bill.

On October 28, the Attorney General addressed the annual convention of the Theater Owners of America. Quite pointedly he broached the "public accommodations" section of the Administration's Civil Rights Bill by stating "the controversy chiefly affects those of you who have theaters in the Southern and Border States." This was followed by an appeal for voluntary desegregation and responsible leadership.

The fall of the year saw a dropping off of the demonstrations, the violence and the ugliness. The assassination of President John F. Kennedy on November 22 brought it to a complete halt.

No protest was heard throughout the land when on November 27 Lyndon B. Johnson told Congress in his first presidental address to that body:

> No memorial oration or eulogy could more eloquently honor President Kennedy's memory than the earliest possible passage of the Civil Rights Bill for which he fought all this long year. We have talked long enough in this country about equal rights. We have talked for 100 years or more. Yet, it is time now to write the next chapter— and to write it in books of law.
>
> I urge you again, as I did in 1957, and again in 1960, to enact a civil rights law so that we can move forward to eliminate from this nation every trace of discrimination and oppression based upon race or color. There could be no greater source of strength to this nation both at home and abroad.

No one expected the dissenters to remain quiet for long, and their protests resumed shortly after Christmas. But on February 10 the Civil Rights Bill was approved 290 to 130 by the House of Representatives and sent to the Senate.

Greater hope was held out for the passage of the bill by the Senate when the Gallup Poll announced on February 2, 1964, results of a January survey on the "public accommodations" section: 61 per cent of the American people were in favor—up from 54 per cent last August. But, 72 per cent of Southern whites were still against it; however, this was down from 82 per cent the previous June. The results of the poll were interpreted as an encouraging sign inasmuch as the public facilities part of the Bill was acknowledged from the beginning to be one of the most controversial aspects.

Robert Kennedy did not give another speech until January 21, 1964, when he was the recipient of a Doctor of Laws degree bestowed by the University of the Philippines. He told his audience, "If there is anything to be gained . . . by the life and death of President Kennedy, it's the fact that we must participate."

He did not give a full-scale address until March 17 when he appeared at the annual dinner of the Friendly Sons of St. Patrick of Lackawanna County, in Scranton, Pennsylvania. In this talk the American struggle for civil rights was compared to the epochal attempt of the Irish to be free.

It was not until the middle of April that the Attorney General was ready to resume a normal speaking schedule. In a sense, this was one of the most interesting periods of his public life. In the background was the historic civil rights debate in the United States Senate with a growing belief that the Bill submitted to Congress by his brother would pass. One reason for the optimism was that the leader of the Republican minority, Senator Everett McKinley Dirksen, was working diligently on amendments which would insure its acceptance by the two-thirds majority needed. Intimately involved in conferences with Senator Dirksen during this time was Robert Kennedy, whose efforts were appraised by Mr. Dirksen as "circumspect and very competent."

In the following months Mr. Kennedy's speeches broadened considerably in scope. While his approach to civil rights never was narrow and parochial, the Attorney General during the late Spring of 1964 presumed the passage of the Civil Rights Bill and stressed, therefore, compliance and social progress.

Perhaps his most provocative speech of this group is the last of this collection, his commencement address at the California Institute of Technology on June 8. His thesis: "Our greatest national responsibility is to strengthen and enlarge the opening to the future."

part i SKETCHING A BLUEPRINT

In late March 1961, two months after Robert F. Kennedy took his oath of office as United States Attorney General, a young Southerner visited his office. Jay Cox, then a law school student at the University of Georgia, asked Mr. Kennedy to address their Honor's Day convocation. Mr. Cox was acting in his capacity as president of the Student Advisory Council of the Law school and, therefore, in charge of the annual Law Day program. The event would be held May 6, on the University campus in Athens, Georgia.

The Attorney General accepted the invitation. He then called into his office John Seigenthaler, his administrative assistant, and his press secretary, Edwin Guthman, former Nieman Fellow at Harvard and a Pulitzer Prize awardee for national reporting in 1950. Mr. Kennedy dictated the essence of what he intended to say, and from then on the three worked on the speech. From time to time other individuals were contacted for their expert opinions, for the Attorney General had decided to use the occasion of his first major address to make known his approach to the civil rights issue. But while many individuals contributed to its composition, the speech remained—through seven revisions—Mr. Kennedy's.*

On the morning of May 6, the Attorney General was driven from the airport to the campus by some law school students. When asked why he had chosen to discuss civil rights, Mr. Kennedy replied that to have chosen any other subject would have been hypocritical on his part.

The significance of his choice of topic is not to be underestimated. While it had been accepted practice in the North to condemn segre-

---

* The process of preparing speeches outlined here was typical. James Symington succeeded John Seigenthaler when the latter became editor of the *Nashville Tennesseean* in May 1962, and practicing attorney John E. Nolan, Jr., became Mr. Kennedy's administrative assistant when Mr. Symington left in May 1963 to practice law in Washington, D.C.

gation, no top-rung Administration official had ever done so in the Deep South.

The timing of the speech was critical because it was to take place only four months after Negro students Charlayne Hunter and Hamilton Holmes had been suspended by the University of Georgia in the wake of student riots.

Athens, Georgia, while ostensibly quiet, was not unanimous in welcoming the Attorney General. Sidewalks were painted "Kennedy go Home" and "Yankee go Home," and police arrested five segregationist demonstrators.

Robert Kennedy was tense during the early morning flight to Athens even though his speech had received the most careful preparation. The day before, May 5, was devoted entirely to a word-by-word study of the address for possible reactions. The intent of the speaker was to be clear and unequivocal but not offensive. In retrospect, the speech of May 6 was his blueprint for the future with respect to his posture toward the civil rights issue.

At eleven o'clock that morning as he faced a wait-and-see capacity audience composed of 1,600 law school students, alumni, dignitaries and their families and friends, the Attorney General was prepared to take his message before the White South.[*]

The speech was begun on an amiable note. Mr. Kennedy alluded to the honors just given to outstanding law school students and observed that he, too, as a graduate of the University of Virginia Law School had been given a prize as the student who had the fifth best sense of humor. This, according to Jay Cox, "eased tension a lot." He then began to read his prepared speech commencing with conciliatory common ground.

As he went into the body of the address he referred to three important problems with which the Department of Justice was confronted: the professional racketeer; the "respectable" citizen who cheated on taxes, price-fixing, etc.; and civil rights. The first two were treated briefly; civil rights took up more than half the speech.

Basically, the address was a plea for cooperation: "We need your

---

[*] University of Georgia student Charlayne Hunter represented the *Atlanta Inquirer* and was the only Negro present. In September 1962 she told this writer that during periods of discouragement the memory of the Attorney General's speech gave her the courage to continue.

help—we need your assistance." Mr. Kennedy made clear his preference for local self-help. He told his audience that his Department had already had many conferences with responsible public officials and civic leaders in the South: "We are trying to achieve amicable, voluntary solutions without going to court."

But the Attorney General did make crystal clear his intent if local efforts were ignored or ineffective. According to Anthony Lewis of *The New York Times,* his language "was firm and his voice was even firmer" as he declared:

> We are maintaining the orders of the Courts. We are doing nothing more nor less.
> Our position is quite clear. We are upholding the law. . . .
> In all cases I say to you today that if the orders of the Court are circumvented, the Department of Justice will act.

Throughout the address there was much that was conciliatory. Where conflict could be avoided, this was done. Whenever a more prudent choice of language could be utilized, it prevailed. But when, ultimately, further dilution would mean compromising basic tenets, the line was drawn.

No applause was heard throughout the speech. After the final word was spoken, the audience rose and clapped for thirty seconds. Whether this ovation was due to simple courtesy, or whether it was evoked by the Henry W. Grady quotation which ended the talk ("a stroke of genius," wrote a University of Georgia professor, delivered as it was in Athens, Grady's home town), or whether it was a tribute to Kennedy's candor in giving that speech in the South ("rather than in New York," as another Georgia faculty member wrote later), or whether it was an acknowledgment of the law of the land, no one can say with certainty. That it was not given as a sign of complete espousal of the speaker's stand may more closely approximate the truth.

The emotional potential of that topic was, of course, practically unlimited. Yet direct emotional appeal was not used; in essence the speech was an appeal to reason. While the common denominator of the talk was people, Robert Kennedy alluded to them only in terms of the rights due them as citizens. Ralph McGill, publisher of the *Atlanta Journal and Constitution,* observed: "Never before, in all its travail of by-gone years, has the South heard so honest and understandable a speech from any Cabinet member."

During his address, the Attorney General alluded to the impact of internal problems on our foreign policy. "In the worldwide struggle," he said, "the graduation at this University of Charlayne Hunter and Hamilton Holmes will without question aid and assist the fight against communist political infiltration and guerilla warfare." Commenting on the speech, *The News and Courier* of Charleston, South Carolina, contended that Mr. Kennedy portrayed White Southerners as pawns in an international propaganda game: "Southerners will be forced to surrender their constitutional rights so that Ed Murrow's U.S. Information Agency may butter up rapists and cannibals in the Congo and other faraway places."

Most of the nation's press was still focused on Astronaut Alan B. Shepard's epochal flight into space the day before. As a result the address of the Attorney General was overlooked by a great many of the nation's newspapers. Those which showed awareness of the Athens event evidenced reaction in a variety of ways. Very few of the papers—even in the Deep South—took exception to the address. Most carried it as a modest news item. The *Atlanta Constitution* was lavish with praise, and the *Philadelphia Inquirer* referred to it as a "notable speech because of what he said and where he said it." The influential Negro *Courier* said the address was of "historical import and significance" because it was "one of the most forthright statements ever uttered on the status of contemporary race relations in the United States of America by a high ranking Federal official."

As word of the address spread, Mr. Kennedy received many letters and telegrams praising the speech. The Reverend Martin Luther King, Jr., said that the speech "probed the deep meaning of the struggle of democracy to perfect itself," and he praised it as "a symbol the White South needs today." Roy Wilkins, executive secretary of the National Association for the Advancement of Colored People, wrote the Attorney General of his "profound appreciation." Said Mr. Wilkins, "No news story could deal adequately with the sweep and emphasis embodied in the address as a whole. I know I speak for the entire Association in extending our compliments and our heartfelt thanks."

If this first speech on civil rights was his blueprint for civil rights action, the next few he delivered might be said to represent an inking in of some of the details.

Against the background of racial terror in southern towns such as Anniston and Montgomery in Alabama, and Jackson, Mississippi, the Attorney General made a Voice of America broadcast on May 26 in which he quite frankly forecast even more such incidents. But he also pointed to prejudice as a universal weakness of man the world over, not just a shortcoming of Americans. And he told his listeners that in spite of appearances, progress had been made and would continue to be made:" We are not going to accept the status quo."

The part of this speech which received the most attention by American news media occurred near the end, when the Attorney General told of the struggle of the Irish for status in this country until now there was an Irish Catholic as President of the United States. Then he added, "In the foreseeable future a Negro can achieve the same position that my brother has."

Mr. Kennedy's next speech, delivered June 7 at a United Press International Editors and Publishers conference, made more explicit the scope of his view of the civil rights issue. He made clear that it involved the whole country, not just the South; not just the element of race, but wherever a citizen's rights were obstructed: "the denial of civil rights that occurs when democratic procedures are ignored or flaunted in labor unions; when business and labor act in collusion to deny workers their rights; and where people live in fear because criminal elements have gained an inordinate amount of power."

On June 21 he specified the interrelationship involved when he said: "If one man's rights are denied, the rights of all are in danger . . . if one man is denied equal protection of the law, we cannot be sure that we will enjoy freedom of speech or any other of our fundamental rights."

Delivered at the Law Day Exercises
of the University of Georgia Law School, May 6, 1961

For the first time since becoming Attorney General, over three months ago, I am making something approaching a formal speech, and I am proud that it is in Georgia. Two months ago I had the very great honor to present to the President, Donald Eugene McGregor of Brunswick, Georgia. Donald McGregor came to Washington to receive the Young American Medal for Bravery. In twelve bad hours, he led a family of four to safety from a yacht which broke up in high seas off the Georgia coast. He impressed all of us who met him with his quiet courage. And, as the President said, Donald McGregor is a fine young American—one of a long line of Georgians who have, by their courage, set an outstanding example for their fellow Americans.

They have told me that when you speak in Georgia you should try to tie yourself to Georgia and the South, and even better, claim some Georgia kinfolk. There are a lot of Kennedys in Georgia. But as far as I can tell, I have no relatives here and no direct ties to Georgia, except one. This State gave my brother the biggest percentage majority of any state in the union and in this last election that was even better than kinfolk.

We meet at this great University, in this old State, the fourth of the original thirteen, to observe Law Day.

In his Proclamation urging us to observe this day, the President emphasized two thoughts. He pointed out that to remain free the people must "cherish their freedoms, understand the responsibilities they entail, and nurture the will to preserve them." He then went on to point out that "law is the strongest link between man and freedom."

I wonder in how many countries of the world people think of law as the "link between man and freedom." We know that in many, law is the instrument of tyranny, and people think of law as little more than the will of the state, or the Party—not of the people.

And we know too that throughout the long history of mankind, man has had to struggle to create a system of law and of government in which fundamental freedoms would be linked with the enforcement of justice. We know that we cannot live together without rules which tell us what is right and what is wrong, what is permitted and what is prohibited. We know that it is law which enables men to live together, that creates order out of chaos. We know that the law is the glue that holds civilization together.

And, we know that if one man's rights are denied, the rights of all are endangered. In our country the courts have a most important role in safeguarding these rights. The decisions of the courts, however much we might disagree with them, in the final analysis must be followed and respected. If we disagree with a court decision and thereafter irresponsibly assail the court and defy its rulings, we challenge the foundations of our society.

The Supreme Court of Georgia set forth this proposition quite clearly in 1949 in the case of *Crumb* v. *the State* (205 GA. 547-552). The court, referring to U. S. Supreme Court decisions, said there and I quote:

> And whatever may be the individual opinion of the members of this Court as to the correctness, soundness and wisdom of these decisions, it becomes our duty to yield thereto just as the other courts of this State must accept and be controlled by the decisions and mandates of this Court. This being a government of law and not by men, the jury commissioners in their official conduct are bound by the foregoing ruling of the Supreme Court of the United States, notwithstanding any personal opinion, hereditary instinct, natural impulse or geographical tradition to the contrary.

Respect for the law—in essence that is the meaning of Law Day and every day must be Law Day or else our society will collapse.

The challenge which international communism hurls against the rule of law is very great. For the past two weeks I have been engaged, for a good part of my time, in working with General Taylor, Admiral Burke, and Mr. Dulles, to assess the recent events in Cuba and determine what lessons we can learn for the future.

It already has become crystal clear in our study that, as the President has stated so graphically, we must reexamine and reorient our forces of every kind. Not just our military forces, but all our techniques and outlook here in the United States. We must come forward with the answer to how a nation, devoted to freedom and individual rights and respect for the law, can stand effectively against an implacable enemy who plays by different rules and knows only the law of the jungle. With the answer to this rests our future—our destiny—as a nation and as a people.

The events of the last few weeks have demonstrated that the time has long since passed when the people of the United States can be apathetic about their belief and respect for the law and about the necessity of placing our own house in order. As we turn to meet our enemy, to look him full in the face, we cannot afford feet of clay or an arm of glass.

Let me speak to you about three major areas of difficulty within the purview of my responsibilities that sap our national strength, that weaken our people, that require our immediate attention.

In too many major communities of our country, organized crime has become big business. It knows no state lines. It drains off millions of dollars of our national wealth, infecting legitimate businesses, labor unions and even sports. Tolerating organized crime promotes the cheap philosophy that everything is a racket. It promotes cynicism among adults. It contributes to the confusion of the young and to the increase of juvenile delinquency.

It is not the gangster himself who is of concern. It is what he is doing to our cities, our communities, our moral fiber. Ninety percent of the major racketeers would be out of business by the end of this year if the ordinary citizen, the businessman, the union official and the public authority stood up to be counted and refused to be corrupted.

This is a problem for all America, not just the FBI or the Department of Justice. Unless the basic attitude changes here in this country, the rackets will prosper and grow. Of this I am convinced.

The racketeers, after all, are professional criminals. But, there are the amateurs—men who have law-abiding backgrounds and respectable positions, who, nevertheless, break the law of the land. We have been particularly concerned lately in the Department of Justice about the spread of illegal price-fixing. I would say to you, however, it is merely symptomatic of many other practices commonly accepted in business life.

Our investigations show that in an alarming number of areas of the country businessmen have conspired in secret to fix prices, made collusive deals with union officials, defrauded their customers and even in some instances cheated their own Government.

Our enemies assert that capitalism enslaves the worker and will destroy itself. It is our national faith that the system of competitive enterprise offers the best hope for individual freedom, social development and economic growth.

ly one Negro in the guard of honor. At the Bureau of
Negroes were used only for custodial work.
eral Government is taking steps to correct this.
leaders from the East who deplore discrimination in
long to institutions where no Negroes or Jews are al-
their children attend private schools where no Negro
enrolled. Union officials criticize Southern leaders and
iscrimination within their unions. Government officials
ate clubs in Washington where Negroes, including Am-
not welcomed even at mealtime.
belief is that if we are to make progress in this area—
e truly great as a nation, then we must make sure that
ied an opportunity because of race, creed or color. We
mple, to take action in our own backyard—the Depart-
ce—we pledge to move to protect the integrity of the
dministration of justice. In all this, we ask your help—
assistance.
you today and I shall come to you in the years ahead
ason and the rule of law.
is spirit that since taking office I have conferred many
ponsible public officials and civil leaders in the South
nations. I shall continue to do so. I don't expect them
e with my view of what the law requires, but I believe
respect for the law. We are trying to achieve amicable,
tions without going to court. These discussions have
voting and school cases to incidents of arrest which
violence.
ought to be helpful to avert violence and to get volun-
e. When our investigations indicate there has been a
w, we have asked responsible officials to take steps
correct the situation. In some instances this has hap-
t has not, we have had to take legal action.
versations have been devoid of bitterness or hate.
n carried on with mutual respect, understanding and
ional unity is essential and before taking any legal
where appropriate, invite the Southern leaders to
vs known in these cases.
merican people, must avoid another Little Rock or

Thus, every businessman who cheats on his taxes, fixes prices
or underpays his labor, every union official who makes a collusive
deal, misuses union funds, damages the free enterprise system in the
eyes of the world and does a disservice to the millions of honest
Americans in all walks of life.

Where we have evidence of violation of laws by the "respect-
ables," we will take action against the individuals involved, as well
as against their companies. But in the end, this also is not a situation
which can be cured by the Department of Justice. It can only be
cured by business and unions themselves.

The third area is the one that affects us all the most directly—
civil rights.

The hardest problems of all in law enforcement are those involving a conflict of law and local customs. History has recorded
many occasions when the moral sense of a nation produced judicial
decisions, such as the 1954 decision in *Brown* v. *Board of Education*,
which required difficult local adjustments.

I have many friends in the United States Senate who are Southerners. Many of these friendships stem from my work as counsel for
the Senate Rackets Committee, headed by Senator John McClellan
of Arkansas for whom I have the greatest admiration and affection.

If these Southern friends of mine are representative Southerners
—and I believe they are—I do not pretend that they believe with me
on everything or that I agree with them on everything. But, knowing
them as I do, I am convinced of this:

Southerners have a special respect for candor and plain talk.
They certainly don't like hypocrisy. So, in discussing this third major
problem, I must tell you candidly what our policies are going to be
in the field of civil rights and why.

First let me say this: the time has long since arrived when loyal
Americans must measure the impact of their actions beyond the limits
of their own towns or states. For instance, we must be quite aware
of the fact that 50% of the countries in the United Nations are not
white; that around the world, in Africa, South America and Asia,
people whose skins are a different color than ours are on the move to
gain their measure of freedom and liberty.

From the Congo to Cuba, from South Vietnam to Algiers, in
India, Brazil and Iran, men and women and children are straighten-

ing their backs and listening—to the evil promises of communist tyranny and the honorable promises of Anglo-American liberty. And those people will decide not only their future but how the cause of freedom fares in the world.

In the United Nations we are striving to establish a rule of law instead of a rule of force. In that forum and elsewhere around the world our deeds will speak for us.

In the worldwide struggle, the graduation at this University of Charlayne Hunter and Hamilton Holmes will without question aid and assist the fight against communist political infiltration and guerrilla warfare.

When parents send their children to school this Fall in Atlanta, peaceably and in accordance with the rule of law, barefoot Burmese and Congolese will see before their eyes Americans living by the rule of law.

The conflict of views over the original decision in 1954 and our recent move in Prince Edward County is understandable. The decision in 1954 required action of the most difficult, delicate and complex nature, going to the heart of Southern institutions. I know a little of this. I live in Virginia. I studied law at the University of Virginia. I have been privileged to know many able Southern soldiers, scholars, lawyers, jurists, journalists and political leaders who have enriched our national life. From them I have drawn some understanding of the South, but my knowledge is nothing to yours.

It is now being said that the Department of Justice is attempting to close all public schools in Virginia because of the Prince Edward situation. This is not true, nor is the Prince Edward suit a threat against local control.

We are maintaining the orders of the courts. We are doing nothing more nor less. And if any one of you were in my position you would do likewise for it would be required by your oath of office. You might not want to do it, you might not like to do it, but you would do it.

For I cannot believe that anyone can support a principle which prevents more than a thousand of our children in one county from attending public school—especially when this step was taken to circumvent the orders of the court.

Our position is quite clear. We are upholding the law. Our action does not threaten local control. The Federal Government would not

be running the schools in Prin
running the University of Geo
sachusetts.

In this case—in all cases-
of the court are circumvented

We will not stand by or b

Here on this campus, not
ordeal. And when your mom
"force" were overridden by th

And for this, I pay my re
ture and most particularly to
University of Georgia. And I
not those who cry panic. For
prevail.

I happen to believe that
belief does not matter—it is t
decision was wrong. That does
respect the law. By facing thi
to all the world that we Amer
solving this problem—under t

An integral part of all this
antee the ballot to every Ame
well as in the South. The righ
grant. The spirit of our democ
our laws require that there be
full freedom to vote for all.
participation of all its citizens.

The problem between the
for all sections of the United
there has been a great deal of
I found when I came to the D
no further to find evidence of t

I found that very few Neg
level. There were 950 lawyers
in Washington and only 10 of
ment the lawyers of the Depa
action to end discrimination,
practiced within the Departme

At a recent review for the

there was o
the Budget,
The Fe
Financ
the South b
lowed and
students ar
yet practice
belong to p
bassadors,
My fir
if we are to
nobody is o
pledge, by
ment of Ju
courts in th
we need yo
I come
to advocate
It is in
times with
on specific
always to a
they share
voluntary
ranged fro
might lead
We ha
tary comp
violation
themselve
pened. W
These
They have
good will
action, w
make thei
We,

another New Orleans. We cannot afford them. It is not only that such incidents do incalculable harm to the children involved and to the relations among people. It is not only that such convulsions seriously undermine respect for law and order, and cause serious economic and moral damage. Such incidents hurt our country in the eyes of the world. We just can't afford another Little Rock or another New Orleans.

For on this generation of Americans falls the full burden of proving to the world that we really mean it when we say all men are created free and are equal before the law. All of us might wish at times that we lived in a more tranquil world, but we don't. And if our times are difficult and perplexing, so are they challenging and filled with opportunity.

To the South, perhaps more than any other section of the country, has been given the opportunity and the challenge and the responsibility of demonstrating America at its greatest—at its full potential of liberty under law.

You may ask, will we enforce the Civil Rights statutes.

The answer is: "Yes, we will."

We also will enforce the antitrust laws, the anti-racketeering laws, the laws against kidnapping and robbing Federal banks, and transporting stolen automobiles across state lines, the illicit traffic in narcotics and all the rest.

We can and will do no less.

I hold a constitutional office of the United States Government, and I shall perform the duty I have sworn to undertake—to enforce the law, in every field of law and every region.

We will not threaten, we will try to help. We will not persecute, we will prosecute.

We will not make or interpret the laws. We shall enforce them —vigorously, without regional bias or political slant.

All this we intend to do. But all the high rhetoric on Law Day about the noble mansions of the law; all the high-sounding speeches about liberty and justice, are meaningless unless people—you and I —breathe meaning and force into it. For our liberties depend upon our respect for the law.

On December 13, 1889, Henry W. Grady of Georgia said these words to an audience in my home state of Massachusetts:

This hour little needs the loyalty that is loyal to one section and yet holds the other in enduring suspicion and estrangement. Give us the broad and perfect loyalty that loves and trusts Georgia alike with Massachusetts—that knows no South, no North, no East, no West, but endears with equal and patriotic love every foot of our soil, every State of our Union.

A mighty duty, sir, and a mighty inspiration impels everyone of us tonight to lose in patriotic consecration whatever estranges, whatever divides. We, sir, are Americans—and we stand for human liberty!

Ten days later Mr. Grady was dead but his words live today. We stand for human liberty.

The road ahead is full of difficulties and discomforts. But as for me, I welcome the challenge, I welcome the opportunity and I pledge my best effort—all I have in material things and physical strength and spirit to see that freedom shall advance and that our children will grow old under the rule of law.

Excerpts of Voice of America Broadcast, May 26, 1961

I think the whole world, as well as all the people of our own country, are aware of what has happened in Alabama over the last two weeks. It is a matter of great concern to all of us. It is disturbing in particular to the United States Government. We are disturbed about the fact that beatings took place and about the fact that people's rights were not being protected. Police and police officials of states and cities in this area were not properly guarding the people because of color. We sent 500 representatives of the United States Government to help and assist these people.

Prejudice exists in the United States and we have many problems and difficulties like that. The United States Government has taken steps to make sure that the Constitution of the United States applies to all individuals.

We have made mistakes in the past for all the world to see. Any time we make an error—every time something occurs—everyone knows about it. But, I think people should understand that good things happen in this area. The incidents in Alabama were caused by a small group. They do not represent the people in the South. They certainly do not represent the attitude of the United States Government or the American people.

We took steps and have prevented it. That is what is important. I'm not saying to you that these incidents have ended. I would be less than frank if I told you that. We will have more.

But it also is important to remember that in many areas of the United States there is no prejudice. It has disappeared in many areas, and Negroes have made tremendous gains over the last 30 years. It is not only the policy of this administration but of past administrations—in the administrations of Dwight Eisenhower, Harry Truman and Franklin D. Roosevelt.

Negroes hold high positions in the United States Government. Some of our leading judges are Negroes. Negroes are United States Attorneys and among the top law enforcement officials in the country. Negroes are mayors of cities. They have made tremendous economic gains. There are Negro presidents of universities. There are Negro lawyers, doctors and dentists, holding leading positions, in almost all communities throughout the states.

We are not going to gain ground against prejudice by just passing laws. Because prejudice exists with people throughout the world—not with people of this country. It exists in all areas of the world. It is not only a matter of color. In some areas Protestants are against Catholics or Catholics against Jews, or Jews against other people. And this prejudice will continue to exist. It never will be perfect because people are human and human nature is not perfect.

But we have tried to make progress and we are making progress. That is what is so important.

We are not going to accept the status quo. We would not accept the riots and we will not accept them. We acted to send people into Alabama in order to end them.

This is the feeling of the American people and of the United States Government. And we are going to continue to make progress. We are working hard at this problem.

You have problems and difficulties in your areas. We have them here. Our society is set up so that everyone knows about our successes and they know about our failures. When Commander Shepard went into space, if he had failed everyone would have known about it and everyone knows about the riots in Montgomery.

But let me say again that the important thing is that the U. S. Government and the vast majority of the American people are working to eliminate prejudice and discrimination. But as I said it never will be perfect.

My grandfather came to this country many years ago. He was brought up in Boston and when he went out to look for a job there were signs on many stores that no Irish were wanted. Now after some 40 or 50 years, an Irish Catholic is President of the United States. That progress has been made over the last fifty years. And we feel that the same kind of progress will be made by the Negroes. There is no question about it. In the foreseeable future a Negro can achieve the same position that my brother has.

We will make progress in this country.

Delivered before the 1961 Conference
of UPI Editors and Publishers
Washington, D.C., June 7, 1961

I am very glad to be able to come here today and report to you about the activities that we are undertaking in the Department of Justice.

The United Press International is extremely well represented here in Washington. Mr. Lyle Wilson is one of the most respected veterans. He has seen a lot of people come and go in office in Washington and I wish I could interview him sometime. Over in the Justice Department Miss Sue Wagner represents the UPI. I have been impressed by her reporting, particularly her coverage of the Justice Department's role in the recent events in Alabama. She is an honest reporter. I have been impressed by her ability and that of other reporters to ask a tough question.

I have a deep awareness of the role that the press plays in our society. I firmly believe that freedom of information is one of the most important weapons we have in the great struggle for freedom now going on around the world.

As I told the American Society of Newspaper Editors in April, we will let the record speak for itself three or four years from now. You will make the judgment at that time and so will the people of the United States. But I would like to report briefly to you this afternoon about some of the things we have undertaken.

In the Criminal Division, we have revamped and beefed up the Organized Crime and Racketeering Section. We are attempting to get a maximum federal effort against organized crime. We are coordinating all federal investigations into racketeering. We are pooling all available information about known hoodlums and racketeers. This work is being done in the Department with the valuable assistance of Mr. J. Edgar Hoover and the FBI.

We have submitted eight bills to Congress which we need if the Federal Government is to meet its responsibilities in law enforcement. The effect of these bills in general would be to prevent hoodlums and racketeers from using interstate commerce, interstate communications and interstate travel, and to give the FBI additional effective weapons to aid and assist local law enforcement officers. These bills are aimed primarily at the well entrenched racketeers who operate on an interstate basis and who are beyond the reach, in many instances, of local law enforcement officers.

The press has commented favorably on these bills by and large, but nowhere have I seen these bills listed in a newspaper or magazine boxscore of "important" legislation now before Congress. We know they are extremely important.

I testified about these bills before the Senate Judiciary Committee on Tuesday and spoke about them yesterday at graduation ceremonies of the 67th Session of the FBI Academy. But, as I said yesterday, we now need more than general support and talk. We need positive support and we need action.

Organized crime is reaping huge profits illegally and using this money to increase its power, so the need for action is clear. We believe with these bills we could sharply reduce these illegal profits and could cut these hoodlums and racketeers down to size.

We have been extremely active and there has been awakened interest in the Antitrust Division of the Department ever since seven top executives went to jail in the electrical price-fixing cases. We have found from our investigations that there is serious price-fixing in almost every major community in the United States and I think this must be a matter of great concern to businessmen and to the American public. I feel very strongly that price-fixing and bid-rigging are extremely serious and extremely harmful to the American system of free enterprise. We intend to investigate vigorously, and we expect to move not only against the companies or corporations which have been responsible but also against the individuals who have participated.

We also have been investigating violations of the anti-merger provisions of the antitrust laws. The purpose is to make sure that no company has a chance to dominate or control an industry or start in that direction.

We firmly believe that effective enforcement of the antitrust laws is helpful to business. The Antitrust Division is there to help and assist businessmen—even the large businessmen—all businessmen who are victims of conspiracy by competitors and by other groups.

We have problems in all segments of our society and this is a very difficult time for the country. Therefore, I think that the American businessman has to look at his own operations and his responsibilities to his community and his state and his country. He has to make certain that he is living up to all our principles, while we are trying to preserve freedom and convince others that our system is the best. If this is done, the Antitrust Division will have a lesser role to play. That is our philosophy and not only in antitrust matters but in all other matters.

We have become increasingly interested in what the Federal Government can do to deal more effectively with juvenile delinquency and youth crime. The rate of delinquency and youth crime has increased steadily since 1948. We are concerned because we know that 7,500,000 of our youth will drop out of schools in the next ten years before graduation and that 2,500,000 of these dropouts will not have completed the eighth grade. We also know that in the next ten years, 26,000,000 of our youth, 25 years old or younger, will be entering the nation's labor force, which will be demanding more education and more skill.

This is one of the major reasons the President has formed a committee consisting of the Department of Health, Education and Welfare, the Department of Labor and the Department of Justice to develop programs to coordinate a campaign of effective prevention, treatment and control at federal, state and local levels.

Within the Department of Justice, we have just received an appropriation of $500,000 for a pilot project so that we can give more effective help to young federal prisoners in making a successful transition from prison life to the community. This will be administered by the Bureau of Prisons and will include establishment of half-way houses where these young men can go after leaving prison and have guidance in getting reestablished in civilian life.

However, we know that even if we substantially strengthen all of our efforts in the field of correction, that we will not solve the problems. It is only if we have a coordinated prevention program that we can solve this most distressing domestic problem.

Essentially, this is a problem that can be solved only at the local level. The Federal Government can lead and aid and assist. But, it is up to each state, city and town to take care of its own delinquency situations. Here, incidentally, is one obvious answer to the question: "What can I do for my country?"

People can contribute greatly to the strength and vitality of our nation, by taking an interest in underprivileged youths or in public or private agencies which are working in the delinquency field.

There is no single answer, no single cure for delinquency, but there is much that can be done.

Another most challenging task we have in the Department is recommending to the President able attorneys for appointment to 93 Federal judgeships and 91 United States Attorney positions.

We also must submit recommendations for the appointment of 91 United States Marshals. All these are Presidential appointments and in connection with the judgeships the President said, and I quote:

> I want for our courts individuals with respected professional skill, incorruptible character, firm judicial temperament, the rare inner quality to know when to temper justice with mercy, and the intellectual capacity to protect and illuminate the Constitution and our historic values in the context of a society experiencing profound and rapid change.

I might add that this Administration regards the appointment of the United States Attorneys and the Marshals with equal solemnity and we intend to appoint men of integrity, ability and character. We get recommendations from Bar Associations and from many persons, including Senators. We ask the judicial committee of the American Bar Association to comment on persons we have under consideration. We ask the FBI to make investigations, but we make our own inquiries.

Without question, this Administration's handling of domestic affairs will be judged in large part by the caliber of its appointments to these important posts.

Another sensitive domestic area is the Civil Rights field and it will occupy a considerable amount of our time. But, I have said repeatedly that is not a Southern problem alone and the basic issues are not endemic to the South.

Our basic position is that we intend to meet our responsibilities. We intend to perform the duties which we have sworn to undertake —to enforce the law, in every field of the law and in every region of the country. Basically, we believe that we must make progress in this nation toward the goal guaranteed by our Constitution that no one is denied opportunity or discriminated against because of race, creed or color.

Looking back at the recent violence in Alabama, I would say that we will have made progress if the responsible leaders, not only in the South but elsewhere in the nation, have been alerted to the constant need for courageous action on their part to maintain law and order and to fight the gangsters and hoodlums who seek to hold power by corruption, threats or violence. I want to make it clear I am talking about the East, the Midwest and the West as well as the South. Recently, we entered a school desegregation case as a friend of the court in New Rochelle, New York.

We are not concerned only with civil rights in the South. We also are concerned with the denial of civil rights that occurs when democratic procedures are ignored or flaunted in labor unions; when business and labor act in collusion to deny workers their rights; and where people live in fear because criminal elements have gained an inordinate amount of power.

This is a constant battle and responsible leaders of our communities cannot let their guard down.

Just one week before the violence occurred in Alabama, some

newspapers in that area were critical of me because at the University of Georgia I said: "I happen to believe the 1954 decision in the school desegregation cases was right. But my belief does not matter—it is the law. Some of you may believe the decision was wrong. And that does not matter. It is the law. And we both respect the law. . . ."

The tenor of these editorials was that I had temerity to say that because many persons believe the 1954 decision was wrong. The inference, therefore, was that the readers did not need to obey the decision.

To those editors, I can only say, "You can't have it both ways." You can't preach disrespect for the Supreme Court and its decisions and have peaceful solutions to the problems raised by those decisions.

Those who advocate disobedience of our laws, following their thoughts to the ultimate, are advocating that we change our form of government.

The late Arthur Capper, who was a distinguished Senator and editor, said:

> The right of free speech, the right of a free press, is the right to be wrong, so far as opinions and beliefs and advocacy of those opinions and beliefs is concerned.
>
> Of course, this freedom is freedom of expression, of advocacy. It is not freedom of action.
>
> I have the right to maintain that a certain law is wrong; that a certain policy of government is wrong; that the law should be amended or repealed; that the policy should be changed or abandoned; that a certain official or party should be retired from public office.
>
> But, I am not given, nor guaranteed, any right to refuse to follow a legally approved or accepted government policy, nor to refuse to obey a legally enacted statute; nor to urge others so to do, under the guaranty of freedom of speech or of the press.

The responsibility of editors, as outlined so well by Senator Capper does not change in a democracy. When law and order broke down in Birmingham and Montgomery, most of the newspapers in those areas reacted with vigor. Some were critical of me and the Department of Justice, but they faced the issue squarely and they stood for law and order. In this connection, I would pay particular tribute to *The Birmingham News* for its courage and its honesty in meeting the test.

Editors have a special responsibility and I would ask only that you look closely at your own communities. I would ask you to investigate and probe in the best traditions of your profession. When you find a group bent on lawless action or engaged in illegal activities, I would ask you to exercise leadership against those elements.

I think it is very clear that a newspaper can be a major difference in whether an issue is going to be settled in the courts—or in the streets.

Delivered before the Joint Defense Appeal of the American Jewish Committee and the Anti-Defamation League of B'nai B'rith, Chicago, Illinois, June 21, 1961

I am proud to be here with you tonight and I am grateful for the award which you have given me. It is a little like old times for me to be talking at a fund-raising campaign dinner. I have had a little fund-raising campaign experience myself. I hope your campaign is as successful as ours but in the end you will have a little bit more left to spare.

Your organizations make a great contribution to the United States, whether one judges by the intellectual stimulus which *Commentary* provides for all, or by the sensible, persistent fight against bigotry which you wage with invincible weapons of research, fact and truth. It is easy to be impetuous and indignant, and to be quick to cry "foul" whenever bigotry appears. It is quite another thing to act with restraint, to aim at sources as well as symptoms, to combat discrimination and intolerance at the roots. You have pursued the latter course both wisely and well, and I believe your record of accomplishments speaks for itself.

As one of Attorney General Bates's distant successors, I will greatly prize this letter. I prize it all the more, for I am an admirer of Lincoln and I have studied much about the Civil War.

I have been drawn to the Civil War, as have many Americans, because it was a climactic time in our history; a time of incredible courage and bravery; a time when the American people faced a strange and bitter crisis and emerged united and resolved to continue the historic struggle of free men to achieve full liberty and full justice for all.

It seems to me, as I read about the Civil War or visit the battlefields in Virginia and Maryland, that all the really fundamental issues testing free men came together at one climactic moment. I find myself going back to the Civil War time and time again because I get renewed strength and insight into today's problems by studying the tumultuous events of a hundred years ago.

But now we have reached another climactic moment in our history. One hundred years ago the test for the American people was whether the ideals and principles on which this Nation was created could be extended to all and still endure on this continent. Now, one hundred years later, the issues are relatively the same. The scope, however, is worldwide.

It is this enlargement of scope which accounts, I think, for much of the bafflement and confusion of our own time. The issues of the Civil War were vivid and immediate. The appeal to duty was plain. The involvement was personal. The response, on both sides, was unstinted and heroic.

But the enlargement of scale in the century since the Civil War has taken many issues out of the area of direct personal involvement and comprehension. Ours is a time when many things are just too big to be grasped. It is a century which has heaped up enough explosive power to blow up the world. It is a century which has probed into the floor of the sea, which has flung men far into outer space, which now threatens to invade the moon.

When things are done on too vast a scale, the human imagination bogs down. It can no longer visualize such fantastic things and thus loses its grip on their essential reality. Killing one man is murder; killing millions is a statistic. The disclosures of the Eichmann trial remind us all how quickly the world has forgotten the massive horrors which one set of human beings perpetrated against another a short twenty years ago.

Our problems, having grown to the size of the world, if not of the solar system, no longer seem our own. Each day we are required to respond to new crises created by people whose names we cannot pronounce in lands of which we have never heard. After a time, the capacity to respond begins to flag; and we turn, not cheerfully, but almost in despair, to the sports pages and the comics.

And yet I would say to you that the stake is just as personal today as it was a century ago, the obligation just as personal, the capacity to affect the course of history just as great. What we require is not the self-indulgence of resignation from the world but the hard effort to work out new ways of fulfilling our personal concern and our personal responsibility.

The President has said: "Ask not what your country can do for you—ask what you can do for your country." And many writers have said: "Tell us, Mr. President, tell the American people and they will do it."

I think myself that if we have to wait to be told we are indeed in a bad way.

Some of us, I fear, think of sacrifice as a big, once-and-for-all gesture, something dramatic, gratifying—and falling in the main on somebody else.

But the real point about sacrifice, except in times of open warfare, is surely that it tends to be undramatic, prolonged and irritating.

We are not making great progress when we define sacrifice as something the other fellow should do—the businessman who feels that sacrifice should begin on the farms; the farmer who wants the trade unionist to sacrifice; the trade unionist who would take it all out on the businessman.

Let us look at some of the things that can be done, that we here in this room can do.

As a Nation, we have an opportunity at this moment to contribute to what some might consider a national sacrifice—and that is through enacting a strong foreign aid program.

Let me make it clear that I do not regard this program as a sacrifice—I regard it both as a national obligation and as a national opportunity, as well as a program for our own survival.

It is a national obligation because, just as other nations helped us when we were engaged one hundred and fifty years ago in the painful struggle for economic development, so we in our turn must help the underdeveloped nations of our time to achieve economic growth and social progress.

It is a national opportunity because it enables men and women of America to enter into creative partnership with other peoples—to bring to them the benefits not just of American technology but of American values and American ideals—and to learn from them the values and teachings of their own civilizations, civilizations in some cases older and wiser than our own.

There have been mistakes made in the program in the past. There will be mistakes in the future. But, because of this program, millions of people are free, countries are deciding their own destinies.

Furthermore, to insure that this program is administered properly, would any of you be willing to give two or three years of your lives to live overseas to make sure that this program would be of maximum benefit to all without favor or corruption? We need assistance from people such as yourselves in this endeavor, but beyond that there is something that everyone in the room can do.

The foreign aid program is under consideration before Congress this very moment. It needs your support. And I will add in all earnestness that I believe it is entitled to your support.

This is an obligation we cannot avoid. The issue is relatively simple—do we do the job or don't we?

To many persons—but certainly not you people—the foreign aid program may seem remote—that the arguments for its necessity may seem abstract and intellectual rather than immediate and personal.

But surely the challenge which confronts us requires us to convert such issues from abstract necessities into personal concerns.

Many communities in this country now have in their midst students, scholars, engineers and businessmen from foreign lands. And some communities have set up committees to make it possible for our guests to meet Americans, to learn what we are really like. But I doubt whether we have done nearly as much in this area as we should be doing. I wonder, even in so distinguished a group as this one, how many of you have entertained foreigners in your home in the last year.

Our communities can do even more. Why should we not, for example, raise money locally each year to send some of our brightest boys and girls to schools overseas—and receive in exchange children from foreign countries in our schools? And I would add that I would not necessarily limit the exchange to countries on our side of the iron curtain. This program should not have to be done just by the Federal Government or under its direction. Responsive citizens such as you here in Chicago could begin and put into effect such a program.

In the last analysis every issue comes at last to a set of intellectual and moral decisions within the mind and heart of each one of us as individuals.

My experience every day as Attorney General reinforces my conviction that our democracy will stand or fall on the capacity of each individual in the nation to meet his responsibilities.

Most of our fellow citizens do their best—and do it the modest, unspectacular, decent, natural way which is the highest form of public service.

But every day in a shameful variety of ways the selfish actions of the small minority sully the honor of our nation.

The politician who takes bribes—the businessman who offers them—the industrialist who rigs bids and fixes prices—the trade unionist who works with gangsters—the God-fearing American who can't stand the idea of fellow citizens of a different color attending his churches or voting-booths—all have made a series of individual decisions which, one on top of another, degrade the whole character of our society.

The moral future of the nation rests in communities and individuals. One of your fellow townsmen is conducting today an effort of the greatest consequence for the children of the country. I mean the splendid new chairman of the Federal Communications Commission, Newton Minow. Mr. Minow is asking concerned citizens to appear in hearings and express their views about the quality of television programming. He cannot succeed without your support—and he richly deserves that support.

The Freedom Riders and the trouble encountered in Alabama, Mississippi and now Florida highlight a problem which exists far beyond the South. The Freedom Riders are a product of a quickening desire on the part of many Americans to break down discrimination and bigotry. The first groups of Freedom Riders traveled to call attention to segregation laws. It took considerable courage on their part as their injuries demonstrated. But they succeeded in moving the Nation's conscience. Perhaps even more important they also succeeded in calling attention to a fundamental truth of our society.

If respect for law and order is upheld vigorously by the leaders of the community, the law stands as a bulwark for freedom. But if over a period of time the law is challenged and the responsible officials do not stand for law and order, then order begins to give way to violence. Whenever men take the law into their own hands, the loser is the law—and, when the law loses, freedom languishes.

This by now should be clear to all Americans. It should be clear that the smallest county courthouse in Alabama and the august chambers of the Supreme Court of the United States must be dedicated to the same purpose—to maintain the individual's fundamental rights. It should be clear that, if one man's rights are denied, the rights of all are in danger—that if one man is denied equal protection of the law, we cannot be sure that we will enjoy freedom of speech or any other of our fundamental rights.

This was what was at stake when the Freedom Riders ventured into Alabama.

Laws can embody standards; governments can enforce laws— but the final task is not a task for government. It is a task for each and every one of us. Every time we turn our heads the other way when we see the law flouted—when we tolerate what we know to be wrong —when we close our eyes and ears to the corrupt because we are too busy, or too frightened—when we fail to speak up and speak out— we strike a blow against freedom and decency and justice.

Mr. Justice Brandeis said:

> Those who won our independence believed that the final end of the state was to make men free to develop their faculties; and that in its government the deliberative forces should prevail over the arbitrary. They valued liberty both as an end and as a means. They believed liberty to be the secret of happiness and courage to be the secret of liberty.
>
> They believed that freedom to think as you will and to speak as you think are means indispensable to the discovery and spread of political truth; that without free speech and assembly, discussion

would be futile . . . and that the greatest menace to freedom is an inert people.

My faith is that Americans are not an inert people.

My conviction is that we are rising as a people to confront the hard challenges of our age—and that we know that the hardest challenges are often those within ourselves.

My confidence is that, as we strive constantly to meet the exacting standards of our national tradition, we will liberate a moral energy within our nation which will transform America's role and America's influence throughout the world—and that upon this release of energy depends the world's hope for peace, freedom and justice everywhere.

part ii A BEGINNING IS MADE

No one who heard President John F. Kennedy's Inaugural Address on January 20, 1961, can easily forget that ringing prose. Some phrases and sentences have been repeated frequently. One of the most memorable passages occurred after he had indicated the vast amount of work to be done. The President stated that it would not be accomplished in the first hundred days, nor the first thousand days, nor in the life of his Administration nor perhaps even in our lifetime. "But," he said, "let us begin."

In the fall of the same year, the Attorney General—in his speeches—began to allude to the fact that in the area of civil rights the Administration had indeed begun, and that certain accomplishments could be pointed out. This was done through the winter of 1961-62 and well into the spring.

Accompanying the account of progress was an issue used in tandem, the competition between the United States Government and the Communist system of government. While not a new issue—it was included in the speech of May 6, 1961—the Attorney General elaborated upon this matter at great length during this phase. In his speech of December 3, before members of the National Conference of Christians and Jews, the subject of religious intolerance was interwoven into his contrast of this country and the U.S.S.R.

The final speeches of this series occurred after Robert Kennedy returned from his month-long trip around the world on February 28, 1962. In his speech of April 3 the Attorney General alluded frequently to his experiences—as an emissary of the President—in many different countries, but particularly to those in the East.

During that tour he made a point of holding question and answer periods with the college age youth of the places he visited. Actual instances of these exchanges were included in the speeches in this section.

It was on this trip that Robert Kennedy was placed in the untenable position of trying to defend the United States as a country of freedom in the face of charges that American Negroes were being denied their rights as citizens. This searing experience left its mark on the Attorney General, the effects of which included a renewed vigor in his attack on the civil rights problem upon his return.

There was another very significant outcome of this tour around the world. The vigor and potential of the young people he met made a lasting impression on the Attorney General. The critical necessity of giving adequate attention to the youth of the world—as future leaders—is alluded to in a great number of speeches in the rest of this book and remains a vital concern to Mr. Kennedy.

Delivered at the Portland City Club, Portland, Oregon October 6, 1961

Our enemies assert that capitalism enslaves the worker and will destroy itself. It is our national faith that the system of competitive enterprise offers the best hope for individual freedom, social development and economic growth.

Thus, every businessman who cheats on his taxes, fixes prices or underpays his labor; every union official who makes a collusive deal or misuses union funds; every lawyer who makes all or part of this possible damages the free enterprise system in the eyes of the world and does a disservice to the millions of honest Americans in all walks of life.

But, let me say again, this is not a situation which can be cured by the Department of Justice. We can take action and we shall, but in the last analysis the answer lies with the business community, union officials, the lawyers—in other words—the people themselves.

In the sensitive, emotional problems of civil rights there has been major progress in recent months, but we still have a very long way to go. For example, though a number of large school districts were desegregated without violence of any sort last month, the problem is still extremely difficult. Of 3,000,000 Negro children in seventeen Southern and Border States and the District of Columbia, only 213,500 attend integrated schools.

And in the North, Midwest, and West, we have segregation in a far more subtle, and often more sinister and damaging form. So, this is a major problem, a problem for the whole country. It is one that will require our best efforts, ingenuity, tolerance and understanding. The Supreme Court has acted. The Constitution is clear. There are those who might not like it, but it is the law of the land and it must be maintained.

In my estimation, the fact that the important cities of Atlanta, New Orleans, Dallas and Memphis desegregated their schools this fall without disorder and disrespect for the law, provided the world with a convincing demonstration of the American people's respect for the law, and of the progress that is being made in improving the position of minority groups in the United States. But it is only a beginning.

The rule of law in an open society still is a revolutionary ideal throughout much of the world. Our strength to transpose this ideal into reality throughout the world must depend over the years on our dedication to it at home.

And these matters that I have mentioned are, unfortunately, not the only difficulties that show that all is not what it might be here in the United States.

The television quiz scandals of several years ago; the basketball scandals of last year; the corruption the McClellan Committee found in important parts of labor, management, and the bar; the revelations of this past week that more than 30 officers and men of the Denver Police Department were themselves operating active and lucrative burglary rings and this after similar revelations in Chicago last year; the corruption of public officials—all of this must be a source of sorrow and concern to every one of us—just as it is, at the same time, a source of continuous comment and pleasure to the Communists.

These are all matters that cut across every segment of American society. No one group can point to another and say: "There lies the fault."

No one section of this country can say: "We are clean. They are corrupt."

No one financial or economic group can plead innocence.

These are matters which are a reflection on all of us as American citizens.

These are matters which are the responsibilities of all of us.

In meeting that problem, we must all play a role. No citizen can escape from freedom and still enjoy it. We cannot corrupt our own processes of government and law nor allow others to do so. We cannot yield to the temptation to let someone else perform the job, or to remain aloof from what in a free society is everyone's business.

As for me—I welcome the challenge and the opportunity and I pledge my best effort. As Abraham Lincoln said early in the Civil War:

> I do the very best I know how—the very best I can and I mean to keep doing so until the end. If the end brings me out all right, what is said against me won't amount to anything. If the end brings me out wrong, ten angels swearing I was right would make no difference.

Delivered at the National Conference of Christians and Jews Dinner Cleveland, Ohio, December 3, 1961

I am happy to be here tonight to join with you in honoring two distinguished citizens, Dr. Millis and Dr. Glennan, for their service to the cause of human relations. And, of course, I am deeply honored to accept this special citation from your organization* which for more than 30 years has made such an outstanding contribution to the fight against prejudice and bigotry and in behalf of human liberty and civil rights.

During the campaign last year, President Kennedy said:

> I believe in an America where religious intolerance will some day end—where all men and all churches are treated as equal—where every man has the same right to attend or not attend the church of his choice—where there is no anti-Catholic vote, no bloc voting of any kind—and where Catholics, Protestants and Jews at both lay and pastoral levels will refrain from those attitudes of disdain and division which so often have marred their works in the past.

* The NCCJ Brotherhood Award.

This kind of an America is a goal for all of us.

This has been the aim and the objective of the National Conference of Christians and Jews from the very beginning.

As we meet in Cleveland tonight, our minds are full of the headlines about Berlin, Vietnam, test ban negotiations, fallout—and outer space which was visited this week by an American chimpanzee.

While our scientists strive to lead the way to the moon, other Americans are helping new nations to decide their own destiny and keep their newly-won independence, for the race won in outer space is meaningless if we fail in our efforts to extend the cause of freedom around the globe.

With so much of a commitment beyond our shores, we are tempted at times to forget that we still face great problems at home.

Members of this organization are perhaps more aware than most citizens that religious bigotry has existed and still exists in the United States. The National Conference of Christians and Jews was founded in 1928 by Americans who were concerned over the prejudice that had developed during the Presidential campaign that year. But what was not possible in 1928 was possible in 1960 and President Kennedy's election in one sense satisfied the purpose for which your organization came into being. But much more remains to be done.

Though the critical matters facing the nation are war, health, poverty and survival, there still are Americans who would vote against a candidate or for a candidate because of his religion. There still are neighborhoods and organizations and institutions in our society which exclude Americans because of the sound of their name or the color of their skin.

There are sections of the United States where citizens are denied the right to vote because of their race; Negroes still have not been accorded equal employment opportunities in many of our States; in some areas American Negroes, as well as African diplomats and students, are denied decent housing and service and facilities in public places.

These are matters that trouble all of us but while we are conscious of them and concerned about them, let us also consider some of the real progress that we have made.

In October 1960, at Wittenberg College, here in Ohio, President Kennedy declared that the Federal Government must set the example if employment opportunities are to be open equally to members of all races and creeds.

The President pointed out that no Negroes held important positions in the Federal Government; that no Negro headed a Federal Agency or held a policy-making post.

Then the President said:

"I believe we can do better."

Now, a year later, there still is much to be done. However, we have done better.

President Kennedy has named two Negroes to District Judgeships and appointed Thurgood Marshall to the United States Court of Appeals. When I came to the Department of Justice, there were only ten Negroes employed as lawyers; not a single Negro served as a United States Attorney—or ever had in the history of the country. That has been changed. We in the Department of Justice are indebted to the City of Cleveland for giving to us such a competent and able lawyer as Merle McCurdy to serve as United States Attorney. Mr. McCurdy was appointed by the President because he was a lawyer of ability and integrity. That is the significant point.

In fact, all of these men were named to positions of trust in our Government—not because of their race or the color of their skin—but because they are men of outstanding qualifications and proven ability. However, they were not denied the opportunity to serve in these important positions because of their color. This is also important.

Earlier this week, a group of the Nation's leading industrial firms sent their executives to the White House to sign an agreement with the Federal Government to voluntarily concentrate their efforts on the task of providing more job opportunities for qualified Negroes. As the President said, such voluntary actions will benefit not only the companies involved but the country as well.

This September, white and Negro children went to school together in such cities as Atlanta, Dallas and Memphis and Little Rock and New Orleans. There was not a single community where local officials failed to meet their responsibilities. There was not a single incident of violence. Under difficult and trying personal circumstances, there was a recognition of responsibility; a willingness to uphold and live by the law.

Again on Friday of this past week, this same recognition of responsibility was demonstrated by the officials of Mississippi when a mob gathered to intimidate a group of Negro bus riders. It was an explosive situation. But ultimately law and order prevailed. Law enforcement officers met their obligations.

It is important that this whole problem be placed in proper perspective.

We are making progress in this country. The President and the Federal Government are working diligently toward that end. Further, the vast majority of American people are aware of the problem and anxious to do something about it.

Obviously, we are going to continue to face difficulties in this area for a long time to come. The problems will not disappear overnight. But this country will continue to move ahead in this field. We will not accept the status quo. We will continue to make progress. That is what is important.

We live in a free and open society; that is where our strength and greatness lies. We do not hide our faults behind a wall; we do not try to bury our mistakes; we do not conceal incidents, even though they are shameful. We have no secrets from ourselves or from others. If there is an outbreak of violence in some section of the United States, it is flashed around the world in less than an hour and quickly finds its way into the Communist propaganda mill.

And while we recognize our own faults and acknowledge our responsibilities to continue to do better, let us also recognize how much better we have done than the system with which we presently are struggling for men's souls and hearts.

Just consider a little of what has happened in the lands under the Communist regime in the field of civil rights in the last few months.

Yes, we have our problems in Alabama, but to be blunt, we are not shooting old women and young children in the back as the Communists are doing in Berlin. As the newspapers and people of the world freely discuss the errors of a small minority in this country and hold the entire United States responsible, the Communist officials themselves build a wall in Berlin to keep truth and freedom out— and tyranny in. Those who attempt to flee the workers' paradise receive a bullet—not a passport.

Can anybody equate the disturbance in Alabama last spring with the death by starvation of hundreds and hundreds of thousands of Chinese peasants under a farm commune system which has failed?

Consider how many thousands of words have been printed around the world about Birmingham and Montgomery compared to what has been said about this systematic extinction of large numbers of Chinese by their fellow countrymen. How much more has been written about Little Rock than Tibet or even Hungary.

This a free society. Our faults are discussed. Our mistakes make a rich grist for the Communist propaganda machine. This we accept. However, let us all remember also that their failures are seldom even mentioned, their mistakes never fully known and the terror of their system discussed only when it becomes politically expedient. Five years after Khrushchev dies—who will be moving his body?

Last week President Kennedy granted an unprecedented interview to Mr. Adjhubei, the editor of *Izvestia*, and that newspaper with a circulation of four million, printed the text of the exchange.

Tass, the Soviet News Agency which provides news to some 200 million other Russians, printed only excerpts of the interview and paraphrased other parts. The interview was distorted. They carefully omitted three of the President's major points. *Tass* excluded the President's statement that (1) our conflict in Berlin exists because the Soviet Union does not intend to permit reunification of Germany; (2) that Russia violated the Yalta and Potsdam agreements by never allowing the countries of Eastern Europe the right to free elections, and (3) that the Soviet Union broke the moratorium on nuclear tests and prepared for new tests in the atmosphere while still negotiating with us in Geneva on a test ban. And, as a matter of fact, the Russian people have not even been told, to this day, that their Government has set off some 50 nuclear explosions in the atmosphere.

The interview was of great importance and most significant however. For the first time the United States was able to have its position known to at least a percentage of the Russian people. The door to the truth was opened a little in Russia. However, the mere fact that an interview should receive such attention indicates the tightness of the curtain around the Communist orbit.

In this country, as I have said, there is religious intolerance. This Nation and our Government are aware of such bigotry and have condemned it and are fighting it. How different from the Soviet

Union where the Government itself recently deposed a number of Jewish religious leaders from their positions in religious congregations. Other Jewish lay leaders are serving long jail terms for so-called anti-state activities. And only a few months ago the *Communist Party Journal* attacked Jehovah's Witnesses and the Seventh Day Adventists as "poisonous religious narcotics."

In 1955 Justice Douglas and I visited Soviet Central Asia. Historically this had been a deeply religious part of the world. In Bukhara in 1920 before the Communists took control, there were 300 Mosques and religious schools. Now there is only one. In fact, there are only a handful of Mosques to serve the whole of Soviet Central Asia. In Ashkhabad, the capital of Turkmenistan, which has a population of 225,000, and in Stalinabad, the capital of Tadzhikistan, which has a population of 325,000, there are no Mosques and no religious schools. The officials with whom we talked made it clear that the Government considered religion backward.

The Soviet Union charges the West with colonialism. The countries of the West have all made mistakes in this field. But examine the colonial record of the Soviet Union. I am not referring just to Hungary, Poland, Latvia, Lithuania, and the rest but consider the region of Kazakistan for instance. Not only has religion been destroyed, but between 1926 and 1939, one out of every three Kazaks died in the Soviet effort to communize their farms. This process was repeated in many places in Russia. What the Chinese are doing today, the Russians did twenty and thirty years ago with equal harshness and terror.

Though we have much to accomplish in this country let us keep our heads high and meet our difficulties with courage. As a nation we need not apologize, we have much to be thankful for. We have much of which we can be proud.

The fact that free men persist in the search for the truth, is the essential difference between Communism and Democracy. The other road might at times appear to be easier—to be less troublesome—to be more immediately profitable. Our way is more difficult and in these days more perilous. The fact, however, that we would rather live in an open society than hide our troubles and mistakes behind a wall or barbed wire, is evidence of the strength of our Government and our way of life.

Thus, the great challenge to all Americans—indeed to all free men and women—is to maintain loyalty to truth; to maintain loyalty to free institutions; to maintain loyalty to freedom as a basic human value, and above all else to keep in our hearts and minds the tolerance and mutual trust that have been the genius of American life throughout our history.

One of our great poets, Archibald MacLeish, said:

> The American journey has not ended. America is never accomplished. America is always still to build; for men, as long as they are truly men, will dream of man's fulfillment.

Upon you and me, and our fellow countrymen, falls the challenge of protecting, not only our country, but the free people of the world in this hour of maximum need—of greatest danger.

With confidence born and nurtured by knowledge and truth, and with the courage of free men, we shall prevail.

Delivered before the
Philadelphia Fellowship Commission
April 3, 1962

Mr. Tom MacBride, Mayor Dillworth, members of the Commission, I want to say how grateful I am to all of you for this award. I feel, in the company of Mayor Dillworth and Mr. MacBride who have done so much over so many years in this field, that I am accepting this award on their behalf and on behalf of those in the Department of Justice, Bert Maral and all those who struggled like you to accomplish a great deal in this field.

I also feel slightly taken aback by the many fine things that were said about me by Tom MacBride and by the scroll. Whenever I receive an award or am present when other people receive an award it takes me back to my days in high school and in college—which was not so long ago. You know, when the graduating class gave the award for the best athlete and for the best scholarship and for the person who was best in Latin, and best in Greek, and who wrote the best composition—I received a prize for being the fellow with the fifth best sense of humor in my graduating class.

So I am very grateful to you and the members of the Fellowship Commission for honoring me and the members of the Department of Justice. Your work is so valuable and so important!

When the President appeared before the United Nations some months ago, he said that in these very difficult times what we are striving for throughout the world is a world of nations who will live under the rule of law. But in order to have other countries follow our leadership in important fields, we are going to have to abide by the rule of law here in the United States. We are going to have to live by the rule of law, and we are going to have to do it in our day-to-day lives and in our relationships with our fellowmen.

It seems to me that you people, by your efforts and by your work and by your energy, make it possible for us to tell the peoples of the rest of the world that we intend to abide by the rule of law here in the United States; that we are worthy of the leadership that we have undertaken. I have just returned from a trip around the world and it came home to me again and again how important this is, and how important what we do here in the United States is in our relationships with other peoples and with other countries.

Every place, every city, every community, every country that I visited, whether at a press conference or whether I met with students or labor leaders or whatever group; I was questioned about civil rights here in the United States, what progress we are making, what steps we were taking.

When Carlos Romulo, whom you honored some years ago, and who is a great supporter of the United States and a great booster of ours all around the world, came by my office to see me just before he left Washington, he said that we were destined to continue to lead the world. However, he said the one thing that can stop us—the one thing that will stand in our way—is if we do not deal with this major problem that we have here in the United States. People are not going to believe that we live by the Declaration of Independence or the Constitution of the United States if we do not treat our fellow human beings as human beings. He said we have a responsibility and an obligation to do it.

From all of this, the fact that we have these tremendous problems here in the United States—racial problems, religious problems, discrimination against minorities—allows Communists and minority groups, who are antagonistic towards the United States in all of these other countries, to work up ferment against the United States.

Again and again I was asked about civil rights and what steps we are taking. I told them quite frankly that we had major problems in the United States, but that we were making progress.

I told them about when the President attended the inaugural parade and was standing there in front of the White House on January 20th and saw the Coast Guard come by. He turned to the gentleman who was standing next to him. Looking at the Coast Guard, he said, "There's not one Negro in the Coast Guard!"

A couple of weeks later the President greeted the President of one of the new African nations. They went out to the airport and then they walked down and looked at the Honor Guard. There was not one Negro in the Honor Guard!

When I came into the Department of Justice—members of which had gone around the country and had spoken and lectured on what other people should do in other communities, and what steps should be taken towards bringing law suits to insure that everybody has their civil rights—when I came to the Department of Justice, there were only ten Negroes working as attorneys in the Department of Justice. Now these things have been cleared up.

The same kind of situation existed in many, if not all, of the departments in the federal government. One of the first things that President Kennedy did was to give orders and instructions that that situation be remedied.

There are now five times as many Negroes working in the Department of Justice as were working there twelve months ago.

There are now Negroes in the Honor Guard and Negroes in the Coast Guard.

Negroes are holding positions, and important positions, in the government. They are not individuals who were selected just because of the fact that they were Negroes, but they were not denied the opportunity for employment for a position of responsibility because they were Negroes.

We have now and for the first time in the history of the United States, Negroes who hold the positions of District Court Judges. Two of our biggest cities have U. S. Attorneys who are Negroes. These cities are Cleveland and San Francisco.

We have moved, as Tom MacBride said today, in the field of transportation. Two-hundred railroad terminals have been desegregated. Over 100 bus terminals have been desegregated. Efforts have been made to insure that everybody has a right to vote in an election. These are steps that have been taken forward.

However, the mere fact that I have to come up here in January or March of 1962 and say that this is what we have now arranged in the United States of America, one-hundred years after the Civil War —that we now have arranged it so that when Negroes go into a bus terminal they don't have to use separate facilities, and the fact that we even have to talk about the fact that everybody can get a job equally in the Department of Justice—is a reflection on all of us. It is a reflection on us as American citizens.

It is this that leads to misunderstandings and misconceptions about the United States in other countries because the small Communist groups can say: "Well, how can you believe the United States? How can you believe that they believe in equality if they have these racial problems in their own country, if they won't treat minority people equally?"

I was talking to the Chairman of the largest Labor Board in Japan. The question of race came up, and then the question of the United States' position around the world. The Left Wing Socialists had just taken a trip to China and at that time they had put out a communiqué with the Chinese Communist leadership, saying that the great danger in the world was the United States, and that we were imperialistic.

I said to this labor leader, "Do you believe the United States is imperialistic?"

He said, "Yes, I do. It is a different kind of imperialism. It is economic imperialism."

I said, "Do you believe that the Soviet Union was imperialistic when it went into Hungary, or do you believe that Communist China was imperialistic when it went into Tibet?"

He said, "No. The United States is imperialistic because they have economic imperialism."

I asked him what he meant by that—what it was in the United

States? He said, "Well, the United States is run by the Morgan gang and by the Rockefellers."

I said, "Well, not yet it's not!"

You can use guns and bullets and you shoot people down, and you are not imperialistic. But because people have been saying or talking about capitalism for one-hundred years, it has now become a dirty expression and you are going to accept everything that is said about it. "How could it possibly be true in the United States with Arthur Goldberg, the Secretary of Labor, or President Kennedy, backed by the labor organization, as he was, that they are now run by the great monopolistic capitalist that you have described?"

But this was the first time he really had thought about it.

When I went down into Indonesia a young student in the course of questioning me, described the United States "monopolistic capitalism."

I said to him, "What do you understand by that?" because when he made that statement about half of the student body applauded and accepted that description of the United States.

I said to him, "Now what do you understand is going on in the United States that fits that description? You have an obligation, now you are a student and have had the advantage of an education. What is in the United States that fits that description?"

He went and sat down.

"Anybody who laughed, anybody who applauded," I said, "anybody who agreed with that description, come forward and tell me what it is in the United States that meets that description."

Not one of them came forward.

I met with a group of about 50 students just before I left Indonesia. In the course of the conversation they made it quite clear that they wanted to talk about the United States' position regarding West New Guinea, and the fact that we were not against the Dutch in this connection.

I explained that we were trying to bring a peaceful solution between the Dutch and the Indonesians on the West New Guinea problem; that both of them were our friends and that we were trying to get this matter resolved peacefully. About five out of the thirty were Communists. One of them made a point, as spokesman of the group, of the fact that we did not oppose the Dutch on West New

Guinea, and did not, therefore, oppose colonialism; that colonialism was amoral; that the Dutch were amoral because they were a colonial power, and we were amoral because we were supporting the Dutch—we were not against the Dutch.

I said, "Now, if you feel that way, are you against what the Russians did in Southeast Europe? Are you against the Russian position in Latvia, Lithuania and Estonia, or in Poland or Eastern Germany or any other countres in Southeastern Europe or Eastern Berlin? Are you against what the Russians did in Hungary or what the Chinese did in Tibet?"

He said, "As far as Hungary is concerned, that was a question of some militarists coming in and taking over the government, and the people got so aroused about it that they called on the Russian Army to come in and save them. As far as Tibet is concerned," he said, "that is for the support of the people." He said that the Llama picked on the people so the people got the Chinese Army to come in and save them from the Llama. Then he went on to say that the Communist regime in all these countries has the support of the people.

I said, "If that is true, how can you explain the wall in Berlin? For the first time in the history of mankind, a wall has been erected—not to keep bandits or marauders out—but to keep the people in. Now, if that has the great support of the people, the Communist regime, that is, why do they have to put a wall around it to keep their people in?"

He said, "We don't want to go into the details of the matter. Let's get back to West New Guinea."

The significant part of it was that, when I came out about a half-hour later, about five of these students came up and started talking to me. They were very friendly, and they asked questions about the United States.

During the discussion, some points were made by the Communist group, but there was not a flicker of support from any of the other people who were there. When we got into the smaller groups and the Communists were gone, they said to me and to some of the newspaper men:

"That was a good point. Those points regarding Communism should be made more frequently. You are absolutely right about Berlin and about the erection of the wall."

One of the newspapermen said, "Why didn't you say something at the time? Why didn't you speak out?"

The fellow said, "We just don't do that in our circles when we are among students."

They had been intimidated for such an extended period of time that they were afraid to speak out.

Again and again the Communist groups concentrate on the differences that exist between the United States and their countries. They concentrate on the differences that exist on West New Guinea, for instance, when it is Indonesia. When it is Japan, they concentrate on the differences we have in the field of trade; the differences that we have in the field of Okinawa.

Then they go to this question of the problems that we have internally here in the United States, specifically and particularly in the field of civil rights. They point out all the problems and difficulties that exist here. That is what creates the difficulty because, when they can come up with some of these true facts on where we are different or where we have problems, and if we are not making progress, they can get the rest of the students to go along with all the other things that dominate and control the conversation.

We have much that we can do with all these people. We have great assets on our side. In the first place, we have the truth. We can admit that we have problems here in the United States, but we can also talk about the progress that we are making.

We can also talk and make comparisons between the progress that we have made through our free system and the lack of progress under the Communist system. All we have to do is compare West Germany with East Germany, West Berlin with East Berlin, or China with Japan which has made such progress under the free enterprise system.

Then what we have to say is that we in this country are not going to accept the status quo; that we are not a selfish society that is interested only in ourselves, and only interested in a greater economic future for ourselves and for our families, but are interested in one another.

Capitalism has become a dirty word because it is synonymous with selfishness. It is believed that the individual here in the United States and under our system is interested only in himself, and is not interested in his neighbor, is not interested in those who live in his community, and is not interested in those who are less well off.

I say that when societies and groups such as yours, this organization here in Philadelphia, and what these people at the head-table have done in order to help and assist those who are less fortunate, those who are less well off; this is what we have to sell in all these countries. This is what is truly the United States. This is what really is the real character of the United States and of the American people. I say that we can sell this; that we can go out into all of these countries and we can tell the story, and we are going to win.

But we have got to continue to make efforts here in the United States. We have got to continue to make progress in this country and I say that we can make progress because we cannot be satisfied with the status quo.

We have made progress in the field of civil rights, but we have much more that we can do and much more that we will do. It is up to you, to us, to those in government and those who are out of government, those who are in the South, and those in the North, East and West to continue to move forward, to continue to be dissatisfied with the status quo and to say that we are going to continue to make progress. I think that together, joined as brothers, we can continue to move forward and that we can later look back upon this era as a turning-point in the history of the United States, and something that will make this country an even better place in which to live, for all of ourselves and for our children, too. I thank you.

*Delivered at the Annual Luncheon
of the Associated Press
New York City, April 23, 1962*

There have been some comments about the Department of Justice awakening three newsmen in the middle of the night to ask some questions.* I want to tell you the reaction of your reporter, Louis Panos, who covers the Department of Justice for The Associated Press.

* A reference to the steel price crisis of April 10, 1962.

The next evening Mr. Panos came into my office and said: "I am just leaving for home and before I go to bed is there anything you'd really like to know?" Then he said, "Don't call me, I'll call you."

I want to assure you that we do not make a practice of calling reporters at two or three o'clock in the morning. But to tell the truth, when I get called at two or three in the morning by a reporter for the Associated Press—and it happens—I am not too sure it wouldn't be a good idea.

I am grateful for your invitation to be here today because I have a high regard for newspapermen who accept their responsibility to probe tirelessly for the truth.

I do not believe that newspapermen are self-appointed judges of what's right or wrong, or what's good or bad. But I believe in and greatly admire those who are competent to seek the truth and inform the people. In my opinion, the newspapers are equal to the courts—and sometimes ahead of the courts—in our system—in protecting the people's fundamental rights.

Since my recent trip around the world, I am even more aware of the tremendous role that a free press plays in a free society, and of the absolute necessity that newspapers make a concerted effort to get the truth to the people.

The Associated Press is distributed in more than 100 languages in 89 countries around the world. Those statistics tell clearly what heavy responsibilities and burdens you gentlemen bear.

But on my trip—wherever I visited—in Japan, Indonesia, Thailand, Germany and Holland—I found a great deal of misinformation and misunderstanding about the United States and the American people.

This was especially true among the students with whom the Communists, though small in number, have done a more effective job in spreading the Communist line than we have in telling the truth about our economic and social progress and about our fundamental beliefs as free men.

.   .   .   .   .

They know we have made great material progress but they have difficulty understanding our federal system of government.

They do not understand that the American people have great concern about their fellow Americans and about their fellow human beings.

They do not know that the American people are dedicated to making progress toward our national goals as set forth in the Declaration of Independence and the Constitution, and that the American people are fiercely determined to remain free.

So, we have a great problem but we have a great opportunity, and, in my judgment, unless we are able in the next decade to convince the people of foreign countries—and particularly the students —that we are true to our ideals and that prosperity and decent health can be achieved in a system that preserves individual liberty, we will lose the cold war no matter how much money we spend on aid.

But I believe that if we get busy and enter this battle for the minds of tomorrow's leaders with all the skill, vigor and dedication at our command, we will win hands down. I believe we have so much going for us—despite what success the articulate, highly disciplined Communist cadres have had.

The President said in his State of the Union message that "our overriding obligation in the months ahead is to fulfill our own faith ... for if we cannot fulfill our own ideals here, we cannot expect others to accept them. And when the youngest child alive today has grown to the cares of manhood, our position in the world will be determined first of all by what provisions we make today—for his education, his health, and his opportunities for a good home and a good job and a good life."

The importance of the President's statement came home to me again and again on my trip.

Every place, every city, every community, every country that I visited—whether it was a press conference, a talk with students or a meeting with labor leaders or businessmen—I was questioned about problems here in the United States—what progress we were making, what steps we were taking.

.   .   .   .   .

On my trip when I was asked about civil rights, what steps we are taking—and it happened again and again—I said quite frankly we had major problems but that we were making progress.

I told them about the progress we are making—that dramatic strides have been made in guaranteeing that all our citizens are able to exercise their fundamental freedoms equally. I cited instances of this progress such as the fact that for the first time in the history of the United States Negroes hold positions of District Court judges; that two of our biggest cities—Cleveland and San Francisco—have United States Attorneys who are Negroes; that Negroes occupy other high places in the government and that they are not selected just because they are Negroes but because they had ability and integrity and they were not denied the opportunity for employment because they were Negroes.

I said that while we have made progress there was much more we could do and much more that we will do; that the problems and difficulties and even the violence they would read about and hear about meant that we were moving ahead—that the American Government and the American people were dissatisfied with the status quo.

Sometimes I was asked about racketeers and hoodlums. Again I could cite the progress that has been made. In January 1961 the Department of Justice began a major effort against organized crime and racketeering. Federal law enforcement investigations are now being coordinated effectively and we are pooling information from the files of Federal and local law enforcement agencies about more than 700 top racketeers. Five of eight bills which we submitted to Congress were enacted and had an immediate effect in lessening gambling profits which finance all other forms of organized crime.

I wish I could stand here today and tell you we have organized crime on the run; that in every city throughout the United States it has been brought to the point where it can be controlled by the local authorities. The important racketeers and hoodlums are well aware of the pressures that have been placed upon them and they are uneasy. However we have a long way to go and much to do, but we have made progress.

But the fact that we have these problems and difficulties in civil rights and law enforcement and other areas is what leads to misunderstandings and misconceptions about the United States by the small Communist groups who then say, for example, "How can you believe the United States? How can you believe that they believe in equality if they won't treat minority people equally?"

What we must do is make it clear that we in this country are not going to accept the status quo; that we are not selfish people interested only in ourselves and our pocketbooks, that we are interested in our fellow citizens.

Capitalism has become a dirty word because it is synonymous with selfishness. Many people in foreign lands believe that Americans are interested only in material gain, that they are not interested in their neighbors, not interested in their communities and not interested in those that are less well off.

Many of you through your newspapers and your civic efforts have assisted your fellow citizens in many ways and you are well aware how much effort Americans expend on improving their churches, their cities and schools and aiding those less fortunate. This is what is truly the United States. This is what is truly the real character of the American people.

This is the story that deserves banner play overseas. This is the story that we must tell and I think we have many other assets as well.

In the first place we are not afraid to admit that everything is not perfect within our borders—that this is a strength of America and not a weakness. One of our greatest assets in this struggle is that we have the truth on our side.

We can stand to hear conflicting ideas and voices of dissent, not only among our citizens, but among our Allies and the non-aligned nations.

We encourage free inquiry and free experiment.

We believe that the state exists to serve the people.

All this distinguishes us from our adversaries, and it was my experience that there are not only reservoirs of good will toward America in the countries I visited but that we—not the Communists —share the common aspirations of people to be free and to be masters of their own destinies.

So, I believe there is a great deal we can do now to help these young people know the facts about us and our way of life. It will not involve large sums of money to do the job but it will require understanding and effort and hard work.

First, we can send groups of men and women to all nations to lecture—not just about the United States and our form of government, or even democracy generally—but to talk also about history and philosophy and literature, and even more practical matters.

These individuals should make tours of as many universities as possible and should confer with labor leaders, farm and cooperative leaders, newspaper editors, businessmen and government officials, as well as students. The people who would be sent should know the history of the United States, the philosophy of their government and be articulate in their understanding of the American people. In recent weeks, two men who have heard me discuss this problem have volunteered to speak at universities on trips they are making to the Far East. One is a young, leading businessman and the other is a top labor official. I know they both will make a favorable impression and they will help.

But I would like to see many more people go—Senators, Cabinet members, Congressmen, Governors, university professors, playwrights and poets travel for this purpose. I would like to see Walter Lippmann tour the Far East for a month, speaking on a number of subjects and answering the questions of students and intellectuals.

Secondly, our government information agencies and services can talk more about the fundamentals in the United States. They explain the social progress being made in this country; what great contributions charitable organizations are making in medicine, sociology, education and all walks of life—both organizations like the Ford, Carnegie and Rockefeller Foundations. I propose that our information agencies speak quite frankly and openly about the problems and difficulties we have in our country, while at the same time strengthening the efforts being made by the government and the American people to deal with these problems and move ahead.

Third, we should encourage other free countries of the world to set up their own peace corps with the understanding that our organization will cooperate closely with them.

There is much, for instance. that young Japanese could do in Southeast Asia. I am convinced they would be willing to do it.

Many young Germans, Frenchmen, and Dutch are as anxious as young Americans to help their fellowmen and others less fortunate economically.

Among all of the students with whom I have talked, I found an idealism and a thirst to make the world a better place in which to live. This is a tremendous potential and it must be harnessed and utilized.

Your organization, going to 89 countries, can do so much in bringing the truth—good or bad—but the truth—to all the people.

And you individually, as publishers of the greatest free press in the world, can do so much in your own communities.

Raymond Clapper said, "Never overestimate the facts that the public has, but never underestimate the ability of the people to draw their own conclusions from the facts."

Hard, digging reporting—the type that made it possible for the McClellan Committee to unveil the full danger of organized crime in America—is absolutely essential. Thirty percent of the leads which the McClellan Committee received came from newspapers. This information did not always come from the large newspapers. It came from newspapers who recognized their responsibility to their local areas and made it their business to know what was going on in their communities.

There are so many internal problems which the press can help solve, which in the last analysis relate to honest, efficient administration of government—whether it is in a city, county, state or federal agency.

It is virtually impossible for even the most alert administration to be fully aware of all the corruption or laxity that can creep into our Government. But, an alert press can make a major difference not only in eliminating wasteful or corrupt practices, but in insuring that justice prevails.

Our greatest strength in international affairs is our integrity in handling our own affairs at home. And if you are diligent and do your job and if we do ours in cleansing our cities, counties, states and Federal Government of waste, mismanagement, corruption and intolerance we will triumph. For even with the problems and difficulties which we have now, we stand out in a category of the highest integrity measured by other nations today. Continuation and improvement of that record can be our greatest assurance in the long sweep of history.

So we need your assistance. But most of all we need your vigilance.

We are willing to make the sacrifices that are needed and we have always had the toughness, courage and perseverance to see the job through. We have the will to win. Therefore, I know we will win.

Delivered at the Law Day Ceremonies
of the Virginia State Bar
Roanoke, Virginia, May 1, 1962

It gives me particular pleasure to take part in this annual observance of Law Day in Virginia. I am not only a resident of Virginia, but I came here 14 years ago as a student—and I hold Mr. Jefferson's university at Charlottesville largely responsible for any gaps or lapses in my knowledge of the law.

Above all, I am glad to be here because, like every American, I am in the debt of those great Virginians who, from Washington, Jefferson and John Marshall, have taught us the role in a free society.

The state of which I am a native has also made its contributions to our national traditions of justice. John Adams in the original draft of the Massachusetts Constitution spoke of "a government of laws, and not of men."

If the members of this Bar will forgive me, I fear that from time to time in our history we have tended to construe this as meaning a government of *lawyers* and not of men. Yet the law, after all, cannot exist without lawyers. And, de Tocqueville said, the legal profession, when it is faithful to its highest ideals, is "the only aristocracy that can exist in a democracy without doing violence to its nature."

It is surely significant that so many of the Founding Fathers of this Republic were lawyers. It is significant, too, that the men in Virginia and Massachusetts and the other colonies who led the Revolution in 1776 were the same men who wrote the Constitution in 1787.

That generation was acutely aware that liberty and law are inseparable and that liberty under law, freedom with justice, is the highest goal of our society. Today we inherit that insight as it has been tested and strengthened in the cruel history of our own century.

The struggles and the passions of the first half century have left their mark; but they are behind us. A new society has taken form, developed and been shaped by the leaders of both of our major political parties. It is a society loyal to the Revolutionary concepts of Jefferson, Madison and Washington—concepts based on the importance of the individual—and it is a society which believes that government has positive responsibility to make individual freedom more than a legal fiction. It is a society which has an inherent belief in justice.

"Justice," said Daniel Webster, "is the great interest of man on earth. It is the ligament which holds civilized beings and civilized nations together."

As the law officer of the United States Government, I have a particular responsibility in the field of justice. And yet, in the last analysis, my responsibility is no greater than that of any other citizen of our democracy. As the inscription on the Department of Justice building in Washington puts it: "Justice in the Life and Conduct of the State Is Possible Only As It First Resides in the Hearts and Souls of the Citizens."

The ultimate relationship between justice and law will be an eternal subject for speculation and analysis. But it may be said that in a democratic society law is the form which free men give to justice. The glory of justice and the majesty of law are created not just by the Constitution—nor by the courts—nor by the officers of the law—nor by the lawyers—but by the men and women who constitute our society—who are the protectors of the law as they are themselves protected by the law.

Justice, in short, is everybody's business—and the breakdown of justice is everybody's business too. The defiance of law, the violation of law, are infectious. Those who challenge the law in one or another of its aspects weaken the whole legal structure of society. For one man to disobey a law he does not like is to invite others to disobey another law which he may regard as indispensable to his own livelihood—or life.

We all know these things in the abstract. In the last few years the question of the rule of law has become to many a new and concrete concern, in part because of the Supreme Court's decision in the case of *Brown* v. *Board of Education.*

This decision represented an interpretation by a unanimous Supreme Court of the meaning of the American Constitution. At the same time, it called for substantial changes in customs and practices in particular parts of the country and, therefore, it has raised questions and roused protests.

Some of the protest has been addressed to the role of the Supreme

Court itself as the final arbiter of our constitutional system. This is a powerful role—but let no one suppose that it came about lightly or by accident. It was a role foreseen by the authors of the Constitution, and this role of the Supreme Court was established by one of the greatest of all Virginians, John Marshall.

Because no constitution is self-expounding, there must be some agency to expound it. And the job of exposition is not that of citing a rigid and unchanging set of theorems, like repeating a mathematical table.

"We must never forget," said Marshall, "that it is a *constitution* we are expounding . . . intended to endure for ages to come and consequently to be adapted to the various *crises* of human affairs."

In following Marshall's injunction, the Supreme Court has acted as the conscience of the nation. It has been one great means by which our constitutional framework has responded to the ethical imperatives of our people.

In doing its work, the Court has aroused protest throughout our history. Not a word has been said in criticism of the Court in the last eight years which was not said often before in our national past.

This, of course, is precisely why we have a Supreme Court—to adjudicate disputes laden with concern and emotion. The American Constitution would indeed be a sterile document if the Court in its labors did not recognize the truth so well stated by Justice Cardozo, "The great generalities of the Constitution have a content and a significance that vary from age to age."

The 1954 decision placed a great and exacting responsibility upon the Federal judges. I think it is appropriate on Law Day to pay tribute to the skill, devotion and courage with which they have met this responsibility.

They have had to consider cases in an atmosphere of perplexity, pressure and sometimes panic. They have confronted complex issues with conscience and candor. In many cases, they have handed down decisions which were unpopular among their neighbors. In some cases, their rulings may have been contrary to their personal views. But they have faithfully recognized that their obligation is not to express private or local preferences but to record the law of the land.

When people criticize the courts for invading spheres of action which supposedly belong to other parts of our constitutional system, they often overlook the fact that the courts must act precisely because the other organs of government have failed to fulfill their own responsibilities.

This surely is the moral of the recent decision in *Baker* v. *Carr* the Tennessee reapportionment case. For half a century the urban voters of Tennessee had been systematically underrepresented in the state legislature—and for half a century political and legislative remedies had proved inadequate to reestablish the substance of democratic equity. And the same unfair situation exists in many other states.

In *Baker* v. *Carr,* the Supreme Court held that a system of apportionment could be so unfair and irrational as to require cognizance under the 14th Amendment. Exactly what judicial standards will emerge no one can say as yet; but, if legislatures continue to evade their primary responsibility, there can be no alternative but to work these standards out, as so many of our constitutional principles have been worked out, on a case-by-case basis.

The responsibility for maintaining the rule of law, in short, is not just the responsibility of the courts alone. In fact, the courts by themselves never can be effective enough to enforce the law in a free society. If the rule of law is to survive in a democracy, it must have other and deeper wellsprings. It must be recognized by the common consent of our people—and it must be carried out by the other agencies of government, federal, state and local, as well as by all our citizens in their daily lives.

Historic decisions like *Brown* v. *Board of Education* and *Baker* v. *Carr* should not be accepted grudgingly for they offer opportunity as well as imposing obligations.

The obligations are to respect and execute the law.

The opportunity is for individual citizens and state and local governments to identify law and liberty as a living reality. If this is done, states' rights will not be eroded. They will be strengthened. If states solve their problems and difficulties within the framework of our Constitution, states' rights will be given new vitality.

And, in the last analysis, if this is done, the opportunity to rise to the full potentiality of our democracy will be grasped by all people, and the rule of law will be made a common undertaking—not only here in the United States—but among free men all around the world.

I know of nothing more important, for as the President said at the United Nations last September, what we are striving for in these very difficult times is a world in which all nations will live under the rule of law.

But in order to have other countries follow our leadership in important fields, we are going to have to abide by the rule of law here in the United States. We are going to have to live by the rule of law, and we are going to have to do it in our day-by-day lives and in our relationships with our fellowmen.

Some people in the world today do not see law as the instrument of freedom and justice. Too frequently the whole tradition of *stare decisis* appears to tie the law to the status quo; and a written constitution means little to a man who cannot remember his last meal and does not know where his next one is coming from.

I recently returned from some weeks in Asia where I had ample opportunity to discuss the world with young men and women for whom hunger and poverty have been familiar realities. Those talks reminded me again of the extent to which emphasis on law, as such, and constitutionalism as such, often seem the self-righteous excuse used by those who have to justify their exploitation of those who have not.

I found much greater misunderstanding about our system of government and the real aspirations and motivations of the American people than I had expected. In some countries, articulate, disciplined Communists have been able to seize on weaknesses and inconsistencies in our system and distort or magnify them out of all proportion, with the result that great misconceptions about America go virtually unanswered.

In Indonesia and Japan, for example, I found bright, alert young leaders accepting Communist descriptions of the United States which were seventy-five and one hundred years out of date.

In Africa, Asia and South America, the number of educated young men and women is increasing dramatically. Education is equipping these young people to fill leadership roles in their countries and they will be the leaders of the 1970's and the 1980's. In Japan today there are more than 600,000 college students. In Indonesia there are approximately 30,000, where before the war there were only a few hundred.

There is a great deal that we can do to convince them that freedom is the way of the future. We can and must do better in making available to them the facts about us and our way of life—to make it clear that we will not accept the status quo; that we are not a selfish people interested only in ourselves and our pocketbooks; but that we are tough, industrious people who are interested in our fellow citizens and in advancing the cause of freedom.

We must impress upon them that our system of government has made great progress in the last sixty years; that our way of life is far different from what Marx described 100 years ago, and that this progress has been made under the banner of freedom.

If we do not meet this problem head on—if we are not ourselves imaginative, dedicated, willing and self-sacrificing—the struggle for the minds of the leaders of tomorrow will not be won by the Communists, but lost by us.

As we act to meet this challenge, let us resolve here not to do so only to convince people across the seas, but because we are dedicated to the proposition that liberty and law are inseparable; that we truly believe social progress strengthens and enlarges freedom.

Let us never forget that we are the descendants of the greatest revolutionaries the world has ever known—men who succeeded in this country by overthrowing a more powerful nation's rule and in establishing this Nation because they were more aware of their goals, more vigorous in pursuing them, more tightly bound together and more combative in spirit.

And, finally, let us do so because ours is the better road—the road of law applied to immediate problems, gradually altered as the ways of life change, enforced by courts of law open to the public with the blinding glare of the free press upon those who judge and are judged.

We do not say that our courts are perfect; that our judges all possess the wisdom of Solomon, or that our prosecutors are all without selfish interests or even malice. But what we must be able to say is that, on the whole, our judicial system does provide justice and does recognize equality under the law.

The travail of freedom and justice is not easy; but nothing serious and important in life is easy. The history of humanity has been a continuing struggle against temptation and tyranny—and very little worthwhile has even been achieved without pain.

So, as we unite on this May 1 to celebrate the rule of law—while men and women in remote parts of the world march in disciplined ranks to celebrate the rule of arbitrary power—let us with courage and confidence rededicate ourselves to the vision of John Marshall— the vision of a free republic in which free men freely use law and government as the means of solving problems within a framework of equity and justice.

And let us be constantly aware that what we do here in the United States—first remaining militarily prepared so that there can be no doubt about our ability to defend ourselves; second, making social progress in such domestic areas as employment, health and civil rights; and third, remaining true to our ideals of justice under the law. How well we do in all of these areas in the next ten years, may well determine our future position in the world for many years thereafter.

part iii A LONG, HARD LOOK

During the first year of the Kennedy Administration, the President did not recommend civil rights legislation, contending that progress could be made without it. The Attorney General concurred. But the start of the second year, January 25, 1962, saw the majority leader, Senator Mike Mansfield of Montana join with Senator Everett McKinley Dirksen of Illinois to introduce a bill designed to ban unfair literacy tests used to prevent qualified citizens from voting. This bill was advocated by the Attorney General from its inception.

On May 5, 1962, in a speech to members of the American Jewish Committee, Robert Kennedy expounded at length as to the need for the passage of this bill. Thus was the Administration fully committed to new civil rights legislation even though on so limited a scale. Congress, however, did not pass it. Parenthetically, it might be added that the same fate met bills submitted from time to time by other Congressmen of both Houses and from both major political parties.

Other signs of change were seen. After more than a year of concentrated service to the cause of civil rights—with considerable success—the President and his Attorney General could see more clearly the extent of the problem.

Robert Kennedy now referred to the civil rights struggle as "the paramount internal issue in this country" and as involving "a long term process." The extent of the effort being made to deal with this issue, he pointed out, was indicated by the fact that the President, the Federal Government, and "the vast majority of the American people" were anxious to move ahead in this field. But he also warned that there might be "some setbacks and some difficult turns," and that the struggle would go on "for some years to come."

In indicating the vastness of the problem, he was not vague in discussing what had to be done. Nor was he reticent when it came to making specific and practical suggestions as to what the members of his audience could do to help quicken progress. For example, in his address before members of the National Insurance Association on July 26, 1962, he gave his listeners a list of possible actions they could perform. And at the Seattle World's Fair on August 7 he asked the members of his audience not to deceive themselves about the difficulties which lay ahead and then stated his conviction: "We cannot stand idly by and expect our dreams to come true under their own power. The future is not a gift. It is an achievement. Every generation helps make its own future. This is the essential challenge of the present."

Two of the speeches delivered in this phase are given to law audiences. On August 6 the Attorney General spoke as a fellow lawyer to the House of Delegates of the American Bar Association, making a plea for the indigent's right to counsel and justice. In his speech of September 29, Mr. Kennedy elaborated on this theme and other "causes" when, in his most winning manner, he urged law students at the University of San Francisco to display courage and charity in their dedication to justice.

Delivered before the American Jewish Committee
New York City, May 5, 1962

It is a great pleasure to be here tonight as a guest of the American Jewish Committee. As you know, the Committee was established in 1906 to work for the fundamental aspirations of the American People —the truths that Jefferson enunciated in the Declaration of Independence. It has lived up to its ideals and I congratulate you.

Among its founders were such distinguished Americans as Louis Marshall, Jacob Schiff, Julius Rosenwald, Adolph Lewisohn, Cyrus Adler, Meyer Sulzberger and Felix Warburg—all men who contributed greatly to the advancement of freedom and equality of opportunity that are so essential to the realization of the American dream.

And their work has been continued by such outstanding Americans as Senator Lehmann whose selfless public service and staunch dedication to his principles and beliefs are an inspiration to all of us.

This organization has made an outstanding contribution to this country and to the American people. It is the kind of contribution so typical of America and the type of voluntary service by individuals in the interests of their fellow human beings that is a hallmark of the American character.

I am also happy to be here to pay my respects to Judge Thurgood Marshall. It would be difficult to name another individual who has worked harder than Judge Marshall for the protection and realization of those civil liberties and civil rights that Jefferson so happily phrased.

As pleased as I am, in one sense, I was sorry to see Judge Marshall elevated to the bench. He was a fighter in the front ranks, both courageous and competent.

We need men of his caliber in this struggle—which, in my opinion, is the paramount internal issue in this country and which must be fought and won within the framework of our democratic system.

As a judge, he now becomes an arbiter of the requirements of our Constitution and of the responsibilities of our citizens. He brings the same integrity and good judgment in interpreting these matters as he has demonstrated throughout his career.

The eradication of racial and religious prejudice in the United States—and in the rest of the world as well—is a long-term process.

What I think distinguishes the United States is the great effort now being made to deal with this problem. The President and the Federal Government are working diligently toward that end. Further, the vast majority of the American people are aware of the problem and anxious to do something about it. And I do not exclude any section of the United States. The vast majority of the people—North, East, South and West—want to get something done and more ahead in this field.

How different from the Soviet Union where the attacks on religious and racial minorities are hidden from public view; where the government itself recently deposed a number of Jewish religious leaders in religious congregations; and where only a few months ago the *Communist Party Journal* attacked the Jehovah's Witnesses and Seventh Day Adventists as "poisonous religious narcotics."

We live in a free and open society and we do not hide our faults behind a wall or try to bury our mistakes or conceal incidents, however shameful. As a result, the whole world knows that we have racial and religious intolerance. The great effort being made by the American Government and the American people to eradicate it is not as well known or understood around the world.

Legal action in this battle is a prime concern of the Department of Justice. We move, sometimes not as fast as we would like, but we move with all the speed we can.

And in the past sixteen months we have dislodged stones in our path which, I believe, in the future will become an avalanche destroying forever the prejudices and injustices that exist today.

We are focusing our efforts at this time on mobilizing support for legislation which will end abuses in the administration of state literacy requirements.

This legislation would ban the unfair use of literacy tests to prevent literate persons from voting. The right to vote is basic to our system of government and the history of the United States demonstrates that as minority groups have achieved the vote their lot has improved. Intolerance and prejudice have not disappeared, but when a minority has made itself felt at the ballot box, there has been greater opportunity for advancement and discrimination has gradually disappeared.

We are taking this legislative action even though we feel a great deal of progress has been made in the last year in lessening discrimination through administrative work.

In the field of transportation alone, more than one hundred bus terminals and more than two hundred railroad terminals have been desegregated.

There has been a major drive to eliminate discrimination in employment. The Vice President's Committee has been particularly effective in this effort.

Further, race and religion have been no bar to employment for responsible positions in the Government.

For example, Negroes of ability and integrity have been appointed for the first time as United States Attorneys, District Judges and to many other important offices. They haven't been hired because they were Negroes, but they were not denied the opportunity to hold these positions because of their color. That is what is important.

Much of the Administration's effort has been done quietly in talks and meetings with local officials in areas where there have been violations of civil rights. In the vast majority of cases, local officials have taken action to correct the situation.

For six months prior to the opening of school last fall, we met with school officials in areas where it was predicted that there would be difficulties and troubles when schools were desegregated for the first time.

Nothing was published about these meetings. Nothing was written about them. That should not be, nor was it the objective. We were interested in having these schools opened last September without violence, and that's exactly what happened.

However, despite this progress, we have come to the conclusion that there is need for legislation—and that the most pressing need and the one with the best chance of success is in eliminating discrimination in voting. That is why we are making a major effort at this time to eliminate the unfair use of literacy tests and that is why I would like to talk about it for a few minutes.

Why is such legislation important? In four cases in which the Department has participated, just this week, unfair application of literacy tests was the means used in each case to deny a substantial number of American citizens the right to vote because of their color.

In one case a Negro, who has a National Science Foundation research grant, was declared "illiterate" and, therefore, denied the right to vote.

In the files of the Department of Justice are hundreds of examples of similar situations. College professors, school teachers and ministers have been declared illiterate while white applicants in the same districts who have attended only the second or third grade have been declared literate and permitted to vote.

The method and means of discrimination take many forms. In one district, Negro applicants who stated their names in four different places on one application form were rejected because they failed to insert it in a fifth place.

In another state, some Negro applicants were asked to explain "due process of law" to a registrar who had no legal training. Needless to say, none succeeded. Whites on the other hand were not asked a similar question.

In still another state, a Negro college graduate was denied registration because he mispronounced a Latin phrase in a state constitution.

So the legislation we advocate recognizes a fact of our national life—that persons who have completed the sixth grade are qualified to vote and are fully capable of intelligent participation in the democratic processes by any reasonable standard fairly applied.

States' rights to set voting standards would not be affected in any way whatsoever. All that this legislation would do would be to prevent any person who had at least a sixth grade education from being declared illiterate—because of his color—but if a state wanted to require that its voters have completed the eighth grade, the tenth grade, or be college graduates, it would have every right to do so. Just as long as it established criteria which it applied straight across the board and did not use for the purpose of preventing a certain class of persons from voting, we would have no quarrel, it would be perfectly legal.

We can and are taking action to remedy the situation through the courts on a county-by-county basis and we have made significant progress. A year ago, the Federal Government was actively attacking voting discrimination in only about a dozen counties. Now we are at work in more than one hundred counties.

But, as I said in Roanoke, Virginia, earlier this week, the problem is so deep-seated and so manifestly unfair, that I believe it demands a solution which cannot be achieved by lengthy legislation on a piecemeal basis in the courts.

In one recent case, we had to examine in detail some 36,000 voting records; take testimony from 180 witnesses at the trial and have four lawyers devote full time for several months to prepare the case.

Hundreds of thousands of our fellow Americans are being denied the right to vote through these tests. This bill would be a major step in remedying the situation. It can be done quickly and easily by Congress, for the right to vote is the easiest right to grant.

This legislation would remedy the situation in the South, but it also would remedy a serious problem here in New York where many citizens of Puerto Rican origin are unable to vote.

These persons were educated under the American flag in schools in which Spanish is the classroom language. By virtue of an Act of Congress, the United States assumed a special obligation to the citizens of Puerto Rico. Part of that obligation has been fulfilled by granting them full American citizenship.

This bill would be a desirable and necessary additional step by removing discrimination based solely on the language in which they have been educated, in the schools for which we have a heavy responsibility.

They are literate citizens, and they can be intelligent voters. The numerous Spanish-language news media available here in New York and in the United States amply inform their readers and listeners about public issues.

In my opinion, we have a national obligation to eliminate the causes of their inability to vote.

This legislation is now being debated in the Senate, and there are great problems and difficulties in getting past procedural hurdles. There is no doubt that a majority of the Senators favor the bill.

Because of the extremely difficult procedural problems the easy thing to do would be not to press for its passage at this time.

But Senator Mansfield is making a strong effort. The critical votes are expected to come within the next two weeks. Regardless of the outcome, we will continue to press for this legislation until it is passed.

President Wilson once said: "I believe in democracy because it releases the energy of every human being."

In these times we need the vigor and the faith of every American as we seek to advance the cause of freedom in a period of perilous cold war. To thwart thousands of our fellow Americans from participating fully in the processes of our Government is to weaken that vigor and to dilute that faith, and we cannot afford it.

But, this is only one aspect of the fight which we must win.

We want and must always want a world of free men. Our record testifies to our desire to see men of different races achieve their own destinies in such fashion as they choose—while respecting those principles of regard for life, individual liberty, and happiness to which we are dedicated. But if we are to remain the leaders in the fight for freedom, we must achieve here at home a full measure of freedom and social progress for all Americans.

In this struggle, our greatest assets are that we have the truth on our side and that we believe that the state exists for the individual —not the individual for the state.

These are the things which we can offer which our opponents can never match. They can compete with us in material progress—in getting to the moon and constructing the Aswan Dam in Egypt and in building mills and power plants in India. But they must wall their people in, conceal their failures, and hide their weaknesses and mistakes.

And so, our ability to give greater meaning to our basic principles here at home is as important as the race for outer space, the race for equality, if not for superiority in nuclear weapons. And I urge you constantly to concern yourselves with it.

Our future outside our borders will in large part be decided by what we do within the United States. The History of Jewry for over a thousand years has been a history of tribulation, but never during those years a history of spiritual bondage. Its ideas about the relationship of man to the state are those of the democratic world.

As it has requested, vainly at times, tolerance, so it in turn bears a message of tolerance, of charity toward all. This is the fight you have been waging for over fifty years and you can take pride in what you have achieved.

But since your ideals are not only those of Judaism, but of America, the importance of your efforts to us of a different faith must not go unnoticed.

All of us must be one with regard to our support of the basic principles of freedom. They are the reasons that make for loyalty to our United States; they are the reasons that should govern our actions abroad as well as at home.

Life, liberty, and happiness, without qualification, without discrimination on grounds of race or religion, must continue to be the credo of American life and it should be plainly exportable.

Barriers have been created against it; witness, as I have witnessed, the Berlin Wall. But barriers to ideas, as all history has demonstrated, are eventually futile.

You have dedicated yourselves to the ideas of truth and justice, whatever the barriers. May God bless you as we all thank you in the furtherance of your undertakings in behalf of these great principles.

Delivered before the
National Newspaper Publishers Association
Morgan State College, Baltimore, Maryland, June 22, 1962

I would like to talk with you tonight about the biggest domestic news story of our time.

You are deeply involved in this story. Your readers demand news about it; you are personally affected by it; and you can have a great deal to do with how it turns out.

The story broke almost a hundred years ago. Negroes were emancipated and shortly thereafter the Constitution was amended to guarantee them the full rights of citizenship. But not since that time has so much been happening in the field of civil rights.

It is an unhappy thing that it has taken so long to implement fully the Thirteenth, Fourteenth and Fifteenth Amendments, but this is not the time to deplore the inaction of the past. It is the time to do something about it.

And we are doing things about civil rights.

I know that some are unhappy that the story is not breaking fast enough, but things are happening; the pace is quickening.

First, we are moving to make sure that every American is free to exercise his right to register and vote.

There are now investigations and court actions going on in almost a hundred counties. There are also follow-up actions to insure that court orders are carried out and that those who come forward to assert their rights are not intimidated. Eighteen court suits have been instituted to order registrars and voting officials to allow qualified Negroes to vote.

One example of voting rights action is typical of the pattern. Macon County, Alabama, is a rural county, but it is the home of famed Tuskegee Institute and thus, the home of many distinguished and well-educated Negroes.

Yet at the beginning of 1961, only a handful of Negroes were allowed to vote in Macon County. On March 17 of that year we obtained a voting rights injunction. Today there are over 2,600 Negroes registered to vote in Macon County and they are voting.

This progress doesn't come about with the wave of a magic wand. It takes work. In one voting case, we had to examine in detail some 36,000 voting records, take testimony from 180 witnesses at the trial and have four lawyers devote full time for several months to prepare the case.

The ramifications of their vote are just beginning to be felt. When they are joined at the polls by Negroes over all the state, the South and the country, I think the civil rights of all our citizens will be better protected.

But we are moving ahead on other fronts as well. Negroes are now serving in important posts in the government—not just jobs created for them or jobs which deal with minority groups.

For the first time Negroes are serving on the United States District Court in the continental United States and the United States Attorneys in two of our largest cities are Negroes.

Progress like this requires affirmative action to overcome centuries of blind adherence to tradition and prejudice. When we came to the Department of Justice, which is responsible for enforcing the laws including those which deal with civil rights, we found that there were only ten Negroes employed as attorneys. Today there are five or six times that number.

These men were not appointed because they were Negroes. They were chosen because we need dedicated, able people in our Government, and we are not foolish enough to deny ourselves the services of such people because of the color of their skin.

Private industry is also beginning to comprehend the folly of racial barriers. President Kennedy announced this afternoon that thirty-three more companies have come forward with affirmative plans to assure equal employment opportunities in their hiring and promotion systems. In all, eighty-five companies with close to five million employees have such plans.

This progress has been brought about by the work of the President's Committee on Equal Employment Opportunities under the leadership of the Vice-President. They will continue to work to see that there is more.

Where voluntary action is not forthcoming from those who do business with the government, we are taking action.

In the field of education, the Federal Government is taking an active role assisting local officials to expedite school integration. We are not waiting until the situation gets to the point where troops are the only answer. Last year, for the first time, the school opening season passed without violence but with desegregation.

Where the Government has standing to do so, we are insisting that local officials move quickly to end segregation in their schools.

Tremendous progress has been made to eliminate racial segregation in interstate transportation.

Hundreds of bus and rail terminals have been desegregated over the past year.

I can announce tonight that fourteen of the few airports still maintaining racial segregation have abolished it voluntarily in the recent months.

Six of these are in Mississippi—Natchez, Jackson, Meridian, Tupelo, Hattiesburg, and Columbus.

Two are in Louisiana—Baton Rouge and Pineville; two in Arkansas—Fort Smith and Texarkana.

In addition, Columbus, Georgia; Raleigh-Durham, North Carolina; Greenville, South Carolina; and Mobile, Alabama have taken voluntary action.

This week we filed suits to enjoin two of the last holdouts from maintaining segregation and within a very short time, it will be possible to fly to any airport in the country without seeing "White" and "Colored" signs.

In all these problems—in voting, in schools, in employment, in transportation—we seek voluntary compliance. We meet with the responsible officials and try to work out the situation with them.

In many, many cases, this procedure achieved progress. Public and private officials throughout the South deserve credit for what they have done in the face of often difficult circumstances.

But I want to make it clear that when we cannot get voluntary action we will continue to go to court to enforce the laws of the United States on discrimination just as we enforce them on narcotics, gambling or anything else.

This progress does not mean that all is well. As you know, there is much more to be done.

All our schools are still not open to everyone who seeks admittance. All jobs are not awarded on merit alone. In some places the way to the ballot is still not easy for the Negro.

Even though there has been no civil rights legislation in this or the last session of the Congress, we are not wavering in our determination to press for needed legislation. We do need laws to help us, particularly in the field of voting rights where unfair literacy tests are a major barrier to voting.

You can help in this effort. The Congress as well as the Executive is responsible to your demands if you make them known effectively.

There has been far too much hypocrisy in the field of civil rights. It is easy enough to give rousing speeches or call for legislation which has no possibility of passage.

But the President is anxious to accomplish things, not merely talk about them. When he saw the Coast Guard march by in the Inaugural Parade and did not see a Negro in the group, he took action to see that this was corrected. When he reviewed an honor guard greeting a visiting African dignitary at the airport and did not see a Negro in the unit, he took action to correct this.

These are but examples of the things that can be done with existing laws, and they are being done. In my opinion, the vast majority of the people of this country—North, East, South and West—want to move ahead in civil rights, and this government is responsive to the wishes of the people.

Newspapers can generate action in this country. They not only record current history, they help to determine what course it will take.

This is particularly true at the community level. Where there is an aggressive, vigilant, honest newspaper there is likely to be a progressive, clean community. Where the newspapers are fat and lazy, the community is in danger of becoming a backwater festering corruption, vice and indifference.

You who serve the Negro communities have a particularly heavy responsibility.

Timothy Thomas Fortune, was a distinguished newspaperman of the 19th century who served as editor of the *New York Age* and as a member of the editorial staff of the *New York Evening Sun*. He summed up the role of the Negro newspaper this way:

> Some declare that colored newspapers are a nuisance; and so they are, in a measure, just as the colored people are a nuisance, in

so far as they have a grievance which they persistently obtrude upon the notice of others, who either have no such grievances themselves, or do not wish to be reminded of the fact that they have one. As long, however, as men are struck, they will cry out in protest or indignation until the wrongs are avenged.

You must continue to perform this function of crying out in protest of indignation, but you have an added responsibility as well.

Your coverage of this big story of our time, the civil rights story, will determine, in large measure, the attitude of the Negro community.

If your stories are sensation-seeking, slanted or vindictive, the Negro community will mirror this attitude. If you dwell upon the remaining flaws and do not report the progress as well, disillusionment will follow.

I do not suggest that you be soft on prejudice and discrimination. You have a duty to bring these facts to light wherever they appear, and attack them vigilantly.

But I do suggest that you also have a duty to report in full the progress that is being made and the work that is going on. It is easy enough to crusade against wrongdoing; it is sometimes difficult to give credit when credit is due.

For instance, when officials in the South enforce segregation, when they make arrests in racial cases or when there is police brutality, it is reported in depth and it should be.

But by the same rule, when officials in the South bring about desegregation, and often they do this in the face of strong local opposition, they should be given credit.

One of the most exciting developments in the civil rights story has been the work of citizens committees in Atlanta, Dallas, Memphis, and other cities. These bi-racial committees have brought integration to their schools in a peaceful, orderly manner.

Solid, plugging committee work may not have the headline appeal of an incident of violence, but it is far more important. This kind of news should be reported, as well as the violence, if the story is to be in proper perspective.

And as newspapermen, you have a responsibility to give your readers the full story.

Responsibility is the key word. We in this country are proud of our free and open society. It is one of the safeguards of our freedom.

If there is a racial incident in any corner of the United States, within hours it is flashed around the world. The Communists seize upon it for their propaganda mill.

We don't hear of the East Europeans who are daily whisked away to jails for seeking only a fraction of the freedom we enjoy.

But we would not have it any other way. Our newspapers must be free to report every facet of American life for this is not only a freedom guaranteed to them but a guarantee of freedom for all Americans.

With liberty for the press, as with all liberties, comes responsibility. Newspapers occupy a position of trust to the public to report to them all the news—not just that which they wish to read or that which an editor thinks they should read.

Your trust with the Negro community is an important part of race relations in the United States today. This is a time of great excitement.

Long delayed gains are being won. The process has accelerated to a point where ferment is inevitable. This ferment is bound to cause emotional upheavals and some bitterness—from those who think the process is too fast and those who think it is too slow.

The exertion of leadership and the exercise of responsibility always bring some scorn from radical elements in our society. But the transition we are making must be made within the patterns of law which are set by our Constitution and within the framework of our Federal system. So the responsibility for exerting leadership is not something that can be avoided, but something that must be faced.

Radical charges, impossible demands and unwarranted accusations will not help. They will hinder the efforts of those who are trying to make real progress.

Sensationalism will add acrimony to controversy but it will not help settle problems. There are enough color problems without adding that of "yellow journalism." Full knowledge of the facts presented fairly and objectively will help by bringing about understanding.

So I urge you to continue to banner across your front pages any discrimination in schools, voting, or employment.

But I also urge you to banner across the same pages the news that the "For White Only" signs are coming down; that Negroes are registering and voting as never before; and that new employment opportunities are opening up every day.

Your responsible reporting will do your readers a great service and it will do the Nation a great service. If the story is told fully and well, understanding and cooperation will be much easier, and we need understanding and cooperation to make progress. You are in a position to help provide it.

Newspapermen and those of us who are charged with enforcing the law are, in a sense, in the same business. We gather facts. We seek the truth. I hope we can work together more closely on the story in which we are both interested.

I hope that you as the leaders of the Negro newspaper world will consider yourselves as an unofficial advisory committee to the Department of Justice in the enforcement of civil rights.

We are available 24 hours a day to hear anything of importance you have to report to us. We are also available to give you the information you need to do your job.

You are a group of newspapermen to whom a great opportunity has been given. You are on top of one of the biggest news stories of our time.

The story will go on for some years to come. There may be some setbacks and some difficult turns. I cannot predict all the developments. But I can tell you how it will end.

No American will be denied his human rights or his Constitutional rights because of his race, creed, or religion.

And when the final line of this story is filed, I hope that Negro Journalists will be able to say with pride that they helped solve our major domestic problems by meeting their responsibilities as newspapermen.

Delivered before the National Insurance Association
Los Angeles, California, July 26, 1962

I am extremely happy to be here with you tonight to participate in the 42nd Annual Convention of the National Insurance Association. I would like to join in paying my respects to President Theodore Jones and the past presidents of this fine organization.

In 42 years your Association has made an enviable record. Your progress and similar progress which we see all around us has convinced me that the day is not far off when no American will be denied full rights of citizenship because of the color of his skin or because of his beliefs. I say this because the record shows that gains are being made faster than at any time since the Civil War.

In the past year and a half, the Federal government has been able to move forward in the civil rights field with heartening success in at least four areas.

First, on the key issue of voting, a much greater effort is being made to win the franchise for Negroes in the South. This is basic to all the rights of citizenship and from it all other rights flow.

Under the Civil Rights Acts of 1957 and 1960, the Department of Justice has the responsibility of assuring that the ballot is not denied to qualified voters because of race, creed, or color.

A total of thirty court actions have been brought to uphold this right, twenty in the past fifteen months. Investigations have been carried out or are under way in over one hundred counties.

. . . . .

We sponsored a bill which would have prevented any states from using so-called literacy tests to prevent qualified individuals from voting. Unfortunately, this bill failed, but we will make an effort to have similar legislation enacted next year; and meanwhile, we will continue to investigate and bring cases where necessary.

A second area of progress has been in employment. More and more Americans are being hired on merit and not being denied a chance to work because of the color of their skin.

This has long been the policy of the Federal Government, but we are taking action to see that equal employment opportunity is not just a pious declaration but a reality.

. . . . .

Private industry is also coming to learn the folly and inefficiency of discrimination.

Eighty-five major companies who do business with the government have been persuaded to develop plans assuring equal opportunity in hiring and advancement for their employees. This has been accomplished in cooperation with the President's Committee on Equal Employment Opportunity. This is only one part of the Committee's activities. Its compliance program has been established on a strong basis and reaches far beyond anything of this type ever done by the Federal Government or any state. Where voluntary action is not forthcoming, the Committee is moving to see that discrimination is eliminated.

For example, the compliance staff of the Vice President's Committee has just completed an agreement with four refineries in Lake Charles, Louisiana. These plants, with the approval of the previous administration's committee on equal employment, had completely segregated facilities—even parking lots—and in job opportunities had excluded Negroes entirely from fifteen out of seventeen categories.

One of the categories open was that of laborer and for the other category, Negroes, but not whites, were required to have high school educations. Under the new agreement all seventeen of the job categories are open to Negroes on their merits, both by the refineries and by the unions involved, and Negroes are now working in jobs which had been completely closed to them before.

Another agreement was just concluded this week in Birmingham, Alabama, with the largest industrial unit in that city—Tennessee Coal and Iron. Under this agreement a dual system of seniority is going to be eliminated for the first time and Negro employees are standing on the same footing in layoffs and promotions as their white fellow employees. The completely segregated employment offices have already been integrated.

A positive approach also is being taken toward school desegregation.

We are not waiting until violence occurs when the meeting of force with force is the only alternative. The Federal Government is protecting the integrity of court orders and working with local citizens and officials to bring about desegregation peacefully and with respect for the law.

Last year, for the first time since the Supreme Court decision, school desegregation was accomplished without violence. This just didn't happen. The credit belongs to local officials and citizens but I am proud of the assistance the Government was able to provide.

Segregation has virtually disappeared from interstate transportation.

However, much remains to be done and this Administration understands its responsibility to continue working hard to remove racial discrimination in other areas. The job will not be completed until every American has full access to all rights of citizenship in every corner of the land. I am firmly convinced that this day is coming because the vast majority of American people in the South, as well as in the North, East and West, want to make progress and they are not satisfied to accept the status quo.

On Washington's birthday in 1861, President-elect Abraham Lincoln spoke in Independence Hall on his way to Washington. He spoke of the men who wrote and fought for the Declaration of Independence. He said its essence was its promise "not only of liberty to the people of this country, but hope of the world . . . that in due time the weights should be lifted from the shoulders of all men and that all should have an equal chance."

This is more true today than it was 186 years ago. On my recent trip around the world, wherever I spoke—in every meeting with officials, students, businessmen, and labor leaders, I was asked about the civil rights problems here in the United States. We are not going to be able to convince people in other lands that we mean what we say in the Declaration of Independence and in our Constitution if a large number of our citizens are denied their full rights.

So we have a clear-cut responsibility, I, as Attorney General, and you, as businessmen who have been highly successful in your careers. First and foremost, we must work to attain the vote for all our fellow citizens. But the problem is greater because the achievement of full legal and political rights will create new challenges. And these cannot be met by legal action or by the courts or even by legislation. Essentially, these challenges involve our young people.

With automation and the increasing demand for higher and higher skills, the young people who have not completed their schooling will be at a great disadvantage. From this group will come the greatest number of malcontents, criminals and persons who will have little faith in freedom and democratic ways.

A high percentage of the dropouts come from Negro and other minority groups. A recent study of youth employment problems in

New York City shows that while the overall unemployment rate for high school graduates and school dropouts is between 15 and 20%, in some low income minority neighborhoods, the number of unemployed out-of-school youths is as high as 70%.

President Kennedy recently said:

> Our youth are our greatest resource and the social and economic implications of protracted unemployment among the one million young job seekers today the many millions who will enter the labor force in the next few years demand immediate attention and action.

I urge you to interest yourselves in this problem, which is so important to the future well-being of our youth and our country. As men who have been successful, you can command attention and respect. Businessmen in every community—working with social, educational and religious organizations—can make a great contribution by helping our young people as they prepare themselves for the world of the 60's and the 70's. Here are a few things that you can do specifically and which I pledge tonight to work with you in trying to accomplish:

—Work for better schools and job training in your communities;

—Encourage high school students to stay in school and encourage those who have left to return, even to night classes;

—Arrange for loans for students who need them;

—Give high school students guidance as to the trades to prepare for and the training needed for these trades;

—Provide both high school and college students with information and guidance on possible future careers and help with the selection of schools and courses to prepare for these careers;

—Help graduates find jobs by providing guidance and contacts.

These are just a few suggestions, and I'm sure you can find many, many more.

I hope that those Americans who are desirous of doing something for their country will give increasing attention to the millions of young people who need guidance and assistance. The Federal Government, under the President's leadership, has taken a number of steps to widen employment opportunities for youths and to assist local communities in employing all their resources to meet this problem. We want to make sure that every American has a chance to develop his talent. Education is basic but the Federal Government cannot do this job. It must be done at the local level by men and women like yourselves.

And that is why I feel it is a privilege to come here and talk with you about these problems because they involve us all.

The great French Marshal, Lyautey, once asked his gardener to plant a tree. The gardener objected that the tree was slow-growing and would not reach maturity for one hundred years. The Marshal replied, "In that case, there's no time to lose. Plant it this afternoon."

Our youths have long lives ahead of them. Today an America of equal opportunity for all its citizens is just around the corner and we have no time to lose. Let's plant our trees this evening.

Delivered before the
American Bar Association House of Delegates
San Francisco, California, August 6, 1962

I am delighted to have this chance to speak today before this convention of the American Bar Association. Our system of judicial administration requires the closest possible cooperation between the Department of Justice and the lawyers of the land; and as Attorney General, I appreciate the opportunity to discuss matters of common concern with the distinguished representatives of the bar whom I find in this room today.

Every department in the Executive Branch regards its mission as indispensable to the functioning of our democracy. But I cannot help feeling that the Department of Justice has a special and urgent responsibility, for the quest for justice is the very heart of the democratic experiment.

This, in my view, is a central and continuing obligation of the Attorney General's office as it must be for every lawyer. In meeting that responsibility I am heartened by the knowledge that we have the support, not only of our whole ethical and political tradition, but more particularly of the men and women who must see that the system operates and expands in this modern society of immense and unforeseen problems, of men, like yourselves, trained in the ideals and processes of Anglo-Saxon justice.

It has never been more important than it is today that free society display its capacity for justice. For here at home and all around the globe our system stands on trial before the world—our beliefs and our actions are pitted against a determined and resourceful and disciplined adversary—while in our own land urbanization, automation, the demand for equal rights in an age of bigness, all bear down upon us with a host of new and pressing problems.

Today, the advances of technology have become so rapid that frequently they tend to outstrip our capacity to deal with their impact upon our social and industrial system. Land urbanization has intensified a host of old problems, besides introducing new ones.

Automation is causing a situation in many areas of our country similar to 19th century England when the handicraft of a feudal age was replaced by the machine-craft of the industrial age. The rise of associational activity has brought its special problems into the field of monopoly and restraint of trade, into the organizational activities of labor unions, and into the dark and dirty world of crime.

The very complexity of modern life makes it easy for individual liberties to be disregarded. More and more American people must rely on the law for the protection of these liberties.

It is here that you and I have such a heavy responsibility. For it rests on us to be certain that the legal protections so necessary for the individual do not become merely fine declarations in the lawbooks but that they actually have some real and genuine meaning for the human beings to whom they have been granted. This task requires the care and attention of the whole legal profession.

At the Department of Justice, we are just part of this effort and as such have our limitations.

We recognize for instance that the line between what the Federal Government can and should do and what state and local authorities can and should do is often shadowy. Frequently it is the sum total of these efforts that counts. For this reason it is vital that we work closely and continuously with local authorities in achieving our common objectives.

No issue brings the role of the individual into sharper focus than that of civil rights. I am proud of the record of the Department of Justice in recent months in striving to assure all citizens the full rights guaranteed them under the Constitution of the United States.

Assistant Attorney General Burke Marshall and his aides are performing a distinguished service in this respect—a service which goes far beyond instituting and prosecuting cases in the Federal courts. We have not filed a single civil rights case without first going to the local authorities. We have informed them of what appears to us to be a violation of the law, for, the Constitution being the law of the land, the local authorities—judges, prosecutors and lawyers—have an equal obligation to protect and defend it.

In the majority of cases, the local officials have taken action and nothing further has been required of the Federal Government. There are no front page stories, but there are changes; there are results and they are brought about by local officials—not the Government in Washington. In the long run this is what is of real importance in this country.

Sometimes the local authorities have disagreed with us about the law, and we have gone to court. On other occasions, local authorities were unwilling to remedy the situation, or could not because of what they believed to be the political facts of life, and so court action was necessary.

In all this effort Burke Marshall has been in the forefront, negotiating, prodding, advising, persuading—working with explosive problems and devising solutions which fulfill the law of our land and the ideals of our nation. This is the historic role of the lawyer in the fullest sense.

I am proud, too, of those Federal judges who have seen and done their duty under difficult circumstances. A judge's popularity or unpopularity is of no proper concern to him in the performance of his judicial duties. Yet to do that duty—to give an honest reading of the Constitution and of the law of the land—may and often does require great courage.

I might add that this is also the sworn obligation of every lawyer. If the bar has done much to assist in the orderly realization of constitutional rights, I would be less than candid if I did not tell you that I believe more can and should be done.

Another area of concern to every private citizen—and to every lawyer—is the war against organized crime. Crime is not only a cause of economic waste, but far worse that that, it is a reproach to the moral pretensions of our society, and advertises to the world the gap between our pronouncements and our performance.

The battle against crime must have a top priority in protecting individual rights. We have heard much about the rights of the individual and with this I have no quarrel, but the general public also has some rights that need to be protected. We have made some encouraging gains in the last twenty months.

The Criminal Division for the first time is spearheading a coordinated drive by all Federal law enforcement agencies to reduce the entrenched power and wealth of organized crime to the point where it can be controlled by local authorities. Desperately needed legislation has been enacted in a bipartisan effort. Intensive investigations are being conducted into the corruption of public officials where unfortunately the inroads of organized crime are particularly frightening. We are moving forward in a systematic way but we have far to go.

A third field of prime consequence to individual rights is the protection of the competitive forces in our system of private enterprise. This is, perhaps, the most technical and complicated field with which the Department is concerned.

Obviously, there are certain areas of the Antitrust law where the guidelines have been set so definitively that no excuse for transgressing them properly can be made. This is true, for example, of conspiracies to fix prices or to apportion territories. In such cases there can be no hesitancy on the part of the Government to act.

In many other areas, however, there are complex economic situations which require deep study and understanding when action is contemplated. The Antitrust laws should be vigorously enforced but they are weapons which should be utilized to help the consumer, the businessman both large and small, and to protect and preserve the free enterprise system. That is our intention. That is our effort.

In all of these matters, as well as the many others that come within our mutual area of responsibility, I cannot help but be concerned as to whether, despite the efforts of dedicated public officials and conscientious lawyers—there is in fact equal justice before the law here in the United States. I am speaking now of a concern for whether there is true equality in the administration of justice.

I ask you—do members of ethnic or political minorities or people who speak our language imperfectly or who have low mentality or disturbed minds; or the largest group, those who are poor really receive the same protection before the courts as the rest of our citizens? I say that all too often they do not.

I need hardly say to this audience that everyone in this land—whether immigrant or pauper, alleged crook or Communist—is innocent until proven guilty and is entitled to as fair a trial and as competent representation as, say, leading citizens accused of price-fixing in business or of corruption in labor.

It seems to me that our obligation—your obligation as attorneys in private practice and my obligation as Attorney General—is to make the assurance of fair and equal treatment to all before the law one of our first concerns.

Judge Learned Hand, speaking at the 75th Anniversary of the Legal Aid Society of New York, said if we are to keep our democracy, there must be one commandment: "Thou shalt not ration justice."

Let me discuss with you just a few of the areas which must cause us all concern. One is the problem of the representation of indigent defendants. This is not a problem of charity, but of justice.

Mr. Justice Black points out in *Griffin* v. *Illinois*, "There can be no equal justice where the kind of trial a man gets depends upon the amount of money he has."

This is true not only at the time of trial, but during the entire range of legal procedure until the last issue is resolved.

Over a year ago, I asked a distinguished committee, headed by Professor Francis Allen of the University of Michigan Law School, to study what could be done to protect the rights of indigents in the Federal courts. The committee has found that much is being done in certain areas of the country. But its study shows that much, much more needs to be done.

Last year, almost thirty percent of the defendants in the 34,008 criminal cases in Federal court could not afford counsel. In the District of Columbia, where the Federal District Court hears all felony cases, over half the defendants had to be assigned attorneys. The situation in the states is comparable.

Federal and most state jurisdictions now hold that the right to counsel at trial is an affirmative right which must be extended by the Government when the defendant cannot provide his own.

Last June, the Supreme Court called for argument upon the question of right to counsel and whether the decision in *Betts* v. *Brady* should be overruled.

The recent decision in *Mapp* v. *Ohio* suggests by analogy that a majority may now hold that the Fourteenth Amendment requires states to provide counsel for indigent defendants in all cases involving serious crimes. And a recent decision by the Oregon Supreme Court has held that in serious crimes the state must not only provide counsel but experienced, competent counsel.

The provision of counsel is indispensable to a democratic system of justice. But translating this principle into practice is difficult. As with most problems, one of the stumbling blocks is lack of money.

And as Professor Allen's committee discovered the problem does not end by merely providing an attorney. There are the added frequently expensive problems such as bail, pretrial investigations and appeal.

The problem of bail for instance is one that has received too little attention. Professor Allen's committee has established conclusively that the question of whether a man will be kept in jail pending trial or be free is directly influenced by how wealthy he is.

A study of cases in the Southern District of New York indicates that over one-third of those required to post bail of $500 or less could not do so. When the bail was set between $500 and $1500, over half were unable to post it. And there is reason to believe that many of those unable to provide bail presented no substantial risk of nonappearance. Their poverty deprived them of their liberty.

Further, the problem of establishing innocence during the crucial pretrial period was made that much more difficult.

Bail protects the interests of society in assuring a defendant's appearance at trial and it also protects the interests of the individual in allowing him to be free to establish his innocence.

But the indigent defendant who cannot offer security for his appearance is denied this opportunity. He cannot provide for his family and for his defense, and cannot take an active part to prove his innocence.

Preliminary studies in the Southern District of New York also indicate that those who cannot make bail are more often convicted and receive stiffer sentences than those who can.

The rights of the indigent after the trial is over—in the appeal stage—is equally a matter of concern.

A series of court decisions in the last twenty years has greatly expanded the responsibility of society to help the indigent perfect his appeal. He is now pledged virtually the same treatment as one who can pay, and this is as it must be.

But, again, the problem of translating this right into reality is difficult. Appellate work is time consuming and requires the highest professional ability.

It usually is an undue burden to call upon counsel, who has contributed his services at trial, to continue on appeal without compensation. Competent new counsel is sometimes difficult to obtain. In this connection I wish to congratulate the bar of the city of San Francisco on what effort it has made in providing counsel for indigent persons on appeal.

We have come a long way since 1876 when a group of German immigrants banded together in New York to form the first Legal Aid Society, but we have not come far enough.

Since 1937, the Department of Justice and for many years the American Bar Association have supported legislation which would appropriate funds to help indigent defendants in Federal courts.

Now 25 years later it is still pending before the judiciary committees of both houses of Congress. The time to translate good intentions into law is long overdue. I ask for your help as a group and as individuals in working for its enactment.

I recognize that much has been done in many local areas to cope with this problem. I congratulate you on what you have done. Yet, the problem is far from solved. Whatever device is used, it is to the bar that society must turn for legal services to be provided for the indigent. It is inescapably a responsibility of the legal profession—a responsibility that none of us can avoid.

Another problem which is closely related and in some ways is even more difficult is the defense of those who do not fall in the category of indigent but who have limited resources available for their defense. Over forty percent of our families have incomes of less than $5,000 a year. These families cannot bear the cost of a complicated and extended trial and appeal which could easily equal their annual income.

Indeed, it can be the case that an indigent defendant, through the services of a first-rate volunteer attorney, may receive a better defense than one who pays a small fee and gets incompetent or indifferent counsel.

Legal services, particularly defense in criminal cases, are not like houses or automobiles where those with more money can buy better products without affecting the basic functioning of society. When one defendant cannot afford a complete defense justice is being rationed.

Today the cost of adequate defense can be high. Psychiatric and highly technical issues require expensive research, investigation and expert witnesses for the defense as well as for the Government.

In a recent case in which the Government was involved the defendant spent nearly $500,000 in legal and accounting fees in defending himself. He is now in prison. But the point is that we must be certain that the average citizen of a family income of $5700—the national median—can afford comparable efforts to protect his freedom. There is no question that a man prepared to spend $500,000 is far more likely to retain his freedom than a man who can afford only a few thousand dollars.

The amount of money which can be expended on defense should not affect the outcome of the trial. If justice is priced in the market place, individual liberty will be curtailed and respect for law diminished.

There is no easy answer to this problem; again, it lies with the bar itself. Professor Allen's committee is continuing its study of the problem and will have recommendations to make before the end of the year. I would like to ask for recommendations and ideas from the bar. I think they could be most important, and from all of this I would hope that we could develop methods whereby our finest legal talent would not be reserved solely for those who could pay without difficulty and an occasional indigent defendant.

I would hope from this effort that leading lawyers and legal scholars would be in court on a regular basis pleading for defendants of moderate circumstances. As long as a man is handicapped before the bar of justice because of his poverty, our task as lawyers is not done.

I thank you for this opportunity to speak.

Fortunately, no generation of lawyers as yet has lost that desire for a just society that will preserve the dignity of man and his individual right to search for happiness.

This association and its kindred associations in our fifty states and hundreds of counties and cities will, I feel sure, keep that desire aflame.

Let us as lawyers—as Americans—as Theodore Roosevelt said, "Boldly face the life of strife, resolute to do our duty well and manfully; resolute to uphold righteousness by deed and by word; resolute to be both honest and brave, to serve high ideals, yet use practical methods. Above all, let us shrink from no strife moral or physical."

A bar dedicated to the preservation of our basic freedoms, pledged to the search for truth, is a main bulwark of our democratic society which can aid mightily to achieve what President Kennedy recently described as a "world of law and free choice, banishing the world of war and coercion."

Delivered at the Seattle World's Fair
August 7, 1962

Mr. Gandy, I want to express my appreciation to you and to the Directors of the Fair not only for your generous invitation to me to speak here this afternoon but for this memorable day you have given my family. It truly has been a day to remember. I only wish we could devote several more days to the Fair, but your state has competing attractions. Tomorrow we are going salmon fishing, and after that we will have four days of camping in the Olympic Mountains.

I have waited a long time for this visit to the Pacific Northwest. Mr. Justice Douglas has often assured me that it is the most beautiful and exciting part of the United States; and, as a mere Attorney General, who am I to argue against the Supreme Court?

Moreover, there are, I believe, about as many graduates of the University of Washington in Washington, D.C., as graduates of Harvard—and they are worse than Texans in their enthusiasm for their native state.

And, in any case, as a citizen of Massachusetts I must agree with one of our great Massachusetts—and American—writers, Henry D. Thoreau, who said a century ago: "Eastward I go only by force, but westward I go free."

Westward I go free—these words sum up the historic experience of the United States. The Pacific Northwest, in a sense, is America's last frontier—and it is therefore especially appropriate that Seattle should hold this great fair with a startling preview of the frontiers of the future.

From its earliest beginnings, Seattle has distinguished itself by its determination to move ahead, defying odds and obstacles to reach for achievement. This can be seen by the fact that the University of Washington was founded here in 1861, long before statehood, at the outset of the Civil War, and only ten years after the first settlers landed at Alki Point. It was demonstrated again, after the Northern Pacific had picked Tacoma as its western terminus, when the residents of Seattle began with their own hands to build a railroad toward the East—the railroad which eventually brought the Great Northern here.

Through the years this has been your tradition and your faith. This fair is only the latest expression of the imagination and drive which mark your city and the whole Northwest.

You remember the poem about Kit Carson and his men:

> Though we travel far and travel light
> And now on summer grass,
> The mountain men ride west again
> To find a newer pass.
>
> We mark the fords and map the routes,
> For pioneers on rails—
> We mountain men ride west again
> To blaze the newest trails.

This is the spirit of the Pacific Northwest and of pioneer America —the unceasing search for new frontiers. And it is, I may perhaps add, particularly refreshing to come from the other Washington to a region of the country which is not mired in the past, not constantly looking backward over its shoulder, not timidly content with the status quo, not weighed down by doubt and foreboding, not fearful of the future—but instead is peering boldly and joyfully ahead into the 21st Century.

This Fair has on vivid display some of the fantastic resources which science and technology have placed at man's disposal. It must

55905

inspire us therefore to think beyond the present, to visualize how man can put these vast new powers to the service of freedom and opportunity and humanity.

As your great mountains lift our hearts above the cares of everyday existence, so the Fair lifts our minds and our sights and subordinates the irritations of the present to the potentialities of the future.

Above all, it inspires us to visualize the kind of world and the kind of nation we want to have in the 21st Century. If we are going to move ahead as a society, we must first of all know where we are going.

Every man must have his own vision of things to come. But many Americans, I believe, share broad and deep hopes for the world —the hope of a world without war—of a world where peoples now suffering in poverty and oppression can win a better life for themselves and their children—of a world where the imagination and energy of mankind are dedicated, not to destruction, but to building a generous and spacious future.

And many Americans too, I think, share broad and deep hopes for our own land—the hope of a land in which every child born has a decent opportunity for education, medical care and employment— of a land where intolerance and segregation become a memory, and a Negro child born in a cotton field in Alabama is as secure in his rights as a white child born here in Washington—of a land where poverty is a thing of the past, and every American has a free and equal chance to realize his own individual talents and possibilities.

If this is the vision of the future—if this is the direction in which we want to move—the next thing we must consider is how we propose to get there, and what obstacles lie in our path. For such a vision is never self-fulfilling. We cannot stand idly by and expect our dreams to come true under their own power. The future is not a gift: It is an achievement. Every generation helps make its own future. This is the essential challenge of the present.

Let us not deceive ourselves about the difficulties which lie ahead in the world. The earth today is divided by a great global civil war. It is shaken by the aspirations of long submerged peoples for independence and justice. It is shadowed by the frightful menace of thermonuclear destruction.

In such a world, the vision of a world without war seems remote

—so remote as to fill some with despair and to produce a longing for drastic and definite solutions, whether through unilateral disarmament or through nuclear war.

I do not share this despair, and I reject these quick and easy solutions as mirages. The road to peace may be long and tortured. But it can be successfully traversed.

In the first stages, the preservation of peace requires, above all, the preservation of our own nation's capability to defend peace. This was brought home clearly to me on my trip around the world last winter.

A high official in Indonesia told me that his country would lose its independence if the United States' Seventh Fleet, with all it implies, was removed from Far Eastern waters.

In Berlin, I saw crowds cheering with an intensity I had never seen before—men and women whose whole existence was staked in their trust in the military power of the United States. When I hear men of good will urging us to abandon our military strength, I can only think of the people whom such action would deliver to the enemy, and of the human misery which would result.

We have taken major steps in recent months to strengthen the frontiers of freedom. The proof of our progress is that the reservists who were called up last summer at a time of crisis are now returning to their homes all across the country. Where a year ago the situation in South Vietnam was dark, the forces of natural independence now have a fighting chance.

We must maintain our military strength so long as our adversaries maintain theirs. But, at the same time, we must be unceasing in our quest for ways to place military power under international control.

We must strive day and night to devise the machinery which will limit and eventually abolish national arms and destroy forever the means and opportunities of aggression. Our representatives in Geneva and the United Nations are themselves pioneers in pushing back the wilderness of war and moving toward the security of peace.

There are obstacles, too, to the achievement of our hopes within our land. Our cities have grown out of control; the very productivity of our agriculture becomes a source of embarrassment; automation threatens to replace men by machinery; our population continues to grow. Enrollments in our colleges are going to double in just ten years. The annual cost per student, now averaging $650 a year, is going steadily upward though almost half our families earn less than $5,000 annually.

In the next decade twenty-six million young people will be coming on the labor market. Seven and a half million of these young men and women will not have finished high school and two and a half million will not have completed the eighth grade unless we do better than we are doing now. These young people will be entering a labor market constantly demanding better education and higher skills.

As our population increases, ever greater attention must be given to the protection and conservation of our natural resources and of our wilderness areas—like the Olympic National Park which I look forward to visiting on Thursday.

The obstacles are great, but to men and women who crossed the mountains of the Northwest anything was possible. It is idle to say that the wealthiest nation known to history cannot afford to educate its children, take care of its old people and offer equal opportunities and productive employment to all its citizens. In recent months, we have begun to move to close the gap between our needs and our performance in a number of these areas.

We still have far to go, and there will always be new frontiers opening up before brave men. But we are definitely on the march. Our nation is pulsating with a new vitality and a new determination. We have established new goals in our national life, and we are moving constantly ahead to transform those goals into human reality. This is the beginning of a great new epoch in our history—an epoch of faith, and an epoch of fulfillment.

In the last analysis, our success, both at home and abroad, will depend on ourselves—on our steadfastness and courage and intelligence as people—on the strength of our determination to give full meaning to the Declaration of Independence and the Constitution and to advance our own revolution of liberty, justice and progress.

We know that freedom has many dimensions. It is the right of the man who tills the land to own the land; the right of the workers to join together to seek better conditions of labor; the right of businessmen to use ingenuity and foresight to produce and distribute without arbitrary interference in a truly competitive economy. It is the right of government to protect the weak; it is the right of the weak to find in their courts fair treatment before the law. It is the right of all our citizens to engage without fear or constraint in the discussion and debate of the great issues which confront us all. We understand this regardless of the extent to which we may differ in our political views. We know that argument in the open is one of the sources of our national strength.

Above all, here in Seattle, where our last frontier looks forward into a challenging future, we cannot but invoke the image of the men and women who came West by covered wagon and fortified by their spirit, we can boldly confront the great new frontier which today extends into the vast reaches of outer space. The future demands of us today the resolution, the sacrifice, the courage and the faith of the pioneers.

I believe that the President spoke for all of us when he said at his Inauguration:

> In the long history of the world, only a few generations have been granted the role of defending freedom in its hour of maximum danger. I do not shrink from this responsibility—I welcome it. I do not believe that any of us would exchange places with any people or any other generation. The energy, the faith, the devotion which we bring to this endeavor will light our country and all who serve it—and the glow from that fire can truly light the world.

Delivered at Dedication of Kendrick Hall
University of San Francisco Law School
San Francisco, California
September 29, 1962

Judge Harris, Mr. and Mrs. Kendrick, very distinguished guests and alumni, ladies and gentlemen:

It is a privilege to be with you and in San Francisco, even briefly, this evening. The occasion is an auspicious and historic one for the University and I am proud to be a small part of it. It is an added pleasure to see so many old friends and associates.

I am advisedly aware that you have spent two long days now celebrating your law school's golden anniversary. I suspect that the greatest virtue in any more oratory will lie in its blessed brevity. If I had any doubts on this score, Father Callahan's letter of invitation delicately enlightened me. He mentioned that Father Connolly was recovering from a spinal disc operation and also that the affair did not have to last too long. I am not clear whether he was whispering a hint, a hope or a prayer. You can never be sure with Father Callahan. But I'll try to keep in mind that any old place in a speech is a wonderful place to stop. I would not want any speech-induced discomfort of Father Connolly to become a widespread affliction of this assemblage.

Now judges, lawyers and law officials are honored to attend many functions of their profession. I personally have not attended many in California lately, but only in part because one of your indigenous political figures started spelling carpetbaggers with a K.* But I have enjoyed and gained from the trips here I have made, and I do particularly enjoy those occasions that bring me to the law schools.

The reason is that I find them not only stimulating but reassuring. In our circle, we have all heard increasingly expressed the nostalgic regret for what may be termed "the lost horizon" of the lawyer in the last half century. As occasional critics have noted, my own memory doesn't reach back quite that far. But I have become accustomed to the lament that lawyers of late have tailored their talents to the merely tangible and the temporary, that they have not sustained the great traditions of the past.

The charge pending against the legal fraternity as a whole is that we have lost our far-sighted vision, that we are no longer steeped in the law's great philosophies and lifted by its lofty purposes, that creativity and imaginations are in ever shorter supply. Whatever is left of these qualities, reads the indictment, hides in our nation's law schools.

Even the law schools are supposed to have succumbed to the restrictive practicalities of a "strictly business" world. The law schools

---

* An allusion to a comment made by Richard M. Nixon during his California gubernatorial campaign.

have moved in the direction of vocational institutions. Curricula have become mere compendia of case law.

In an age when countries and even continents are shucking boundaries as though they were chains, lawyers stand accused of narrowing their boundaries and allowing their vision to feeble into a state of myopia.

I am sure the law schools are too subborn and contentious—and just maybe too idealistic—to accept this indictment. And I hope and have faith that the broader charges are equally untrue. But this is too serious an indictment for a plea of *nolo contendere*. For if it is true we have lost not only a horizon but a heritage.

It is fortunate that the Jesuit founder of this University in 1855 did have the long-range view. If Father Anthony Mareschi, a secret agent from Turin, Italy, out of Santa Clara College, had consulted a close-thinking lawyer with a strictly business bent that long ago October about opening a school here, he would have received discouraging counsel.

The 35,000 inhabitants of vigilante-ridden San Francisco were largely broke. They were recovering from five major fires. There were runs on its banks, and business failures.

As a practical matter, there were very few students with or without the price of tuition. Father Mareschi would have been counseled to defer his dream.

Instead, he kept his own counsel and his vision. He opened the doors, thirty students came in, and a great university was born. A great courage was vindicated.

The new college prospered and it was not too long before its arch rival, Santa Clara College, founded in 1851, was abetting a population explosion by advertising: "If more than two brothers enter the college each additional one pays only $200 per session."

And so it went, I'm told—quantity at Santa Clara, quality at S. F. U.

I note with some curiosity that the opening of your law school fifty years ago coincided with the opening of school classes at Folsom Penitentiary. I assume well rounded lawbreakers and lawmakers ultimately emerged from each. I should add *respectively,* I suppose.

The emerging scholarly felon presumably gained a new horizon but the question is, Did the emerging law student widen his? I think we have an answer to this and the earlier charges in this evening we are sharing.

Tonight we are here to celebrate your fiftieth anniversary and to dedicate your new law school, Kendrick Hall. At their best, anniversaries are more than occasions for nostalgia, and the dedication of buildings can also be re-dedications to first principles. I'd like to talk about two such principles—courage and a concept of citizenship—which between them refute and will continue to refute the charges in our earlier indictment.

The late Justice Jackson and others have said courage is the most important attribute of a lawyer. It is more important than competence or vision. It can never be an elective in any law school. It can never be delimited, dated or outworn, and it should pervade the heart, the halls of justice and the chambers of the mind.

Tonight, it is in our presence in a close and personal way. It may be said to be personified by the name engraved on your new law school, Kendrick Hall.

Beyond his benefaction and generosity, there is, in Mr. Kendrick's life, a source of inspiration and an example of courage which could well enrich all of us.

If he will pardon me this personal reference, on March 29, 1917, at the age of forty-one, and five days before the outbreak of World War I, he wrote the War Department "it is my belief that I still owe service to my country." He expressed his preference for service in the line. His enlistment accepted, he served with great distinction in the battles of Saint Mihiel and in the Meuse-Argonne offensive. He was wounded and awarded a Purple Heart. After the war, Major Kendrick served ten years in the Army Reserve. He has, in the intervening years, continued to served his country and community.

Major Kendrick had three children at the time of his enlistment. One of them, Charles Warren Kendrick, was born on April 16, 1917, several weeks after his father's offer to serve.

Twenty-two years ago yesterday, *The San Francisco Examiner* of September 28, 1942, recited the acts of heroism of the son. Charles Warren Kendrick, a Harvard law student and a Marine Corps fighter pilot ace, was in the first wave of the first offensive action in the Pacific in World War II. He shot down five enemy planes and his squadron, 224, held Henderson Field in the Solomons for six weeks without reinforcements or support. He died twenty years ago this next week and Admiral Nimitz's citation "for heroism and extraordinary achievement in aerial combat with the enemy," concludes: "His courage throughout was in keeping with the highest traditions of the Naval Service."

I might add that his courage was also in keeping with the highest traditions of the legal profession. Our history books are filled with the examples of lawyers who demonstrated both physical and moral courage.

In 1735, one of the best-known lawyers in the Colonies was Andrew Hamilton. He was sick and he was ailing but he made the tiring trip from Philadelphia to New York to defend—without pay— an impoverished immigrant printer named John Peter Zenger against charges of seditious libel, charges levied by the Governor of New York.

Hamilton's defense more than won freedom for his client. A hundred years later, it formed the basis for the English-speaking world's definition of criminal libel, a cornerstone in the structure of guarantees for a free press.

In 1770, the prosperous and respected John Adams was pilloried as a traitor and turncoat by his fellow Bostonians when he defended a British officer and eight soldiers for firing on a crowd of Boston civilians. Adams, despite some 100 hostile depositions and catcalls in court, won acquittal for most of his clients, but he judged his political career to have been ended irrevocably by the episode. Even after he was elected President, he remembered the action as one of the finest of his life.

In 1846, William Henry Seward, also a highly successful lawyer, became a social outcast and his children were stoned on their way home from school when he defended—unsuccessfully—an insane Negro, already convicted of horse theft, who had massacred an entire innocent family in New York. It was a political miracle unlikely to to repeated today that he later became a United States Senator and eventually Secretary of State.

In 1895, Clarence Darrow gave up a profitable career as attorney for a powerful railroad to defend Socialist Eugene Debs and other officers of the American Railway Union against charges of criminal conspiracy, evolving out of the union strike against the railroad for which Darrow was counsel. For an attorney much sought after by large corporations to renounce all that to defend a poverty-stricken labor leader was unthinkable. But it took Darrow only one day to decide to defend Debs.

"I didn't want to take it," he said later ... "but when I saw poor men giving up their jobs for a cause, I could find no sufficient excuse, except my selfish interests, for refusing."

Incidentally, Darrow's defense of Debs did not ruin his career. He went on to achieve lasting fame as a defense counsel and his anteroom was filled with people wanting to retain him.

In 1924, Homer Cummings, the state prosecutor of Connecticut, asked for the dismissal of an indictment against a young itinerant laborer named Harold Israel.

Dozens of eyewitnesses had identified Israel as the man who had shot a popular Catholic priest. Israel himself had confessed, though he repudiated it a week later. He owned a gun of the same caliber as the murder weapon and he had left town, unexplainably, shortly after the murder.

As a topnotch prosecutor, Cummings had tremendous political prospects. But he turned them all down because after much investigation he believed Israel innocent.

In 1942, after eight months of war and many military reverses, Harold Medina, then one of New York's best known trial lawyers, accepted an assignment to defend a former German national charged with high treason.

Medina worked on the case for three years off and on, for no fee, because, as he said, "It was wonderful to be in there pitching for justice."

All these attorneys rose above the interests of their pocketbooks. They were men who freely stepped across the boundary of their own legal speciality, often at the cost of their popularity.

They served in a role which, throughout history, has challenged the finest of our lawyers—that is the role of the citizen. By that I mean a great deal more than the right to vote, or to obtain a passport, or even to speak and worship freely.

Since the days of Greece and Rome when the word "citizen" was a title of honor, we have often seen more emphasis put on the rights of citizenship than on its responsibilities. And today, as never before in the free world, responsibility is the greatest right of citizenship and service is the greatest of freedom's privileges.

Lawyers have their duties as citizens but they also have special duties as lawyers. Their obligations go far deeper than earning a living as specialists in corporation or tax law. They have a continuing responsibility to uphold the fundamental principles of justice from which the law cannot depart.

The work of an eminent Texas attorney, Leon Jaworski, President of the American College of Trial Lawyers, shows what one lawyer can do. About five years ago, he called in a small group of outstanding Texas lawyers and persuaded each of them to join with him in taking one unpopular case each year.

One of my great disappointments in our present efforts to deal with the situation in Mississippi as lawyers, has been the absence of any expression of support from the many distinguished lawyers of that state. I realize in that difficult social situation that to defend the fundamental principles of respect for the law and compliance with federal court orders would be unpopular and require great courage.

I also understand that many of them may not agree with the decision in *Brown* vs. *The Board of Education*, but whether they agree or not, they still have their obligations as lawyers and they have remained silent.

However, I might also note that there have been no pronouncements in this matter by the American Bar Association.

Ladies and gentlemen, your law school has a proud origin, a proud record of achievement and now a proud name for its next era. I congratulate you.

I am also confident that the graduates who come out of Kendrick Hall in the long years of its future will be men dedicated to the highest ideals and richest traditions of their heritage. And they will be lawyers courageously dedicated to the broadest horizons of citizenship and service. We will be waiting for them. We need them.

Thank you all.

part iv CRITICISM MOUNTS

Roy Wilkins, executive secretary of the National Association for the Advancement of Colored People, began to criticize the Kennedy Administration as least as early as May 10, 1961. That was in reference to President Kennedy's decision—announced by Press Secretary Pierre Salinger on May 9—not to send a message to Congress supporting the Clarke-Celler civil rights legislative package.

The President's judgment was based on the fact that there was no pressure on Congress in behalf of the legislation and that an overt attempt on his part to push for its passage would jeopardize his legislative program. Too, he believed that a great deal of progress could be made if the laws already on the books were enforced, and if he could bring his executive powers to bear.

While Mr. Wilkins conceded that the Kennedy Administration had made an excellent beginning relative to civil rights through the Justice Department, by the appointment of Negroes to office, and through the attitude and pronouncements of the President himself, he felt that President Kennedy should throw his weight behind new legislation. "As for practical politics," said Mr. Wilkins, "the record is conclusive that whether a President sponsors civil rights legislation or not, his general legislative program is subject to hatchet treatment by Southerners and their allies."

This basic conflict—to push for immediate civil rights legislation or not—was to remain a source of continuous irritation between the Administration and the leaders of what came to be referred to as the civil rights movement.

Throughout the rest of 1961 there was an increase in the criticism directed at the Administration. While the principal source of the censure was in the civil rights leadership, others began to take it up.

On January 1, 1962, a report of the Anti-Defamation League of B'nai B'rith expressed "keen disappointment" by civil rights leaders in "the President's failure to press for civil rights legislation in 1961."

On that same day, Roy Wilkins was honored in New York for thirty years of service on the staff of the N.A.A.C.P. President Kennedy sent a telegram in which he said, "It is rather the nation as a whole which should be congratulated tonight for having a man like Roy Wilkins to spur it on to the essential goal of securing the full constitutional rights of all our citizens."

The next day, January 2, in his report at the organization's annual membership meeting, Mr. Wilkins referred to President Kennedy's reluctance to press for major civil rights legislation as a "basic error," explaining that "the racial bloc in Congress cannot be appeased, it must be defeated."

The editorial page of *The New York Times* for January 3 presented, probably coincidentally, evidence of the complex nature of the problem as seen by competent observers at the time.

An editorial referred to President Kennedy's "retreat" in failing "to put forward major civil rights legislation and to issue an executive order barring racial bias in Federally aided housing." Yet the same editorial applauded the President's conviction that his principal test in 1962 would be in his attempt to secure passage for "his imaginative proposal . . . to permit a huge expansion in our commerce with the European Market, Japan and the rest of the free world."

On that same page, James Reston expressed the President's dilemma in the first two paragraphs of his column:

> The first question for President Kennedy in the New Year is not whether he can get along with Chairman Nikita Khrushchev, but whether he can coexist peacefully with Chairman Wilbur Mills of the House Ways and Means Committee.
>
> Mr. Mills is not as powerful or unpredictable as Mr. Khrushchev, but he is powerful and unpredictable enough to worry the President, whose tariff, tax and medical care bills have to pass through Ways and Means.

The essence of this conundrum was that what the civil rights leaders were asking for was *legislative* action, the responsibility of Congress. This was the same Congress upon which the President of the United States was literally dependent for enactment of his program. Thus progress in any area of legislation depended upon the personnel and committee structure of Congress. Wilbur Mills, U. S.

Representative from a southern state, Arkansas, was a powerful man; not only was he Chairman of the crucial Ways and Means Committee but he was a member of the House Committee on Committees, a group which appointed members of the House of Representatives to the committees. And President Kennedy believed that the provision of jobs took precedence over every other matter; for a prosperous economy would help all Americans.

Criticism continued, increasing in intensity. At times other racial events took the spotlight—such as the matriculation of James H. Meredith at the University of Mississippi with Federal assistance in September of 1962—but always present and frequently active was the often bitter discussion about the Administration's apparent apathy toward major civil rights legislation.

The President's executive order forbidding discrimination in U. S. Government-aided (Federal Housing Administration and Veterans Administration) housing, issued November 20, 1962, provided only a temporary lull in the criticism, for many civil rights advocates argued that the Order should have included housing financed with conventional mortgages.*

The Mansfield-Dirksen bill introduced on January 25, 1962—designed to prevent discrimination in voting by the use of "literacy tests"—failed to get off the ground. A year later, on February 28, 1963, President Kennedy sent a message to Congress recommending the passage of legislation which would curb such discrimination by the use of literacy tests, expedite voting suits in the Federal courts, allow temporary referees to register Negroes while their suits were pending, provide financial aid for schools which were desegregating, and extend the life of the Civil Rights Commission four years. It would also expand the role of the Commission so that it would serve as a national clearing house providing information, advice and technical assistance to any requesting agency, private or public.

While not much hope was given the immediate future of this request of many parts, the message did put Congress and the country

---

* Experience with the Order for a year and a half appears to confirm that complaint. After conducting a nation-wide survey, the *Wall Street Journal* (July 16, 1964) concluded that the lack of impact by the Executive Order was in its limitations. The survey also found, however, that "neither Negro organizations nor individual Negroes had been particularly vigorous about taking advantage of the opportunities the Order does make available."

at large on notice that the President was getting ready to put the prestige of his office behind an attempt to procure effective and comprehensive civil rights legislation. But even what the President asked for at this time was referred to as "inadequate" by many who hoped for more.

In the meantime, unmistakable signs of recalcitrance and hostility appeared in the South. On January 14, 1963, George C. Wallace was elected Governor of Alabama on a defiantly segregationist platform.

And less than a month later a Negro family of 10 was sent from Shreveport, Louisiana, to Trenton, New Jersey, on a "reverse" Freedom Ride; the family had been told by their White Citizens Council sponsors that they would be met by Nicholas deB. Katzenbach, U. S. Deputy Attorney General of the Department of Justice, who had a job for them. Other Negro families were subjected to this cruel hoax, some of them being sent to Hyannisport on Cape Cod where many of the Kennedys congregated during the summer.

Events were moving toward a climax, and the speeches delivered by the Attorney General during the winter of 1962-63 were given against such a background.

Delivered to the American Jewish Congress
New York City, October 28, 1962

It is an honor and pleasure for me to accept the Stephen S. Wise Award for advancing human freedom. I am deeply grateful to you for choosing me to join so distinguished a list of recipients as President Truman, Prime Minister Ben Gurion and Senator Lehman.

Let me say that I am pleased, also, to accept this award because it typifies a different kind of brotherhood than that occasionally attributed to me—and my brothers.

The significance of this award perhaps, can be measured best by the very association of the name of Stephen Wise in the title with the phrase "Advancing Human Freedom." There is little need for me to recall to this body—which he helped found—the lasting accomplishments of Rabbi Wise.

I would like to think however that some of this accomplishment stemmed from the fact that he was born on St. Patrick's Day. What is more certain is that it stemmed from a consuming love of freedom and justice and great courage in fighting for both. These are qualities characteristic not only of St. Patrick but of Jews throughout history.

"Throughout my life," Rabbi Wise wrote in his autobiography, "it seemed to me that all ministers of religion were for justice in principle, but too ready to be silent about injustice in practice. One of the dangers of all of us is that we are willing to fight for justice for ourselves alone, forgetting that justice will be for all or none."

Rabbi Wise lived according to that declaration, and concerned himself intensely with the welfare of the Jew, the Negro and the Catholic; the unemployed, the ill and the aged, to the honor of his religion and to the progress of his country. Because of the courage, the concern, and the conscience of Rabbi Wise and others like him, our country has made progress toward fulfillment of our ideal of equal rights for all citizens.

In earlier generations, the struggle was against those who insisted that "no Irish need apply" or who crudely typed all Jews as predators of the marketplace. Today, members of all minority groups sit in the highest councils of our land. A Roman Catholic has been elected President of the United States—something which was not possible during Rabbi Wise's life.

True as this progress has been, we cannot pay satisfactory tribute either to our ideals or to the work of Rabbi Wise simply by praising them. Persisting passion and prejudice do not surrender to efforts of the past; continuing and unremitting effort is required.

Such effort has been the policy of this Government for many years and of this Administration since its start. Over the past 21 months, we have made great progress but we still have a very long way to go. However, I think it is important, as a measure of what can be done, to review briefly what has been done.

At the first Cabinet meeting, President Kennedy issued orders that positive action be taken immediately to insure and promote equal opportunity for all persons employed by the Federal Government. Yet in the Department of Justice—the Agency charged with seeing that others comply with the Civil Rights Laws—I found, for example that out of 900 lawyers in Washington, D. C., only 10 were

Negroes. That situation has been changed. There are now six or seven times that many.

The United States attorneys in two of our largest cities are Negroes. For the first time Negroes are serving as District Judges in the Continental United States. A Negro lawyer of great ability was sworn in recently as a member of the Federal Trade Commission. And, as you know, Thurgood Marshall was appointed by the President to the Federal Court of Appeals for the Second Circuit.

All of these men were chosen for ability and integrity, not color, and they are a great asset to the Nation.

The record also shows real progress in many other areas. We are making a widespread effort to end voting discrimination against Negroes in the South. This is the right from which all other rights flow.

The Department of Justice now has brought 32 cases to uphold this right. Ten of these have been filed in Mississippi, where no action had been taken before.

In addition, voting records in some 70 counties in the South are being analyzed for evidence of violations and the FBI has been directed to make investigations in a large number of other counties.

All this activity is bringing results. For example, in Bullock County, Alabama, five Negroes were registered last September. Now there are over a thousand. In neighboring Macon County at the beginning of 1961 only a handful of Negroes were being allowed to register. Today more than 2,800 are registered to vote and they have made their influence felt.

In the last year, virtually every bus station, every railroad station, and every airport in the South has been desegregated as a result of action by the Federal Government. There are many towns throughout the South where these are the first and still the only facilities which Negroes can use without discrimination.

This summer, for the first time, the Department entered a case seeking to forbid hospitals which were built with Federal funds to discriminate racially against doctors and patients. We believe it is unconscionable for any hospital—and certainly one built with tax money—to bring color barriers into questions of health and safety.

Last month, again for the first time, the Department brought suit to require desegregation of a school district financed with Federal impacted area funds. It made no sense for the United States to ask its citizens to serve their country in the Armed Forces and then to put them in a place where their children are discriminated against in school because of their race.

And finally, just last week, we filed briefs with the Supreme Court of the United States on behalf of students who had been convicted in New Orleans and Birmingham, Durham and Greenville, for participating in sit-in demonstrations.

You should be fully aware that in these 21 months the officials and citizens of many Southern communities have moved to end segregation. We make continuing efforts to consult local officials and to persuade them to correct injustices themselves. In many cases this has been done and this has been a major development in advancing civil rights within the framework of law.

We have taken action not only in the field of civil rights, but also in the field of civil liberties. The President recently signed a measure permitting 30,000 residents of countries whose immigration quotas are heavily oversubscribed to come into the United States.

Last week, the President vetoed a bill which would have provided police in the District of Columbia with broad, but probably unconstitutional, powers to seize indecent literature and close stores.

The President after a long struggle going back to the years when he was a Senator also sought and secured repeal of the loyalty oath requirement for teachers or students seeking assistance under the National Science Foundation and National Defense Education Acts. The President said in approving this legislation, "It is highly unlikely that the affidavit requirement kept any Communist out of the programs. It did, however, keep out those who considered the disclaimer affidavit a bridle upon freedom of thought."

I am firmly convinced, on the basis of my experience of the last twenty-one months, that the vast majority of the American people in the South, as well as in the North, East and West, want to make progress and are not satisfied with the status quo.

This progress has been made and is significant because it is right. It is dictated not only by our consciences and our ideals, but also by our laws. The unhappy fact, however, is that neither our progress nor our laws are universally respected.

There are now, as there were during the life of Stephen Wise,

Philistines of bigotry and disobedience. In recent weeks, the Nation and the world, have seen a great tragedy visited on one of our states because state officials refused to obey court orders and accept their responsibilities of leadership.

The President was obliged to act in Oxford, Mississippi, to protect the orders of the Federal courts. When the United States marshals went to Mississippi, it was not to enforce the law for the benefit of a single Negro student, but to enforce the law on behalf of every American citizen, and to make it clear that this is a country which lives by law.

While we must enforce the law with vigor, we must respond to the broader problem of desegregation with understanding. The path of progress in civil rights is both steep and narrow.

Your organization has made a great contribution. In the words of your President, Dr. Prinz: "We do—and must—join forces with many groups in the community in the battle for full equality in a free society for all Americans."

But you—and all of us—must do more. We meet tonight in a time of grave crisis with our attention fixed on the waters of the Caribbean and the once peaceful hills and fields of Cuba.

The confrontation between the United States and the Soviet Union is in reality a confrontation of all people who believe in human dignity and freedom with those who believe the State is Supreme. It is that fact, not the drama of the particular moment, which is of real significance.

In our society, laws are administered to protect and expand individual freedom, not to compel individuals to follow the logic other men impose on them.

The tyranny of communism is as old as the Pharaohs and the Pyramids—that the state stands above all men and their individual aspirations. And this is why we oppose it, because by force and subversion it seeks to impose its tyranny all around the world.

We will not win this struggle merely by confronting the enemy. What we do at home, in the final analysis, is just as important.

Thus, we all must accelerate our efforts to banish religious prejudice, racial discrimination, and any intolerance which denies to any Americans the rights guaranteed them by the Declaration of Independence and the Constitution.

That is what this crisis is all about; that is why our ships are on station in the Caribbean and why American soldiers are on duty tonight in West Berlin, South Vietnam and South Korea.

They are there for the same reason the Maccabees stood their ground against Antiochus—for human dignity and freedom. It has been said that each generation must win its own struggle to be free.

In our generation, thermonuclear war has made the risks of such struggles greater than ever. But the stakes are the same: the right to live in dignity according to the dictates of conscience and not according to the will of the State.

As the President said Monday night:

> The cost of freedom is always high—but Americans have always paid it. And one path we shall never choose, and that is the path of surrender or submission. Our goal is not the victory of might, but the vindication of right—not peace at the expense of freedom, but both peace and freedom, here in this hemisphere, and, we hope, around the world. God willing, that goal will be achieved.

It is the ideal of freedom which underlies our great concern for civil rights. Nations around the world look to us for leadership—not merely by strength of arms but by the strength of our convictions.

"Discrimination," Stephen Wise once wrote, "damns the man who discriminates and it damns the man discriminated against."

This is not the kind of injury our nation can afford. We not only want, but we need, the free exercise of rights by every American. We need the strength and talent of every American.

We need, in short, to set an example of freedom for the world—and for ourselves.

Delivered at Opening of Exhibit
on the Emancipation Proclamation at The National Archives
Washington, D.C., January 4, 1963

One hundred years ago today, in a nation torn by fraternal strife, Abraham Lincoln proclaimed that all persons held as slaves in the area of rebellion "henceforward shall be free." He added, "Upon this act, sincerely believed to be an act of justice . . . I invoke the considered judgment of mankind and the gracious favor of Almighty God."

We cannot think that Mr. Lincoln invoked either that judgment or that favor in vain.

In the long course of the American commitment to freedom and dignity of the individual, no single deed has done more than Lincoln's signing of the Emancipation Proclamation to redeem the pledge upon which this republic was founded—the pledge that all men are created equal, are endowed equally with inalienable rights and are entitled equally to life, liberty, and the pursuit of happiness.

Thus it is altogether proper that we gather on this day, one century later; we Americans, the heirs of Lincoln, to observe the placing of this historic document on exhibit here in the nation's capital for all to see. It is a moment to reflect on how far we have come in these hundred years toward the goal of equality and to appraise the problems and difficulties that still stand between us and that goal.

It is also a time to consider both our common responsibility toward achieving the promise of American life for all our citizens, and the implications of this document for an entire world, struggling everywhere for independence and equality and the full attainment of human dignity.

We have had a great deal of talk in this country in the past one hundred years about equality. Deeds, not talk, are what is needed. It is only relatively recently that we as a nation have again gathered our strength, our will, and our determination to act boldly and vigorously to lift from all our citizens the degrading burdens of intolerance, bigotry and discrimination.

We do so with the knowledge that the ideal of freedom has traveled a long and hard road through human history. Yet the record shows that the ideal persists and has an explosive power greater than that locked up within the atom. It shows that this ideal is the strongest motive of human action—that it fortifies the human will in the face of adversity and force and terror—and that the passion for equal rights for all is the ultimate weapon in the struggle for independence and human dignity.

Today we face a double challenge: achievement of our ideals at home and maintenance of our leadership among the free people around the world. Are not these two challenges really one?

We have the military means to meet and repel any adversary and we intend to maintain that lead in the future. Ours is a strong nation composed of industrious, brave people, who have always had a basic sense of justice. We have always had the courage, the will, and the military power to defend ourselves.

But while our freedom and the freedom of our allies depends upon our armed might now, both will finally depend upon our will and our ability to realize fully—and in fact—the ideals we claim to defend.

In this generation we have seen an extraordinary change in America—a new surge of idealism in our life—a new and profound reality in our democratic order. Much has been done. But much more must be done, first because it is right, and because in making equal opportunity a reality for all Americans, we make it a certainty for each American.

As Lincoln once said, "In giving freedom to the slave, we assure freedom to the free."

And, we must do more because nations which are free and peoples who would be free, look to us for leadership—not merely in strength of arms but in strength of convictions. Americans are on duty today in South Vietnam, South Korea, at the Berlin Wall, and around the world because the freedoms which Lincoln lived and died for belong to all men.

Other countries have discrimination, intolerance and bigotry, too. But because we are a free society—open for all the world to see— and because we ourselves were born of revolution, people of these lands look to us to see whether we can eradicate these plagues.

I have no doubt that we can. The energy which causes people from all sections of the United States to strive for fulfillment of the pledges of the Declaration of Independence and the Emancipation Proclamation is essentially moral energy, and it has no end.

President Kennedy said almost two years ago:

> We dare not forget today that we are the heirs of that first revolution. Let the word go forth from this time and place, to friend and foe alike, that the torch has been passed to a new generation of

Americans—born in this century, tempered by war, disciplined by a hard and bitter peace, proud of our ancient heritage—and unwilling to witness or permit the slow undoing of those human rights to which this nation has always been committed and to which we are committed today at home and around the world.

Ladies and gentlemen, we meet today to honor that commitment and this document that gave it both shelter and force.

*Delivered at the 10th Anniversary Convocation
Center for Study of Democratic Institutions
of the Fund for the Republic
New York City, January 22, 1963*

First I want to congratulate President Hutchins and the Board of Directors of the Fund For the Republic for the imagination and the initiative that have gone into the preparation of this Tenth Anniversary Program—Challenges to Democracy in the Coming Decade.

Secondly, I wish to express my appreciation for being asked to consider with you the question of individual rights and privileges in this troubled time. It is a time of hope, as well, as we have seen in recent months and even days.

But bright as we believe the world could be, we must face it as it is, a world of nation states seeking public solutions to what are inherently personal questions. This is the dimension of the time we live in and which we call the Cold War—a struggle very grand in scope but very personal in importance. For this reason an examination of these personal questions—the rights and interests of individual human beings is as timely as ever before.

Some of you may be familiar with the recent classroom scene in a Russian elementary school. A little boy, when asked to describe the United States, said, "The United States is a sad country where workers and peasants are starving under capitalist exploitation by the cynical ruling classes."

"Correct," said the teacher, "and what is the major goal of the Soviet Union?"

"To catch up with the United States," was the sober reply.

Throughout our parallel histories, I believe the United States, as a whole, has lagged behind Russia in the exploitation of one class by another.

The comparison is an old one. De Toqueville concluded his treatise on America with these prophetic words:

> There are at the present time two great nations in the world which started from different points . . . I allude to Russia and America . . . The principal instrument of America is freedom and of Russia, servitude.
>
> Their starting point is different and their courses are not the same; yet each of them seems marked out by the will of heaven to sway the destinies of half the globe.

In today's terms this may seem a generous oversimplification. We have only to look at the growing power of free Europe, or the snarling giant tiger that is Red China, or the awakened democracy of India, or the rising nations of Africa and Latin America, to know that there are other handholds on the globe, other forces capable of swaying its destiny. It would be quite wrong, and quite unlike a group such as the one assembled here, to become mesmerized by the present confrontation of the Soviet Union and the United States. Yet in this brief moment in time we can see some polarization of allegiance—some to the Communist way—some to the way of freedom.

This is the tug of the Cold War. We should be excused if we venture the opinion we are winning. As the President said last week in his State of the Union Message: "Not a single one of the nearly fifty United Nations members to gain independence since the Second World War has succumbed to Communist control." In one case, a wall has gone up to prevent a great people from accepting the tug of freedom. History will record that while the Great Wall of Old China was built to keep barbarians out, this brooding ugliness by the Brandenburg Gate was built to keep civilized people in. And men may speculate on the current Soviet proficiency in the high jump.

But overall, we are winning—Why? What is it we have that others will reach for, run for, die for? Surely, it is more than houses, cars and dishwashers. Even Communism, with some rearrangement of production priorities and a few other sacrifices by the New Class, could provide these things. No, the attraction of the so-called "Materialist" West is more a thing of mind than of matter. Why then do young foreign students become disaffected with Iron Curtain curricula and seek out our consuls? What is it that brings tears to the eyes of new Americans as they take the oath of citizenship? What is it they sought? What is it men want? Isn't it freedom of conscience and action conditioned only by the legitimate needs of private and public security?

Our civil rights laws and actions are founded on that premise. No recitation of them should be necessary. Observance of them is entirely necessary. Encouraging lip service is paid also in Articles 124 and 125 of the Soviet Constitution to the principles of freedom of religion, speech, press and assembly. But they have gone the way of many a New Year's Resolution. The British have proved a Constitution needn't be written. The Soviets have proved a Constitution must be *more* than written.

This discussion deals primarily with the United States and the Soviet Union—not because we are the only nations involved, but because there is still some reason to believe we are the leaders respectively of the free and Communist worlds.

Our Bill of Rights, particularly in the first nine Amendments, holds out a series of personal promises. The addition of the Fourteenth Amendment increased the commitment of the National Government to insure that those promises are kept. In most respects, our legislatures have followed with the greatest care the mandates implicit in the Bill of Rights and the Fourteenth Amendment. An independent judiciary has served well to correct misconstructions of those principles. And while the matters affected have ranged from freedom of speech and press to questions of search and seizure, and right to counsel—most of these protections were well established from our early times and are invoked today not at all with regard to their validity, which is certain, but to their vitality in a modern society.

But the matter which the very term "civil rights" brings most immediately to mind in our time is the position of the American Negro in American society and the treatment accorded him in all walks of life.

In this respect I would like to glance at the record.

For the headline hunter, the violence at Mississippi has been the most noticeable event of the current period. The historian, however, will record the progress made—not only in the unflinching commitment of the Federal Government to civil rights—but more importantly, and more notably in the amount of voluntary compliance by Southern officials and citizens in this area.

For example, over the past year in *Voting*: In 29 counties in Georgia, Alabama, Mississippi and Louisiana, officials have voluntarily made voting records available to us without need for court action. In about 50 counties in the same states, discriminatory practices have been adandoned voluntarily, avoiding the need for suit.

Where voluntary action was not forthcoming, however, we have brought suit. Under the 1957 Civil Rights Act, the Department of Justice has undertaken 32 suits and 82 voting record inspections.

In *Transportation*: Discrimination in interstate travel has disappeared. Virtually all bus and rail terminals were desegregated in 1961 pursuant to ICC regulations sought by this administration. In 1962 we surveyed 165 airports and found 15 still segregated. All are now desegregated, 13 voluntarily and the other two after suit.

At present, the only such segregated facilities in the country are bus and rail terminals in Jackson, Mississippi, and there we took successful legal action, which is now on appeal.

In *Education*: In 1962, 28 more Southern school districts desegregated voluntarily and peacefully, many after consultation with the Department of Justice.

As chairman of The President's Committee on equal employment opportunity in the Federal Government, Vice President Johnson, pointed out in November that Negro employment in the Federal Government stood at 28,986 at Grades GS-5 through GS-11, an increase of 18.3 per cent over the previous years—although the increase in such job vacancies was only 4 per cent.

In Grades GS-12 through GS-18, the number of Negroes increased from 343 to 1380—a 33.1 per cent increase, as compared with a raise in the number of such jobs of 7.8 per cent. In the private sector 104 major national business firms have signed equal employment pledges under the Plans for Progress Program.

The right to travel, to share public facilities and accommodations, together with the right to equal education—these rights have been given Federal impetus as never before—but again, more importantly, they have received wide public acceptance in a quiet, normal way that hasn't hit the headlines.

The President's Order last November prohibiting discrimination in Federally assisted housing—together with the actions of some 17 states and 55 cities barring discrimination in that area is a milestone on the march. And on this march the American Negro himself has walked well. Much depends on the scope and dignity of Negro leadership; and it is equal to the test.

The trail is long—we've crossed rough terrain; and there's more ahead—much more to do for the American Negro, the American Indian, the migrant worker—minorities yes, as the American people themselves are a minority in this world.

Meanwhile, back in the Kremlin's shadow, what do we find? We find over 100 persons executed in the past year for economic crimes —most of them Jews. We find Christian faiths harassed and Christian peoples persecuted. We find a statement last year by Roman Rudenko, Soviet Public Prosecutor, that the very causes of crime in capitalist countries are absent in the Soviet Union. Then we find a complaint in *Pravda* that Muscovites removed daily, without paying, 77,000 bus tickets from help-yourself dispensers. We find a law branding as treason any unauthorized departure from the country—and the unhappy story of a Jewish woman sentenced to be shot last February for "currency manipulation," after a prior three-year sentence in Siberia for trying to escape to Israel, and long after seeing her two daughters murdered by the Nazis. And we find a 1961 commentary on lawyers in a Soviet paper as follows:

> There are two groups of lawyers. One: Modest, quiet, unobtrusive, who will acknowledge guilt (if his client is guilty) and refer to mitigating circumstances.
>
> The other—working with his vocal cords and elbows, even shedding some tears. His voice going through the whole courtroom—My client's arrest is due to a mistake. When the case was retried at the Public Prosecutor's demand, the same man was found guilty when another lawyer took his defense.

Another unobtrusive lawyer no doubt. Save us from them!

What is the difficulty here? What's missing in Communism's instant Utopia?

An appreciation for the natural rights of man? I should think so.

It suffers from an overdose of Marxism-Leninism and a deficiency of Lockism-Jeffersonism. It would benefit so much from just a little exposure to First Amendment principles.

If freedom is to thrive in any corner of the world, there must be communication and a sense of law. There can be no meaningful discussion of civil rights until these concepts have been examined.

Turning first to communication, if our Constitution had followed the style of St. Paul, the First Amendment might have concluded—"But the greatest of these is speech." In the darkness of tyranny, this is the key to the sunlight. If it is granted, all doors open. If it is withheld, none. But a truth unheard is as much a social force as a tree falling in the lonely forest is sound. Truly *free* speech implies a guarantee of the right to listen. In passing, it was my impression that it was to prevent truth from going unrevealed that the Center itself was established on Eucalyptus Hill. There's no such hill in Russia.

Those matters which a government tries to conceal from the outside world are guides to its personality—but what it would hide from its own people is a reflection of its character. Thus, the secret speech denouncing Stalin in 1956—hidden from the public—told as much about its authors as its subject. More recently, in the past years, mobs of angry people have tested the laws of many nations. We read about the Walloon-Flemish differences in Belgium, violence in Paris and Mississippi. But what did we hear of the wage and price riots in southern Russia—that left hundreds of dead and wounded—what beyond vague references to "rowdiness"—while during that same week both *Pravda* and *Izvestia* highlighted the following earthshaking events:

The stock market dropped in New York.

A group of New Jersey students protested U.S. atomic tests.

Two unknown persons slipped into the Soviet sector of Germany.

This is the fact of Soviet news policy. What is the doctrine? I take it we can still look to Lenin for guidance on Soviet doctrine.

In 1903 he wrote indignantly, "Until freedom of speech and of the press is declared there will not disappear the shameful Russian inquisition which persecuted profession of unofficial faith, unofficial opinions, unofficial doctrines."

Later he wrote, "The periodical and non-periodical press and all publishing enterprises must be entirely subordinated to the Central Committee of the Party."

Thus, today's Soviet leaders have a fairly wide latitude of "Leninist" press policies to draw on.

There is, of course, freedom in the USSR to say the right thing. This was brought home to a young American visitor to Moscow who was earnestly explaining how any American could openly denounce the life and morality of the United States—even ridicule the President.

"It is the same here," said the guide. "A Soviet citizen may also denounce life and morality in the United States and ridicule your President."

Freedom of communication involves both information and expression. I have touched on information. It is crucial to a dynamic society, which communism claims to be. But expression is no less so. Thus we read with concern the Soviet Party's reply last month to Russian intellectuals who had claimed that "without opportunity for different artistic directions, art is condemned to death." The reply said that the Party does not tolerate experimentation in the arts, and "is determining the tasks and directions of artistic creativeness." What sad rebuff! But what a fine claim!

And we shall wait to see if and how a young Soviet poet changes a now famous poem of protest—particularly so since it concerns racial persecution.

The Soviet Government seems to have good working relations with the Soviet press. If the Soviet chief of state should take exception to the editorial policies of a paper, he needn't cancel his subscription; he just cancels the paper. But that is hardly necessary at present.

Soviet papers serve their Party well, rewriting human history even as it rolls off the presses of human endeavor. As the great hand writes, and having written, moves on—the agitation that follows is a team of Soviet historians with erasers. Someone should tell them to relax.

I have tried to explain how difficult it is for me at least to picture the struggle for civil rights where there is a limit on communication. What about limits on law?

It seems to be recognized by some Soviet authorities that terror is inefficient. The so-called Special Board of Ministry of Internal Affairs has been abolished—and with it, its function—which was to send people to labor camps without a hearing, in secret procedures

without right of counsel or appeal. Confessions must now be cor-
roborated by other evidence. And all in all there seems to be a growing appreciation for what the Soviet call "legality"—and a growing
awareness among the Soviet legal profession itself of the obligation
of law to society, and of lawyers to the law. The outcome of this trend
remains uncertain. You may recall that after a great deal of noisy
pride about "abolishing" the death penalty—the Soviet Union in
1961, reinstated it for crimes described as "economic" and specifically
for illegal transactions in foreign currency. Subsequently, two men
were executed under an *ex post facto* application of the currency law.

From Harvard's expert on Soviet law, Professor Harold Berman,
I learned of a conversation he had on this incident with a leading
Soviet jurist. Berman had remarked on the unusual nature of the
trial and sentence and suggested it violated the 1958 Soviet Principles of Criminal Procedure. The jurist replied,—"we lawyers didn't
like that"—a response, Berman noted, which was no less remarkable
for its "we lawyers" as for its "didn't like that.'

I suppose what is needed is more lawyers who don't like things.

The law's slow progress in the Soviet Union may be due, in large
part, to the lack of public debate. Thus the recent "anti-Parisite"
laws by which people not doing "socially useful work" may be
exiled to remote areas for two to five years, went into effect as quietly
as the falling tumblers of a combination lock.

All great questions must be raised by great voices, and the
greatest voice is the voice of the people—speaking out—in prose, or
painting or poetry or music; speaking out—in homes and halls,
streets and farms, courts and cafes—let that voice speak and the still-
ness you hear will be the gratitude of mankind. Man giving thanks—
Jews thanking the God of Abraham for their lives—Siberian Christians thanking the Lord for their children—people giving thanks. It
is a good sound.

And the world is listening, watching, weighing, deciding. . . .

Latin Americans listen to the stifled sounds of Cuba. Macao and
Hong Kong receive the gaunt refugees of Red China and hear the
unspeakable. Europeans watch what they hope is the final chapter in
subjugation on that continent.

Africans can see these things—and there is much to occupy their
own moralists on their own vast continent.

There is ample evidence that dictatorial conduct is not confined to societies ruled by whites. South Africa's Sabotage Bill, and restrictive laws on voting and free speech, are no less encouraging than the Preventive Detention Act of Ghana, which empowers the government to imprison without trial for up to five years all persons suspected of subversion; or Ghana's Dignity of the President Bill passed last year which subjects Presidential detractors to 500 pound fines or three years' imprisonment. (If there is a Ghanaian Vaughn Meader—he's laughing on the inside.)

Wrongs that passed as white no color can make right.

A nation, it is true, must work its own evolution in its own way and at its own pace. Time and tide have favored ours. The best hope we can have perhaps is that governments may listen to the voices of their people—American governments have tried to do that. We have found that when people find a willing ear they are more disposed to lend a willing hand. We think with Jefferson that our government is, "The world's best hope; the only one where every man at the call of the law would fly to the standard of the law and would meet invasions of the public order as his own personal concern." This is a Virginian's answer to the demagogues of today, both foreign and domestic. It is the answer of thousands of Southern citizens and of the U. S. Marshals, most of them Southerners, who held the line at the Lyceum in Oxford.

It is clear that the standard of law in America flies to protect the civil liberty of all American citizens from private as well as public invasions. Thus the Sherman Antitrust and Interstate Commerce Act give protection from excesses of the business community. Other legislation guards the public and the working man from the abuses of labor. And today we face in this country a conspiracy which could be extremely erosive of the rights and liberties of our citizens— organized crime. So when we move against these excesses, we do so on behalf of all our people, and at their call. And the agencies and bureaus of government which answer this call, with the patience and care their work requires, deserve the respect of all Americans.

Finally, we have found that man's handhold on the globe is a precarious one. But we have always believed that. We always thought that our destiny was cradled in another Hand. And when Mr. Khrushchev reported that the Cosmonauts—like the Bolshevik pilots of the early twenties—reported seeing "no signs of God," we can only suggest that they aim—with the rest of mankind—a little higher. In the meantime, there is work to do here on earth—to that day when Caesars render unto man what is man's.

Delivered to the Civil Rights Committee
New York City Central Labor Council, AFL-CIO
New York City, March 9, 1963

I suppose it is inevitable that most of us are near-sighted about national problems. We are able to focus on them only as they apply close to home and we find it difficult to see how they affect people in other fields and other states. One of the curious things I have found since becoming Attorney General, however, is that when it comes to civil rights, we very quickly become far-sighted. We are quite ready to point accusing fingers at the South and are easily outraged by a Little Rock, by the beating of Freedom Riders, or by a Meredith case. Yet we respond to discrimination right around us with blank and uncomprehending stares. The attitude is "the other fellow is wrong" and the more wrong he is, the more that automatically puts us on the side of the angels.

There is no question that segregation in the South is socially, politically and morally wrong. But there is deep-seated segregation in the North, also, and it is just as wrong. Racial discrimination is a national, not a regional problem, and it cannot be solved simply by individual instances of federal action on behalf of Freedom Riders or a single college student. The solution requires the hearts, the voices, the mind and the muscle of individuals and organizations all over the country, public and private. The President said last week, in his Civil Rights Message, "The cruel disease of discrimination knows no sectional or state boundaries. The continuing attack on this problem must be equally broad."

I am particularly pleased to be with you here today because labor, and especially groups like yours, historically have been committed to social justice and social action. For years, unions have been in the forefront of efforts toward equal opportunity for all workers and all citizens.

Last year, Mr. Van Arsdale's Local 3 provided an example of such leadership by including 200 Negroes and Puerto Ricans among its 1,000 new apprentices. The New York Council of Painters also has opened its apprenticeship program to Negroes and Puerto Ricans.

In the past few months, 122 international unions, representing more than 10,000,000 workers have joined with the President's Committee on Equal Employment Opportunity and pledged themselves to union programs for fair practices. The dual seniority problem is the subject of wide and serious attention by labor. Segregated locals are fast disappearing. Indeed, probably at no time in the long history of the American labor movement have so many union leaders given such deep and effective attention to the problem of providing equal opportunity for all, regardless of race.

Yet we would be dishonest with ourselves if we did not admit that some discrimination continues to exist within the labor movement—and by no means only in the South. I am thinking, for example, of a particularly ironic situation that exists right now in Washington. Howard University, a distinguished Negro institution, is building a new gymnasium. At least four of the building trades locals involved, however, have no Negroes working on the project. For that matter, these locals have only a handful of Negro members or apprentices.

The fundamental responsibility for solving problems like this is that of labor itself. Your group and others like it do a great deal to help. The Government also has a responsibility in this field: the work of the Vice President and the Equal Employment Committee is well known to you and the President has directed me to seek legal techniques, rules, and procedures to deal with such discrimination.

But there is a more fundamental responsibility for both you in the labor movement and for us in Government. We are as firmly opposed to discrimination in voting, education and other fields as we are to discrimination in unions. It is in order to help the Nation act more effectively against discrimination that the President last week sent Congress a Special Message on Civil Rights. The Administration's program includes three legislative proposals, concerning voting, education, and assistance to areas and organizations undertaking desegregation.

The first and most important bill deals with voting. The people's vote is the people's voice and when some people cannot vote they cannot effectively speak against injustice and deprivation of other rights.

It's like the story told at the time the 19th Amendment was being voted on by the states. A decided anti-feminist complained to his Congressman: "Can't you do something to stop them scarecrow suffragettes from voting?" The Congressman replied, "You mean my charming constituents of the fairer sex?"

We have worked very hard under existing law seeking to guarantee the right to vote to all citizens. The Department of Justice has filed 35 voting suits, 25 of them in this Administration, challenging discrimination or threats in southern counties against Negro registration applicants. But this is a painfully slow way of providing what is, after all, the fundamental right of citizenship. There remain more than 200 counties in the South where less than 15 percent of the eligible Negroes are registered.

Even where we have brought suit, the cases require extremely detailed preparation. In our suit in Montgomery County, Alabama, for example, it was necessary to analyze 36,000 pages of voter applications and to subpoena 185 witnesses for the trial. Each such suit requires the total attention of four to six of the 40 lawyers in our Civil Rights Division for several months.

It often takes many more months before Negroes finally can register and vote. In Ouachita Parish, Louisiana, for example, the Department filed suit in July, 1961. Although 24,000 out of the 40,000 eligible whites were registered to vote, only 725 of the 16,000 eligible Negroes were registered. Another 5,000 Negroes had, in fact, been purged from the voting rolls.

In the 33 months since we brought the suit, a special election for Congress has passed. A general election has passed. And still not even the date for trial has been set. It may well be 1964 before we finally secure a decision and Negroes can register and vote freely.

This is neither an extreme nor an isolated case. There is a real and immediate need for speeding up the process.

We are asking Congress, therefore, to authorize that voting suits be given preference on court dockets and tried in an expedited manner. This parallels the laws of many states which give priority to election suits in an effort to resolve them before the election is over and the chance to vote is wiped out.

Even if cases can be expedited, there still will be a time lag between the filing of a suit and the issuance of orders against further discrimination. Therefore, we have asked Congress to provide for the appointment of temporary federal referees to determine the qualifications of registration applicants during the time voting suits are pending in court.

In addition to the need for speed in guaranteeing the right to vote, there also is a great need for insuring fairness in determining who is qualified to vote.

Some Southern states use the literacy test to make this determination. As a result, barely literate whites, coached by the registrar, often are registered. Meanwhile, Negroes—like a National Science Foundation graduate student from Cornell, or teachers with advanced degrees—arbitrarily are declared illiterate and thus ineligible to vote.

Other states have used the Constitutional interpretation test. Applicants must copy and explain sections of the Federal or State constitutions. Negroes often are required to copy and interpret long, archaic sections of a state constitution, or are required to explain what "due process" means, to a registrar who knows no law.

Whites, meanwhile, copy such provisions as, "There shall be no imprisonment for debt." One white gentleman, who *was* registered, interpreted that section in these words, "I think that a Neogroe Should Have 8 years in college Be for voting Be couse He dont under Stand."

We should reflect on such examples more in sadness than in irony, because they demonstrate the double burden of injustice inflicted on the Negro. Not only is he prevented from registering and voting, but the method of doing so is a grotesquely unfair test.

There's an acid joke about the Negro who attempted to register in a southern county. The registrar asked him to copy and interpret the 14th Amendment. He did so, brilliantly. "All right, if you're so smart," the registrar said, "recite the Gettysburg address from memory." The Negro did. "Okay, give us the Second Inaugural speech." Again the Negro came through beautifully. Finally, the registrar pulled a Chinese newspaper out of his desk and asked, "Can you read this?"

"That's easy," said the Negro. "It says, 'No Negroes are going to vote in this state this year.'"

We are asking Congress in our proposed voting measure to prohibit specifically the use of different tests or standards for different registration applicants. And we have asked that completion of the sixth grade should be regarded as evidence that an applicant is literate.

We also are asking Congress for two other pieces of legislation, both stemming from a need for assistance as well as enforcement. Our experience has demonstrated that people want to obey the law. In the field of education, for example, the violence last fall at the University of Mississippi should not overshadow the fact that sixty Southern school districts were desegregated last year—peacefully and without fanfare. In many cases the Department of Justice assisted through informal consultations.

Communities in the South not only want to obey the law, but they want and need assistance in doing so. One of the laws we seek would establish in the Office of Education a program of technical and financial assistance to communities in the process of integrating their schools.

Such a program would help such school districts profit from the lessons of others—such as Atlanta, where public and private bodies combined with great success in 1961 to desegregate schools without incident. Many communities lack the background and resources required to minimize tensions both outside and inside the schools and to assure the maintenance and improvement of educational standards.

We have applied the same principle of providing information in our third legislative proposal, for the extension and expansion of the Commission on Civil Rights. Not only community governments, but many organizations, both public and private, both in the North and the South, can benefit substantially from expert guidance and information about how others have handled integration problems.

The Civil Rights Commission has the background and ability to satisfy this need and the President consequently has recommended that it be authorized to serve as a national civil rights clearing house

—providing information, and technical guidance to any requesting agency.

Combined with continued effort under existing laws and policies, this, then, is the Administration's civil rights program. There are those who say this program does not go far enough. It is true that there is other civil rights legislation which might be introduced, such as a bill seeking authority for the Government to initiate school desegregation suits. But I would say to these critics that it is perfectly simple to introduce and support bills that have no chance of passage. But to do so would endanger measures that do have a chance. These critics have no responsibility for action. It is the aim of this Administration to seek action and progress, not merely talk and headlines.

Further, let it be clear that this civil rights program is only that— a program. To sit back and wait for progress to come just because somebody in Washington has asked for new laws, is as starry-eyed as waiting for the day labor minstrels once described when "the mills are made of marble and the machines are made of gold."

It took courage and effort for the labor movement to achieve the economic standards it enjoys today. It will take the same kind of effort to achieve the social ideals we profess in the field of civil rights.

We stand not only for labor or the Negro or minority groups, but for the ideal of freedom and dignity which underlies our society.

I come here today to call on you for your efforts on behalf of the Administration's program. I come to ask you to speak out and act as a body. I ask you to go back to your internationals, your locals and your communities to seek their support, both for this program and for its aim.

"Race discrimination," the President said in his Civil Rights message, "hampers our economic growth by preventing the maximum development and utilization of our manpower. It hampers our world leadership by contradicting at home the message we preach abroad. It mars the atmosphere of a united and classless society in which this nation rose to greatness. It increases the costs of public welfare, crime, delinquency and disorder. Above all, it is wrong."

part v TURNING A CORNER

The period in which the following speeches were given—from March 18 to June 2, 1963—witnessed the most intense conflict in the civil rights struggle in this country to that time. Recrimination and acrimony were directed toward almost every partisan.

During the Spring of 1963 civil rights advocates used the word "revolution" far more frequently as a substitute for "movement." The newer concept, and what it implied, was discussed later in a brief and lucid article by Donald Louis Anderson in *Commonweal* (December 13, 1963). An historical approach to this subject can be seen in Roy L. Hill's *Rhetoric of Racial Revolt* (Golden Bell Press, 1964).

The aggressive Black Muslim movement, dedicated to the separation of the races, was gaining in strength. Malcolm X, their leader in the East, seemed to be as critical of leaders of other Negro organizations, such as Rev. Dr. Martin Luther King, Jr., president of the Southern Christian Leadership Conference, as he was of the Kennedys.

Dr. King publicly expressed the hope that the various leaders of disparate Negro civil rights groups could cooperate toward common goals. Yet he antagonized some by leading demonstrations in Birmingham, Alabama, in early April, a time others considered imprudent because of an impending change in city administration; a change which offered the chance of an improved posture toward integration.

The Birmingham city officials who were still in office fought these demonstrations ruthlessly. Clubs, fire hoses, police dogs, cattle prods, jailings, and any and all other available means were put to use.

As in similar situations, the United States Department of Justice was immediately interested and active but limited by the Constitution in what action could be taken, the police powers in this country being in the hands of local and state governments.

On April 22 James Farmer, director of CORE (Congress of Racial Equality), stated that many Negroes were disenchanted with the Kennedys in that the Administration tended to "appease" Congressmen rather than intervene in civil rights crises.

Adding to the increasing tension was the death of a Baltimore postman, William L. Moore, near Attalla, Alabama, on April 23 as he was making an integration pilgrimage.

On April 24 Attorney General Robert F. Kennedy flew to Montgomery, Alabama, to talk with Governor George C. Wallace. The latter had vowed publicly to defy any Federal desegregation order, if and when issued, to permit Negroes to enter the University of Alabama. The Attorney General had to walk through pickets bearing such signs as "Mississippi Murderer" and "No Kennedy Congo Here" to get to the State Capitol. After a conference lasting an hour and a quarter, the two men agreed on at least one matter: Governor Wallace had not changed his position.

While in the South, Mr. Kennedy consulted with United States attorneys and other Federal officials in Alabama, South Carolina and Georgia. He addressed members of the American Association of University Professors at the University of South Carolina on April 25, the text of which is in this section.

In early May, as the Birmingham crisis worsened, Swedish sociologist Dr. Gunnar Myrdal, author of the classic on the Negro problem, *The American Dilemma,* observed that in his opinion racial strife was inevitable as the progress of Negroes in this country continued. He said that while he believed that segregation in the legal sense would end in the next decade, the greatest peril to the Negro was "economic stagnation," a situation which would make the Negro's position more vulnerable.

In contrast to this position, which was in obvious agreement with President Kennedy's priority treatment of economic legislative and executive measures, criticism toward the Administration's work in the field of civil rights did not lessen.

There was a report on May 25, later verified, that the Attorney General had held a secret meeting with some Negro writers at his family's New York apartment during the evening of May 24. According to the report, novelist James Baldwin had initiated the meeting as a means of bridging what he saw as a gap between the Negroes and the Administration.

Highly respected newsman James Reston discussed this confrontation in his column of June 7:

The [Baldwin] meeting started with a savage comment by one of the Negroes against "the Kennedys." Thereafter, the Administration was blamed for not doing enough to settle the Birmingham problem, for hesitating to move Federal troops into Alabama until a white man was hurt, and for leaving the crisis in Alabama to be settled by Negro demonstrations in the streets.

As a matter of fact, the Attorney General and Burke Marshall had been deeply involved behind the scenes in trying to settle the Birmingham crisis. Marshall opened the New York meeting by explaining what the Justice Department had done to arrange a settlement there, but when he finished after 40 minutes, some of the Negroes laughed at him.

Mr. Baldwin later admitted publicly that the meeting was characterized by "caustic" exchanges. While many of the twelve in attendance—mostly Negroes, none of whom held offices in civil rights organizations—considered the meeting a "flop," Mr. Baldwin believed that the exchange might lead to a national dialogue between Negroes and whites.

It was during this period that preparations were being made to register Negro students Vivian Malone and James Hood at the University of Alabama. The stage was set for a showdown. Governor George C. Wallace stated that he would stand in the doorway, if necessary, to prevent their entry, and the United States Department of Justice was making plans to see to it that the students would be allowed to attend the University.

Anthony Lewis reported in *The New York Times* on May 27 that when the Attorney General was told at the meeting of the 24th that the President should personally lead the Negro students into the University of Alabama he replied that it was "an act" and said "we're not interested in acts; we're interested in results."

Walter Lippman advocated in his column May 28, 1963, that desegregation should be a national commitment, not just a Negro movement. He added "I think this is the direction in which the President, and his brother, the Attorney General, are now moving"; and he recommended that they move boldly.

A "result" which all civil rights advocates could applaud had taken place a week earlier. The United States Supreme Court, in effect, had legalized the sit-in demonstration as a tactical weapon when the convictions of 28 Negroes and three white students were set aside. The cases had originated in Alabama, Louisiana, North Carolina and South Carolina. The Court held that segregationist ordinances and policies of local governments were discriminatory and therefore unconstitutional; thus not applicable to the prosecution of persons who sought services in privately owned stores.

The four prepared addresses delivered by the Attorney General during this time of turmoil took place in southern cities.

On March 18 Robert Kennedy gave the principal address at Kentucky's Centennial of the Emancipation Proclamation. This was a pivotal talk for the Attorney General, one in which he stepped back a bit from the strife of the day and looked at the civil rights movement in perspective. "We are," he said, "turning a corner." But he was not talking in terms of days or months. What he meant was that a great deal of progress had taken place but that the sort of change desired was going to take much more time: "By the end of this decade we will have gone much farther down this road." The rest of this speech constitutes a very well reasoned analysis of the stage of the civil rights movement in perspective.

The speeches of April 25 and May 17 delivered in Columbia, South Carolina, and Asheville, North Carolina, were appeals for understanding and cooperation in the racial struggle. As the content of both was essentially the same, only the text of the April 25th address is included.

The final talk given in this period is a commencement address at Trinity College—composed in an attractive style—in which he recommends specific ways in which the graduates of this Catholic women's college might make personal commitments as steps toward a better society.

Delivered at Kentucky's Centennial
of the Emancipation Proclamation
Freedom Hall, Louisville, Kentucky, March 18, 1963

One hundred years ago, Abraham Lincoln, a son of Kentucky, proclaimed that all persons held as slaves in the area of rebellion, "henceforward shall be free."

We join today, in the Centennial of that proclamation to re-dedicate ourselves to the parallel doctrine that all Americans, of whatever race or creed, shall also be equal.

The Emancipation Proclamation was an act of great courage and great clarity. As Lincoln went to sign it, he said, "If my name goes down in history, it will be for this act. My whole soul is in it. If my hand trembles when I sign this proclamation, all who examine the document hereafter will say: 'He hesitated'."

But Lincoln's hand did not tremble. He did not hesitate. As always, he saw with greater vision than those around him what issues were at stake in the war. He called the Proclamation an act of justice and invoked upon it the "considered judgment of mankind and the gracious favor of Almighty God."

On another occasion, he tied his act to the essence of our national purpose, saying, "In giving freedom to the slave, we assure freedom to the free."

The signing of the Emancipation Proclamation started the clock of progress ticking toward the day when all Americans could live, in practice, according to the national ideal that all men are born free, with equal opportunity to obtain justice and equal opportunity to pursue—and obtain—happiness.

But a quarter century later, the clock practically stopped. For the next fifty years, the doctrine of "separate but equal" lay like a dead hand on the springs of progress. The Nation had not retained nor understood the clarity of Lincoln's purpose.

It was another son of Kentucky who saw most precisely when our nation stopped moving ahead towards equal opportunity for all Americans. Mr. Justice John Marshall Harlan, a former slave owner himself, and an opponent of the enactment of the Thirteenth, Fourteenth, and Fifteenth Amendments to the Constitution, was a native of Boyle County who served on the Supreme Court of the United States for 33 years. His was a dissenting voice on questions of racial equality and the commands of the Constitution, but it, also, was a voice of great clarity.

In 1883 the Court struck down what was to be the last action of Congress in the civil rights field from 1875 to 1957. Justice Harlan predicted in his dissent to that opinion that "we shall enter upon an era of constitutional law, when the rights of freedom and American citizenship cannot receive from the nation that efficient protection which heretofore was unhesitatingly accorded to slavery and the rights of the master."

Thirteen years later, the Supreme Court put its stamp of approval on the practice of segregation. But again the vision of the American ideal was in a Harlan dissent. He saw that segregation "puts the brand of servitude and degradation upon a large class of our fellow citizens, our equals before the law." He said that the practice in the long run "gives no other result than to render permanent peace impossible and to keep alive a conflict of races, the continuance of which must do harm to all concerned."

He said, "Our Constitution is color-blind, and neither knows nor tolerates classes among citizens."

In our generation, that view is no longer expressed in dissent. It represents the view of the majority of our Nation. We can see now, with the vision and clarity of Lincoln and Harlan, the toll exacted by discrimination—whether overt segregation or covert bigotry.

And when we talk about the human rights guaranteed by the Constitution, we must talk about both segregation and bigotry, whether in the North or in the South. Lincoln said, "The North responds to the proclamation sufficiently in breath." There is a very great need for the North to respond to the deprivation of rights in action as well.

Our effort cannot be directed only against open discrimination in one area, while ignoring the real deprivation of opportunity caused by indirect discrimination in another.

As President Kennedy said just three weeks ago:

> The Negro baby born in America today—regardless of the section or state in which he is born—has about one-half as much chance of completing high school as a white baby born in the same place on the same day—one-third as much chance of completing college—one-third as much chance of becoming a professional man—twice as much chance of becoming unemployed—about one-seventh as much chance of earning $10,000 per year—a life expectancy which is seven years less—and the prospects of earning only half as much.

Lincoln described the signing of the Emancipation Proclamation as the central act of his administration and "the great event of the

Nineteenth Century." Today, we can maintain that America's present accelerating effort toward the fulfillment of Lincoln's central act is the great event of our century.

We have come to the time in our history to show the world and ourselves—what our ideals mean in practice: that Americans are generous, not merely affluent; that we are concerned with character, not with color; that, in Lincoln's words about his proclamation we seek progress "not in anger, but in expectation of a greater good."

We have a lot to do. With your help—with the help of Americans of vision and goodwill everywhere—I believe and I pray that we will do so. Kentucky, the mother of Lincoln and Harlan, will be, under the leadership of Governor Combs, in the front ranks of the forward march.

Thus, I am especially happy to be here tonight to participate in this observation, not only of what Lincoln did a hundred years ago, but of what we must do today.

We must make sure that the Negro citizens of all states can fully and freely exercise their franchise. This may take strenuous litigation and great energy on the part of many people. But it is worthwhile as we have found out in the past two years. Under existing law the Department of Justice has filed 35 suits—25 of them in this Administration—to end discrimination against Negroes who seek to vote.

Some Southern states use a literacy test to deny Negroes the right to register. As a result, barely literate whites, coached by the registrar, are allowed to register and vote. Meanwhile, Negroes—including scientists with national research grants or teachers with advanced degrees—are declared arbitrarily to be illiterate and thus denied the right to vote.

The difficulty is that each one of these cases require extremely detailed preparation and many months to litigate. In Ouachita Parish, Louisiana, for example, the Department filed suits in July, 1961. Although 24,000 of 40,000 eligible whites were registered to vote, only 725 of the 16,000 eligible Negroes were registered. In the 21 months since we brought the suit, a special election for Congress has passed. A general election has passed. Still not even the date for trial has been set.

But the results are worth the effort. Where the voting suits have been completed, Negroes have been registered in increasing numbers. In Bullock County, Alabama, five Negroes were registered last September. Now there are a thousand. In neighboring Macon County, 2,800 Negroes are registered today. Only a handful were allowed to register there in 1961.

To speed up this process, the President has asked Congress to authorize that voting suits be given priority on the dockets and be expedited.

We must achieve equal education opportunities for all our children regardless of race. Segregated schools cause educational as well as psychological difficulties and the resulting drain on our greatest resource—the spirit and knowledge of our children—must be eliminated.

We may observe, with as much sadness as irony that outside of Africa, south of the Sahara where education is still a difficult challenge, the only places on earth known not to provide free public education are Communist China, North Vietnam, Sarawak, Singapore, British Honduras—and Prince Edward County, Virginia.

But while the situation at Prince Edward County or the violence which occurred last fall in the University of Mississippi may capture the headlines, the far more important fact is that an increasing number of southern communities, local officials, and citizen groups are working effectively to desegregate their schools peacefully and without fanfare. Last year, for example, 60 southern school districts were desegregated without any difficulty whatsoever.

It should be our goal to make it possible for any child who wishes to do so to enter the same public schools on the same basis as they are made available to children of another race.

We must continue achieving equal job opportunities for all our people. We must do this because we have proved to ourselves and to the world that it is the quality of the man, and not the color of his skin, which determines who can serve on our courts; who can hold high public office; who can exercise great responsibilities in office; who can produce miracles of science or our educational institutions. This has now been shown by example after example, until examples are no longer necessary.

And finally, we must move ahead throughout the country in achieving, for all our citizens, access to public places and the freedom to live where they choose.

President Kennedy said in his message last month: "No act is more contrary to the spirit of our democracy and Constitution than the barring of (any Negro) citizen from restaurants, hotels, theaters, recreational areas and other public accommodations and facilities."

In the past three years alone, many states by law and many cities by voluntary act have ended a century of such discrimination. And last year, as a result of Federal action, virtually every bus station, every railroad station, and every airport in the South was desegregated. It is now possible to travel from Seattle to Key West and not see signs "White Only" or "Colored Only."

Many states and cities as well as the Federal Government through executive order last fall also have moved to open communities to Negro residents. By the end of this decade we will have gone much, much farther down this road.

We are, in short, turning a corner—in a period of great and intense change.

Once again the mark of this change is seen with clarity here in Kentucky. Only today, Governor Combs has issued a Code of Fair Practice, following the establishment of the Kentucky Commission on Human Rights and the Louisville Human Relations Commission. This is a wise and long step for the State of Kentucky. It is also a reflection of how far all the American people have gone in understanding the wisdom of the Emancipation itself, and the dissents of Justice Harlan.

In the last analysis, the changes of this decade are not going to be those of the Federal Government or of the states or the cities. They will come, rather, as is right in a free society, from the people themselves—from their hearts and their minds and consciences.

The Kentucky Code of Fair Practice shows how the states can assert their responsibilities and thus preserve their rights. And my own experience in the Department of Justice over the past two years has convinced me beyond question that the vast majority of the people in all the states—in the North, South, East and West—want to obey the law, and that the American people as a whole demand progress in this field and will not accept the status quo.

The problems that remain are massive. The results of racial discrimination carry on for generation after generation. To face this openly, and to try to meet it squarely, is the challenge of this decade of change.

It is one thing to free the franchise for all our citizens. It is another to persuade everyone that they should register and vote, and still another to learn to exercise the franchise wisely.

It is one thing to open the schools to all children regardless of race. It is another to train the teachers, to build the classrooms, and to attempt to eliminate the effects of past educational deficiencies. It is still another to find ways to feed the incentive to learn and keep children in school.

It is one thing to open job opportunities. It is another to train people to fill them, or to persuade American enterprise to seek Negro as well as white applicants.

It is one thing to free new housing for all citizens regardless of race. It is another to enable more Negroes to have the means to take advantage of decent housing.

The Federal Government, the states, each city, and all organizations which have devoted their energies to the cause of racial justice, should recognize clearly that these are the challenges of the future: that meeting them requires a great outpouring of energies of a very different kind than the instruments of Government and the private organizations have used in the past.

The Emancipation Proclamation had and has great meaning for America. It has brought the American Negro within calling distance at least of all the privileges and protections of our Constitution and Bill of Rights. It has given him the freedom to speak his mind.

But for this reason and for others it is clear that the meaning and reach of the Emancipation are by no means confined to the boundaries of the United States. If it was true, as Jefferson said, that the American Revolution belonged to all mankind, the same may be said —in fact must be said—of the Emancipation.

Its message sweeps like a great tide which will enter and wash out every crevice of unjust privilege in the world. It has meaning for the underprivileged and struggling masses of our own hemisphere. For millions of them are still slaves to hunger, disease, illiteracy, and abject poverty.

Must any nation or group of nations which systematically bring the individual to his knees before the will of the State—which, more often than not, means the whims of a small group of self-centered men.

The bowed heads of the world are no longer those of American

Negroes. They belong, rather, to the unfortunate millions living under communism and other forms of tyranny.

The act we celebrate today must not be considered a purely American experience. It is a torch that men will pass from hand to hand into every dark place in the world where slavery, of one kind or another, exists.

This work will go forward firmly, without malice and with charity not merely because of the Cold War but, as the President has said, "because it is right."

*Delivered at a Meeting of
the University of South Carolina Chapter
American Association of University Professors
Columbia, South Carolina, April 25, 1963*

I am highly pleased and honored to be here with you in the State of South Carolina. This is the state that produced Marion and Sumter, Calhoun and Major Anderson.*

It was just six months ago that Major Anderson made the pictures which alerted this Government and this country to the Soviet missile threat in Cuba. It was his death six months ago this Saturday and the incidents which led up to it which led the President to send notification to Mr. Khrushchev that strong and overwhelming retaliatory action would be taken unless he received immediate notice that the missiles would be withdrawn. And it was within 24 hours of his death that President Kennedy received the message from Mr. Khrushchev that the missiles would be taken out.

I remember when the President received the message about the death of Major Anderson. He turned to several of us who were in the room with him and said, "That's the worst thing about war—the best and bravest are the ones who are killed."

* Major Rudolf Anderson, Jr., U. S. Air Force reconnaissance pilot, was declared missing and presumed dead by the Defense Department on October 27, 1962. Within a week, his body was returned from Cuba where his plane was shot down. A native of Greenville, South Carolina, Major Anderson was one of two pilots credited with gaining the first conclusive evidence of the Soviet missile build-up in Cuba.

And so I'm proud and pleased to be here in your state with you at this university.

We live today in an era of challenge. This is a time of uncertainty and peril; it is also a time of great opportunity.

The decisions we make as a people, as a Government, during the next few years will affect this planet for generations to come. In fact, what the United States does can very well determine the more basic question—whether there will even be generations to come.

All of us are most concerned about the kind of America we want to pass on to our children. Every generation inherits a world it never made; and, as it does so, it automatically becomes the trustee of that world for those who come after. In due course, each generation makes its own accounting to its children.

When our time comes, we want to make sure that we bequeath to our descendants a better and safer world than the one in which we live today—a world in which people will be free from the terrors of war and oppression, free from the handicaps of ignorance and poverty, free to realize their own talents and fulfill their own destiny.

This is the object of our foreign policy and of our defense policy. I will only say that if the free world is to survive, it must accept the responsibility to resist aggression. And aggression in the contemporary world takes a multitude of forms. It, therefore, requires a variety of responses. It is our purpose to develop balanced military forces, capable of countering every form of attack, from the nuclear strike to a guerrilla attack, and then use the interval thus gained to work unceasingly toward disarmament and peace.

To this end, we have increased our Polaris missile procurement by 50 per cent. We have doubled our capability to produce the Minuteman missile; we have greatly increased our ability to airlift troops and equipment from this country to the point of attack; our strength in conventional military forces has been built up from 14 to 19 combat-ready Army and Marine divisions; and we have doubled the number of warheads in our strategic alert forces.

But we have learned that aggression is not limited to nuclear attack or even conventional warfare. We must be ready to meet war by guerrillas, subversives, insurgents, assassins, war by ambush instead of combat. Now, for the first time we have that capability.

To deal with Communist guerrilla attacks and Communist-inspired insurgency, the following steps have been taken:

1. A special committee of high officials has been established in Washington to supervise our counterinsurgency efforts on a continuing basis;

2. By June, some 57,000 government officials will have attended courses dealing with counterinsurgency;

3. The Army special warfare forces are now six times their 1961 strength; and

4. Special warfare training is now carried out in several languages at the Special Warfare Center at Ft. Bragg, the Police Academy and Jungle Warfare Training Center in Panama, and at training centers in Europe, Okinawa and Vietnam.

It is especially appropriate to mention counterinsurgency here in the capital of South Carolina; for your state nurtured the great partisan leaders of the American Revolution—Pickens, Sumter and Francis Marion.

The safety of our nation and the peace of the world constitute one great challenge. Another is our economic growth here at home. This is the issue which is the center of the controversy over the proposals currently before Congress to lower the income tax rates and reform the tax structure.

The objective of these proposals is to speed the rate of economic growth in our domestic economy which requires us to find 30,000 new jobs every week during this decade.

I know that many people are worried about the size of the Federal budget. Yet, the budget is bound to grow as the country grows and as our global responsibilities to defend freedom remain heavy. A century ago, the total population of the United States was about 34 million—just about the number of people we have added to our population in the few short years since 1950.

The growth of public expenditures is not confined to the Federal Government. It is worth observing that in your own state of South Carolina, the state budget has grown twice as fast as the Federal budget over the last 20 years.

This is true of state expenditures generally. Twenty-five years ago the non-defense expenditures in the Federal budget were just about equal to the total state and local expenditures; today, these Federal expenditures are about 60 per cent of state and local expenditures. Since 1948, state and local employment has risen by 81 per cent while federal-civilian employment has risen 22 per cent—less than the rate of growth of the population as a whole.

The program of tax reduction is designed to raise our economy to new heights of activity and productivity. Those who worry about our nation's fiscal position should recall the lesson we all learned in 1959; it is recession rather than reduction which poses the gravest danger to fiscal balance. Another depression would cause a much larger deficit than anything contemplated in the proposed tax cut.

To enlarge the vistas of opportunity, we must also clear away those conditions which deprive our citizens, and especially our boys and girls, of the chance for a decent living.

As Attorney General, I have a number of specific responsibilities in this area. I would like to select just three for mention here tonight: the fight against organized crime; the fight against juvenile delinquency; and the fight for civil rights. I believe that we must make steady progress toward success in each of these areas if we are to build the kind of America which we would be proud to pass on to our children.

I might congratulate you tonight on the fact that there is little or no organized crime in South Carolina. This is true. May it always be so.

Two years ago we faced the frightening prospect of organized crime and racketeering steadily increasing their power in community after community throughout the land. This spreading blight was financed by the enormous profits of gambling. It was expanding most rapidly in narcotics, labor-management payoffs and corruption of public officials.

In 1961 with bi-partisan support, we were able to obtain passage of new anti-racketeering laws aimed against interstate gambling operations, to cut heavily into the gambling revenue which bankrolls organized crime. The FBI has made more than 10,000 investigations under these new laws.

The work of the FBI and all the other Federal investigative agencies is being coordinated for the first time and intelligence is being gathered on the activities of 1,100 of our worst underworld figures.

In the Department of Justice the work of the Organized Crime and Racketeering Section has been greatly expanded. The personnel

Many people are now at work, with the full support of this administration, to wipe out the underlying causes of unrest and turmoil in our Nation's Capitol.

In conclusion, I would like to mention the toughest and gravest internal challenge which the United States faces today—the need to grant full equality of opportunity to the American Negro in his own country.

The Negro baby born in America today—regardless of the section or state in which he is born—has about one-half as much chance of completing high school as a white baby born in the same place on the same day—one-third as much chance of completing college—one-third as much chance of becoming a professional man—twice as much chance of becoming unemployed—about one-seventh as much chance of earning $10,000 per year—a life expectancy which is seven years less—and the prospects of earning only half as much.

I speak of this as a need, not a choice, for that is what it is. We as a Nation have no choice but to make progress towards full equality of opportunity. I have learned in the past two years that the vast majority of our people accept this, as it must be accepted by any American who thinks about the problem in the light of history.

First, because, as the President has said, it is right. We are still a people moved by moral force. We believe that all men are created free and are equal before the law. One of our overriding moral drives now is to make that true for Negroes as well as others.

But the practical needs of the United States and the world today would compel our National Government—regardless of party or personal conviction—to do everything possible to eliminate racial discrimination.

We are committed in the world to the cause of freedom. This is not a matter of words, but of compelling international politics.

In the trip I made last year to Asia and Europe, the one issue which was raised in every meeting, by every group, was racial discrimination in the United States. And it makes sense that this should be so. The fact is that we live in a world that is ridding itself of the patterns of the past, and where immense international power has come to new nations and new leaders who are not white.

But we would have no choice whatever the moral issue, not even if we could live in isolation from the rest of the world.

It has been 100 years since the slaves were freed. During that time in many places little progress has been made to give full liberty to the descendants of the slaves. Now time is running out fast for this country.

We must recognize, as responsible citizens and as responsible government officials, that the Negroes in this country cannot be expected indefinitely to tolerate the injustices which flow from official and private racial discrimination in the United States.

The troubles we see now, agitation and even bloodshed, will not compare to what we will see a decade from now unless real progress is made. I am not speaking of the South alone, for these injustices are not a matter of region.

As years pass, resentment increases. The only cure for resentment is progress. The only antidote to agitation is the effort which state, local, and Federal officials are making to deal both with discrimination itself and with its deep-seated economic and social effects.

So despite the changes that are required, and sometimes resisted, we are fortunate as a nation that these three great needs of our time— the moral drive for equality, the necessities caused by our position before the world, and the surge for equality by Negroes throughout the country—are met in the United States, as has been true of other needs in the past, by recognition in the law.

This great State acted under the law last January when Harvey Gantt was admitted to Clemson College without disorder, without bitterness, and without defiance to the orders of the Court.

I am obligated by my oath of office to uphold and enforce the law. If you were in my position, you could do no less than I. And I deeply believe that in this case the law accurately reflects the needs of the country and of its people.

Over the coming months and years, I am confident that respect for the law will prevail, and that the transition which is enjoined by the law will be made. And that accomplishment will be in accord with the deepest traditions of our history.

As Thomas Paine wrote in 1776, "Yet that we may not appear

defective in earthly honors, let a day be solemnly set apart for pro-claiming the charter; let it be brought forth, placed on the divine law, the work of God; let a crown be placed thereon, by which the world may know that so far as we approve of monarchy, in America the law is king."

Thank you very much.

Delivered at the Commencement Exercises, Trinity College Washington, D. C., June 2, 1963

I consider it a great honor to take part in this ceremony—to be as-sociated, however briefly, with one of the finest liberal arts colleges in America—and I must add too that I find it a great pleasure.

.   .   .   .   .

Remembering my own graduation from college (which, people keep reminding me, wasn't really so very long ago), I think I can imagine something of what you feel this afternoon.

For most of you, I would guess that the main significance of this day is that it marks an ending—the culmination of four unique and memorable years—and that like most endings it is touched with sadness.

But our ceremony, after all, is called commencement. And what commences today, for each of you, is membership in the most vital segment of this country's population—that scant nine per cent of American adults who have received and mastered a higher education.

I suspect there may always be arguments about what constitutes a higher education, but wise men through the ages have at least been able to agree on its purpose.

Its purpose is not only to discipline and instruct, but above all to *free* the mind—to free it from the darkness, the narrowness, the groundless fears and self-defeating passions of ignorance.

And so perhaps it's not too much to say that what we are cele-brating here today is the liberation, the setting free of your minds.

From now on you have earned the right to do your own learning, to develop your own insights and draw your own conclusions, to conduct your own explorations in the life you find around you. Your minds have been freed.

You may sometimes regret it, for a free mind insists on seeking out reality, and reality is often a far more painful matter than the soft and comfortable illusions of the intellectually poor.

But your regret will be nothing compared with your advantage —the measureless advantage you will always have over the vast majority of human beings on this earth.

In the light of a truly freed mind no prejudice can disguise itself as zeal, no bullying can masquerade as leadership, no pettiness can pose as importance.

The freed mind will never confuse a sentimentality with a true emotion, an act of violence with an act of heroism, a slogan with a cause.

Men and women with freed minds may often be mistaken, but they are seldom fooled. They may be influenced, but they can't be intimidated. They may be perplexed, but they will never be lost.

Granting that you have won this freedom of mind, and that you have the courage to accept it, there follows next an almost automatic question.

How are you going to use it? What are you—and I mean each of you, as individuals—what are you going to do with this hard-earned and priceless power?

It seems to me that three choices lie before you.

You can simply keep it, savor it, and never use it in any but an occasional negative or critical way—and this can only be considered a terrible waste.

Second, you can use only that small portion of it that may serve to advance your own status in the economic and social scales—but to do this would clearly betray your failure to grasp the distinction between education and training.

Your third choice is to use your mind to the fullest, for the benefit of others as well as yourself—to take an active, creative part in the community, the Nation and the world you live in.

And that, it seems to me, is not merely the best of the three alternatives but the only one worth considering.

This Nation today needs all the freed minds it can muster, in order to meet the challenge posed by the infinite complexity of problems both at home and abroad, to pit our intellectual strength against the insidious menace of an enemy that goes by many names: discrimination, hunger, disease, ignorance, economic oppression, and political tyranny.

The current crisis in civil rights for example, is not something that can be solved by Government edict. It is an intensely human problem, and its ultimate solution will rest in the ability of men and women everywhere to recognize and follow their own best instincts.

They will need guidance in this quest for right as opposed to wrong, for vision as opposed to blindness, for reason as opposed to hysteria. Our answer to the extremists must be to move quickly in establishing those reforms which all of us know in our hearts, should have been made long ago.

And you, enlightened by your religious and liberal education, will be among those expected to provide the necessary leadership.

The Negro's struggle for equality, for all its urgency, is by no means the only pressing social problem within our shores. We think of ourselves as a rich country, yet the spectre of poverty hangs over many hundreds of thousands of Americans.

I wonder how many of you are aware of this fact: nearly 21 per cent of American families—not individuals, but whole families— are living on total annual income of less than the amount of a single year's tuition and board at this college.

Conditions among the American Indians, seldom publicized, are so poor that I could devote the rest of my talk to them alone, but I'll settle for two statistics.

The infant mortality rate among Indians is nearly twice that of any other racial group in the country; and their overall life expectancy is twenty years less.

And here is another alarming truth about the United States today: one out of every eight Americans is either mentally ill or mentally retarded, and present facilities for their treatment and care are sadly inadequate.

None of these problems is the business of government alone, or of any specialized organization. They are *your* business, all of them; and by you I mean every one of you, personally—especially you whose minds have been freed.

I would remind you of your own Sister Margaret's words, in that inspiring talk she gave last month, when she called on all of us to "show in our deeds what we say in our words," and when she pointed out that "a deep and genuine concern for our fellow men is not proven by the regular contribution of tax-deductible sums to our favorite charities."

The challenge is there to be met; the only remaining question is that of how you, as individuals, will be able to meet it—and this of course depends to a great extent on what your immediate plans are after leaving college.

A recent survey shows that some 62 per cent of women college seniors in this country plan to take up some serious profession or employment before marriage, while the remaining 38 per cent look forward to early marriage as a career in itself. These figures may not apply to this graduating class, but, in any case, I would like to address my next few remarks to each group starting with those of you—the majority, I assume—who now plan active working lives.

Of all the occupations you may follow perhaps you can best meet the challenge in the field of education. Present estimates show that within the next ten years we will need no less than 30 per cent more teachers than we are presently producing, if our educational system is to survive.

Perhaps you can best serve by taking an active part in your Government, or in its agencies—the enormously productive Peace Corps, for example, or the hopefully soon-to-be-established Domestic Service Corps Organization.

Perhaps you will find your place in medicine. Over the next decade, the physical and mental health of our nation will demand as many as half a million more doctors and nurses than we now have.

Your range of service might lie in the ever expanding physical sciences, or in the social sciences, or in economics, or in the law, or in the arts. The choice is yours, to be made according to your own skills and inclinations.

But any responsible use of your freed mind will demand that the choice be made—and that it be made for reasons greater than mere convenience or personal gain.

And now I would like to talk to that other, presumably smaller group of you—those who will be going straight from college into married life.

You have, of course, my blessing. But I'm afraid I must add that you also have my concern. The classic role of wife and mother as *just* a wife and mother is something that belongs, I believe, to simpler times than ours—and to simpler minds than yours.

The bland gospel of "togetherness," so sweetly and solemnly spread by merchants over the mass media of this country, can no longer be dismissed as a minor irritant in our popular culture.

It has come to reflect a real and present danger: a growing concept of ideal family life as containment within an air-tight capsule of coziness and consumership, a bright plastic bastion from which all the range and clamor of the world is shut out—from which reality itself is forever held at bay.

Don't—as those other frightening advertisements used to say—don't let this happen to you.

Consider it imperative, for your own and your husband's and above all your children's sake, as well as the sake of your countrymen, that you continue to make full and generous use of the mind your education has set free.

If only with part of your time and only in the region of your own community, you may find yourself able to work effectively against the forces of darkness around you.

Your opportunities are unlimited, for volunteer workers are urgently needed for a multitude of programs in depressed areas all over the nation.

Right here in Washington, for instance—and mind you, this is only one of hundreds of cities—there are many humane projects whose need for volunteer help is enormous.

To cite only several examples:

Washington Action for Youth, an organization established with funds from the President's Committee on Juvenile Delinquency, is now engaged in a broad program to help overcome the years of neglect that have allowed our capital to reach a crisis point in family deprivation and adolescent unrest.

But hundreds of volunteer workers will soon be needed if the efforts of this group are to succeed.

The Urban League has launched an educational drive that calls for an unlimited number of volunteers to teach at school remedial centers, helping children who are falling behind in their work.

The Urban Service Corps, both in its own remedial teaching project and in its *widening horizons program* this summer, will also need substantial volunteer help.

So will the *area "P" crash program* of the *Junior Chamber of Commerce,* in its counselling work with potential high school drop-outs; and every settlement house in the city urgently requires volunteers to work directly with underprivileged children.

These are only a few of the agencies dealing with problems in Washington alone.

The same story can be told of conditions in almost every other city in America—wherever you live, you must face the fact that your home will be surrounded by a crying need for help—*your* help—in as many ways as there are kinds of oppression and poverty and pain.

If family circumstances do prevent you from taking an active part in the human struggle beyond your doorstep, in your town, your country and the world, then at the very least you can—and it seems to me that you must—take an active interest.

This college and this Nation have every right to expect that much of you. And you, with your freed mind, have no excuse but to expect that much of yourself.

I am sure that all of you, liberally educated as you are, need not be told that we live in a perilous, exciting, potentially disastrous and yet also potentially the best of times.

And I need scarcely remind you that your generation will have plenty to worry about—more, perhaps, than any other in history. My message here is simply that there can be no allowance for your complacency in the days and years ahead, and there will be every reason and every need for your intense, personal involvement.

As people with free minds in a free society, we have literally everything to live for.

And, as we use our faculties to the maximum, as we apply ourselves fully to do God's work we have nothing to be afraid of.

Good Luck! And may God be with you all.

Thank you.

part vi FOR A COMPREHENSIVE
CIVIL RIGHTS BILL

If one day were selected as the most critical in President John F. Kennedy's public involvement in civil rights, that day very probably would be June 11, 1963.

The Birmingham crisis during the previous two months had received worldwide attention. Pictures of brutality and terror were carried by television, newspapers and magazines everywhere. In the minds of many, much of the blame for the racial strife was placed on the Administration. Included, surprisingly, were some intelligent but either unthinking or uninformed individuals who seemed to believe that President Kennedy could transcend the Constitution and, by fiat, bring tranquility to the no-man's-land that was then Birmingham.

And for many weeks Governor George C. Wallace had been claiming that he would not respect a presidential order to desegregate the University of Alabama.

Unlike the Birmingham crisis, a legal showdown with Governor Wallace would not be difficult to win, and by a show of strength President Kennedy could gain the enthusiastic applause of millions of civil rights partisans. But the question was whether the goal—the matriculation of Negroes Vivian Malone and James Hood—could be achieved without making a martyr of the Governor, without bloodshed, and without unnecessarily antagonizing the people of the South.

President Kennedy was able to achieve his end with minimum risk of perilous repercussions by brilliant strategy which consisted of taking just two steps: issuing a proclamation enjoining Governor Wallace from preventing the registration of the students, and federalizing the Alabama National Guard.

That night President Kennedy gained the spirited gratitude of most civil rights advocates by delivering over nationwide television an emotional speech—unique for him—pledging his total effort to this "moral crisis" and asking the cooperation of all citizens to correct racial inequities. The Reverend Dr. Martin Luther King., Jr., said the speech was "one of the most eloquent, profound and unequivocal pleas for justice and freedom for all men ever made by any President." Roy Wilkins, executive director of the N.A.A.C.P., also praised the speech saying it posed the moral issue in racial matters, but Mr. Wilkins expressed disappointment that the President did not emphasize "the most pressing problem confronting Negro Americans"— discrimination in employment.

Then tragedy struck again. Early on the morning of June 13, Medgar Evers, Mississippi field representative of the National Association for the Advancement of Colored People, was fatally shot in the back as he walked to his home in Jackson. Once again outrage was felt across the land. Demonstrations were held in Jackson and fears were voiced that another Birmingham would be set off. Fortunately, this did not occur.

While there seems to be no connection with the Evers tragedy, the Attorney General was himself the object of a half-hearted and generally good-natured demonstration the next day, on June 14.

The Negroes involved—estimated at a few hundred—first gathered in Lafayette Park, across Pennsylvania Avenue from the White House. From there they paraded to the District of Columbia Building and thence to the Justice Department. Encircling the building, they waved their homemade signs reading: "Let Negroes Work in the Justice Department," "Don't Play Politics With Human Rights," and "Why An Almost Lily White Justice Department—It's Not Easter."

After about twenty minutes the Attorney General arrived and the demonstrators mixed a few boos with their cheers. Robert Kennedy was smiling but obviously not pleased. He cited the gains made in Negro employment at "Justice" during his tenure and declared "Any individual can come in here and get a job if he is qualified." After promising to continue to oppose discrimination in hiring, the Attorney General said "But I'm not going out and hire a Negro just because he's not white."

For more than a month well-founded rumors persisted that the President, the Attorney General and other Administration officials were working on a new presidential message on civil rights. On June 10 the 5,500-word request for an omnibus civil rights bill was sent to Congress. A good part of the message consisted of recommendations previously made, but there were some new provisions which civil rights leaders hoped for and were not optimistic about getting.

Perhaps the boldest request was for a law forbidding discrimination in public accommodations. Another would ban discrimination in employment where Federal monies were involved.

A recommendation that had far-reaching implications would make clear that "the Federal Government is not required, under any statute, to furnish any kind of financial assistance to any program or activity in which racial discrimination occurs." Congressmen from southern states that boasted lucrative defense industries and military establishments had reason to fear such a suggestion.

A provision having infinite potential for good would create a Community Relations Service to act as a mediation agency in communities having racial tensions. In this way, it was hoped, problems might be settled equitably and perhaps amicably.

In all, the President's message was the most comprehensive ever sent to Congress on the subject of civil rights and one that so caught the attention of the people that this complex recommendation was referred to thereafter as simply "the Civil Rights Bill."

When on June 19, 1963, President Kennedy sent his message to Congress he passed the point of no return. The heavy opposition which greeted the news reinforced the conviction of some civil rights advocates that as desirable as such legislation would be, the cloture rule in the Senate was just too great an obstacle. A simple majority was simply not enough, two-thirds of the Senators present would have to vote to end the filibuster that was sure to come, and that was an almost impossible goal. For in addition to the opponents of civil rights legislation, some Senators opposed cloture on principle, contending that to end debate in that fashion was to vote against the Senate's privilege of free speech.

On the other hand, John F. Kennedy, now two and a half years in office, had seen much of his legislative program passed and the rest well on the way. So now was the time to try for the kind of civil rights legislation that would be meaningful.

Rather surprisingly, the President's message appeared to have little effect on the number of demonstrations or the vehemence of criticism. Not all the barbs were directed at the Administration, however. Roy Wilkins, executive director of the N.A.A.C.P., indulged in some introspection with respect to the participation of Negroes. On June 21 he was quoted as having decried massive demonstrations not tied to specific purposes: an indication of the strain among Negro organizations. Too, he expressed disappointment in the number of Negroes in New York, and northern Negroes in general, who were apathetic with respect to taking full advantage of their rights as voters.

Another sign of antagonism within the Negro ranks was seen when perhaps their most famous leader, the Reverend Martin Luther King, Jr., was the target of a few Negroes throwing eggs when he visited Harlem on June 30. Because Dr. King had criticized the Black Muslims, members of that group were suspected of the effrontery.

The big event of that summer was the March on Washington of August 28, directed by A. Philip Randolph, president of the Sleeping Car Porters Union, and Negro activist Bayard Rustin. An estimated interracial crowd of 200,000 persons provided a decorous and moving display for the country. For the many diverse civil rights organizations, frequently at odds on matters of objectives and tactics, the "March" was an example of unprecedented cooperation and unanimity.

The President's great popularity suffered in the months following the submission of his civil rights bill to Congress. Democrats began to wonder whether he could be reelected in 1964. The results of a poll published by *Newsweek*, October 21, 1963, showed that President Kennedy would lose 3.5 million votes in a 1964 election because of his civil rights policies.

In a *Saturday Evening Post* article of March 28, 1964, Peter Maas wrote of a discussion he had with Robert Kennedy concerning those frustrating summer and early fall days of 1963. The Attorney General said that he never believed there was any question of the President's reelection, but he quoted his brother as saying at the time, "What the hell. If we're going to lose, let's lose on principle."

President John F. Kennedy wrote a letter for a special commemorative issue of *Ebony* (September 1963) marking the centennial of the Emancipation Proclamation. He said in part: "The year 1863, when Abraham Lincoln struck off the bonds of slavery, marked the first stage in the emancipation of the American Negro. I believe that future historians, looking back on the brave events of recent months, will regard the year 1963 as the beginning of the final stage— as the great turning-point, when the nation at last undertook to carry the process of emancipation through to its fulfillment."

Roy Wilkins appeared to agree with the President's analysis when, in another article in the same issue of *Ebony*, he said rather poetically: "Come what may, we are on our way and the new day already looms in sight."

The speeches given by the Attorney General during this period were marked by a good deal of variety, the topics concerning the moral aspects of civil rights, the problems of Spanish-speaking Americans, the legal implementation of *Brown v. Board of Education*, religious liberty, the concept of freedom, school drop-outs, and the public accommodation section of the Administration's Civil Rights Bill.

Delivered at Ceremonies Celebrating the 175th Anniversary of the Ratification of the Constitution Independence Hall, Philadelphia, Pennsylvania, June 21, 1963

We are here to celebrate one of the greatest documents ever conceived by man.

The Constitution of the United States, in a few thousand words, established a way of life that has built this Nation into greatness as the world's leader and champion of freedom.

It is fitting that our celebration should be held in the great city of Philadelphia, at the very site where the Constitution was drawn up, and where it was finally ratified a hundred and seventy-five years ago today.

And it is fitting too, I think, that we should pause to examine the meaning and the spirit of our Constitution now, at an hour in our domestic history that can only by described as a time of profound national unrest.

The wise and brave Americans who pledged themselves, in their Preamble, that their Constitution would "establish justice, insure domestic tranquility, promote the general welfare . . . and insure the blessings of liberty on ourselves and our posterity"—those patriots had no way of predicting the vast, swollen, infinitely complex society their document would one day come to govern.

Philadelphia, the largest city then, had a total of sixty thousand inhabitants, and there were only six other cities in the nation with populations of more than eight thousand.

The whole country contained only four million people—less than the population of Philadelphia today—and more than one-eighth of those four million were Negro slaves.

No, the signers of the Constitution, for all their foresight, couldn't have dreamed of the America we live in today. The remarkable thing is that their work is as alive and as meaningful for us as it was for them—and as it will be for our grandchildren.

Curiously, the authors of the Constitution were for the most part very modest in their own appraisal of what they had achieved.

"I wish the Constitution had been made more perfect," George Washington wrote, "but I sincerely believe it is the best that could be obtained at this time."

Thomas Jefferson, who was later to caution future generations against looking on the words of the Constitution "with sanctimonious reverence," described it merely as "a good canvas, on which some strokes only want retouching."

And a note of outright gloom was sounded by John Marshall when, some years after the Ratification and not long before his death, he wrote: "I yield slowly and reluctantly to the conviction that our Constitution cannot last."

But it did last.

It even weathered the Civil War, and it has continued to weather our crises and serve to illuminate our progress ever since, to the envy of all other nations on this planet.

In 1878, the British statesman Gladstone said that "The American Constitution is, so far as I can see, the most wonderful work ever struck off at a given time by the brain and purpose of man." And the same sentiments have been echoed time and again around the world.

But perhaps no one has better defined the unique nature, the unique significance of these treasured papers than Woodrow Wilson. "The Constitution of the United States," he wrote, "is not a mere lawyers' document. It is a vehicle of life, and its spirit is always the spirit of the age."

President Wilson's words have proved true through the governmental, industrial and social upheavals of two World Wars and a major economic Depression—for in each of those critical times the spirit of the Constitution did indeed become the spirit of the age.

And what about *this* age?

What about the America we know now, at a time when the inadequate phrase "Civil Rights" has come to reflect an urgent nationwide struggle for equality by the 10½ per cent of our people whose skin is not white?

Clearly, and beyond any possible argument, the Constitution and its Amendments have set forth the basic particulars of "Civil Rights." Negroes were freed from slavery under the Thirteenth Amendment, and granted the right to vote under the Fifteenth.

The time is long past when any sensible American could tolerate the denial of free voting rights to all races, or the existence of "White Only" signs on public facilities—even by the narrowest interpretation, these things are unconstitutional.

And nine years ago the Supreme Court ruled that the old faulty dictum of "separate but equal" schooling for Negroes was unconstitutional too.

But must we now wait, as intelligent modern Americans in a changing society, must we now wait for the Supreme Court to spell out each new particularity of civil rights for us?

Whatever color we are, let us hope not.

Now as always, when the Constitution is too narrowly interpreted on a word-for-word basis, it can too easily become a crutch for reaction, a rationalization, an excuse for maintaining the status quo.

This is the very thing that Jefferson feared, so long ago, when he urged us not to regard the wording of the document with "sanctimonious reverence."

My point is that the Constitution was never meant to specify every detail, every individual right in the relations of man to man in this country.

It was intended to set forth certain duties of government and certain restrictions on government—nowhere in its wording does it pretend to tell us, as individual citizens, how to treat our neighbors.

But what Woodrow Wilson called the *spirit* of the Constitution does, and has always done, just that.

Interspersed throughout the Constitution and its amendments—written in between the lines, if you will—are the basic moral principles of democratic justice by which we all try to live.

Surely we don't need a new Court decision to tell us that the Negro is entitled to decent housing, and that his right to have such housing must not be denied or abridged because of his color.

Surely we don't need a new Court ruling to insure the Negro equal opportunities in employment, or equal opportunities to advance from unskilled into skilled and responsible jobs.

These are moral issues, not legal ones, and their constitutionality is a matter of common sense.

Not in its words alone but in what these words imply, in the underlying truths it teaches—that is how the Constitution has always served us as an inspiration and a guide.

And today that is how it points the way clearly to what thinking Americans have known all along: that racial discrimination is not worthy of us; that the stifling air of prejudice is not fit to be breathed by the people of a nation that takes pride in calling itself free.

The shameful scenes of riot and bloodshed in Oxford, Mississippi, last Fall, and in Birmingham, Alabama, this Spring, were only symptoms of the trouble—outward manifestations of an inner disease. And the infection is by no means localized.

Let no white Northerner delude himself that discrimination is chiefly a matter for Southern concern. It may be true that a Northern Negro is free to register at a Hilton hotel, but how much pride or pleasure can he take in this when he can't buy three meals a day for his children?

In Detroit, where Negroes account for 20 per cent of the population, they account for 60 per cent of the unemployed. In Chicago, one out of every four Negroes with families to support is out of work. And the same frustrating, demoralizing facts are to be found in the Negro ghettos of every other Northern city.

This is a national crisis, and it is immediate.

The Federal Government is doing and will continue to do its part. Indeed, in the past two and a half years more progress has been made in securing equal rights for all Americans—through executive action, legislation, litigation, persuasion and private initiative—than in any comparable period of our history. Yet a great deal more needs to be done.

But in questions of public morality, Federal action alone is not enough. In an era of great social flux and upheaval, it would be idle for anyone to suppose that real enlightenment can be brought about by governmental edict.

The surface eruptions of an internal disease cannot be cured with bandages.

The only way to cure a disease is to attack it at the source; and the sources of this disease, this malignancy that has been allowed to grow within the tissues of our national life, are as minute and various as the cells in any living body.

They are to be found throughout the texture of our society, wherever a meeting takes place between persons of light and dark skin.

That is where the treatment must begin.

There must be active and continued work toward interracial understanding at all levels—in states, in cities, in individual neighborhoods within cities, in towns and hamlets and in homes across the length and breadth of this nation.

Leadership must be taken at every level—by clergymen, by educators, by civil authorities, by newspapers, by businessmen and by labor unions.

But above all, I believe that the moral health of this country depends on individual citizens, white and Negro, who are able to use their minds, able to see, able to act truthfully in a time of evolutionary change.

For too many years the Negroes have been asked to "be patient," and advised that we must all "move slowly in adjusting civil rights to social custom."

The day is long gone when those phrases had any validity—if indeed they ever did.

We know what our goals are and they are clearly in sight. But no one can afford, now, to let the power of his zeal for action be weakened by hysteria.

In these difficult days, when so many avenues of action are open to them, Negro leaders have a greater responsibility than ever before.

Their decisions during the next few months will affect the lives of all Americans for years to come, as well as their own place in history.

We must understand the spirit as well as the letter of the Constitution we are celebrating today—the spirit that "will always be the spirit of the age."

And those of us who are white, as the President said, must look into our hearts—"not in search of charity, or of tolerance, for the Negro neither wants nor needs our condescension. We must look into our hearts and find that one plain, proud and priceless quality that units us all as Americans: a sense of justice."

Thank you.

Delivered at The American G. I. Forum
Chicago, Illinois, August 23, 1963

Early last year, while on a tour for the State Department, I spoke to the students of the University of Indonesia, in Djakarta.

I mentioned that I thought the United States had been unjustified in its war with Mexico—that I didn't think it was a very bright chapter in our history—and, as you may remember, the remark touched off a minor storm of protest here at home, chiefly from Texans.

It didn't seem to matter to most of the angry letter-writers that they were confusing the Mexican War with the Battle of the Alamo and the Texans' fight for independence, which had taken place some years before.

But I should certainly wish to add that many pages of American history have indeed been brightened by our war with Mexico—not so much in terms of territorial gains as in the great gain of human resources. Had it not been for that war, many of you here today would not be Americans, for your birthplaces might have been national territory of the Republic of Mexico. And we are without question a stronger and better nation today because we can number so many Spanish-speaking people among our own.

The contributions made to this country by Spanish-derived culture through the ages are incalculable. Whether you are of

Mexican, Spanish, Puerto-Rican or Latin-American descent, you can well afford to take pride in the achievements of your ancestors.

When the Pilgrims were getting ready for their voyage on the *Mayflower*, Spanish-speaking people had already established a civilization on a great part of this continent for more than a hundred years.

Five of our states, many mountain ranges and rivers, innumerable cities and towns, lakes and parks bear Spanish names; and our national literature, music and art have been greatly enriched by Spanish influences.

But taking pride in one's ancient heritage is always less fruitful—and less American—than taking stock of one's own recent past, his present, and his goals for the future. As Abraham Lincoln once said, "I don't know who my grandfather was, but I am much more concerned about what his grandson will be."

And so it is the current generation of Spanish-speaking Americans that concerns us today—the people who, collectively, have only in modern times begun to rise and free themselves from the status of an under-privileged minority within the mainstream of American life.

Let's take stock of your people: the progress they have made, the problems they face today, and the future they seek.

As is the case with any ethnic minority in our country, the key to social and economic progress has always been education. And for many years, the education of your people was sadly neglected.

It wasn't until after the First World War that any substantial number of Spanish-speaking Americans began to receive high school diplomas in this country, and it wasn't until the great social upheaval of the Second World War that the major strides were made. Military service took the young men away from their minority environment and the G. I. Bill of Rights gave them undreamed of educational opportunities.

Countless Spanish-speaking Americans emerged as teachers, lawyers, doctors, engineers, scientists, technicians, and men skilled at business administration. The "Latino" could no longer be regarded solely as a man to be employed: in many cases he had become the employer.

It was due mainly to better education.

But I must interrupt the main theme of my talk here, because I can't leave the subject of the Second World War without mentioning another proud chapter in your history. If any proof were needed that Spanish-speaking Americans are among our finest citizens, that proof was far more than amply demonstrated in the following list of names:

Joseph P. Martinez of Colorado; Luciano Adams of Texas; Macario Garcia of Texas; José M. Lopez of Texas; José Valdez of New Mexico; Silvestre Herrera of Arizona; Cleo Rodrigues of Texas; Manuel Perez, Jr., of Illinois; Ismael R. Villegas of California; David Gonzales of California; and Alejandro Ruiz of New Mexico.

Each of these men was awarded the nation's highest decoration for gallantry in action, the Congressional Medal of Honor.

And in Korea, half a decade later, that gallant roster was lengthened to include: Eugene A. Obregon of California; Joseph C. Rodriguez of California; Rodolfo Hernandez of California; Edward Gomez of Nebraska; Benito Martinez of Texas; and Ambrosio Guillen of Colorado.

Having so nobly proved themselves in times of war, your people have continued to make rapid progress into places of distinction in many areas of public life.

Mike Garcia, Hank Aguirre, Pancho Gonzales, Rick Casares and Alex Kellner—these are only a few of the top sports figures.

In the performing arts there are such actors as Anthony Quinn and José Ferrer; singers like Andy Russell and the Coronados.

There are many who have distinguished themselves in learned professions, such as Raoul Magan in the law, Walter Alvarez in medicine, and George I. Sanchez in education.

The names of Joseph M. Montoya, Henry B. Gonzales and Edward Roybal are inscribed on the roster of the 88th United States Congress.

Elsewhere in the field of Government service, notable progress for Spanish-speaking citizens has been late in coming. Until 1961, there were very few appointments at the Federal level. The President, in his desire to give equal opportunities to all Americans, has since encouraged the recognition of many Spanish-speaking men in top Government positions—not because they are Spanish-speaking, but because, in each case, they have been the best available men for the job.

.   .   .   .   .

Last month I had the duty to appoint a delegation of leading jurists to represent the Department of Justice at the Third Annual Inter-American Congress of Attorneys General, held in Mexico City. For the first time in history, a United States delegation to an international conference contained a majority—eight of eleven—of Spanish-speaking Americans. And I am proud to report that their participation in the conference was highly valuable in helping to strengthen ties among our Latin-American neighbors.

But to go on with further examples of this gratifying success story is to miss another and equally important point. For all these impressive gains, far too many of your people are still the victims of poverty and of social and economic discrimination.

As much as 50 per cent of our Spanish-speaking population still earns less than the average American per capita income—though this does show a notable improvement over five years ago, when the figure was set at 62 per cent.

And what about education?

The average Spanish-speaking citizen in California, Texas, and New Mexico has been given only a fifth-grade education or less; in Texas the average still is third grade.

Those figures, of course, include the total Spanish-speaking population—adults and elderly people, as well as youngsters. It is beyond question that the present generation of children are receiving a better education than their parents and grandparents.

But if education is the key to all other forms of American progress—and we have clearly seen that it is—can we be content to give our children anything but the best possible opportunities?

The fact is that we are not helping them nearly as much as we could—and I'm talking now about all American children, not only those with Spanish-speaking backgrounds.

Many millions of public school students today, of whatever national origin, face critical educational problems. Schools are overcrowded and understaffed, and the number of dropouts from junior and senior high schools across the country is steadily increasing. More than a million are expected to drop out this year.

And the disturbing thing about these boys and girls who leave school too early, apart from the education denied them, is that they present a serious unemployment problem.

No less than 30,000 new jobs will have to be found every week during the next 10 years if we are to avoid a national depression. Our economy will continue to offer an abundance of jobs for trained employees, but the market for unskilled and semi-skilled workers is rapidly shrinking under the advance of industrial automation.

The problem of unemployable school dropouts is not merely an economic but a social one; idleness and poverty among the young breed resentment and frustration, family disorganization and juvenile delinquency.

What are we going to do about it?

In a recent press conference the President called public attention to the severity of the problem. He emphasized that it can only be solved by all of us—as responsible citizens, whether as individuals or in groups, taking action in our own communities.

Americans have never been a people to depend on Federal edict alone in solving their own domestic problems. The very strength of our democratic system has always been the ability of free citizens to act on their own initiative.

Today, through various programs and expenditures, the Federal Government is actively supporting projects in many cities designed to prevent dropouts, and to initiate remedial education and job training for unemployed youth.

But all these activities are *local* in origin—they have been undertaken by parents, by school principals, by clergymen, by labor unions, by civil leaders and other public-spirited people. They are working in the classic American tradition of self-help and community responsibility.

An organization like yours, concerned with the problems of a specific ethnic minority, and keenly aware of the need for education, is ideally equipped to take on leadership of this kind.

Both as a group and as individual responsible citizens, you must know that there is an active and continuing need for your engagement with this cause—not because you are Spanish-speaking Americans, but because you are Americans.

Let none of us forget that we are living in a time of infinite possibilities. Both domestically and in international relations, America has never before in history had a greater chance to fulfill the dreams of men through the ages—dreams of individual freedom, national prosperity, and world peace.

The test ban treaty may not put an end to the Cold War, but it is a positive step toward honorably peaceful relations with our potential enemies. And history may well show that it was only the first of many steps leading to the ultimate goal of a world free from the threat of nuclear destruction.

In the meantime, we have continued to build our military defenses to a point where no nation can seriously challenge our strength. From within this bastion of might, which all of us pray we will never have to discharge, we can stand without fear as the champion of peace and democracy for all men.

But success in international affairs, no less than in domestic matters, depends on active interest and support not only by our leaders but by all of us. The responsibility of world power, like that of democracy, is something that must be shared by all citizens of the nation that enjoys it—citizens who know how much they have to gain by sustaining it, and how much they have to lose if it should ever fail.

I am confident that as the Spanish-speaking people continue to rise and prosper within our society, the society itself will also prosper in terms of enlightenment, wisdom, and courage.

America today is moving ahead toward the realization of its destiny—moving at a pace unmatched by that of any other time in history. And I would be proud, as would millions of our countrymen, to see the American G. I. Forum in the vanguard of that forward march.

Delivered at the Annual Meeting of the
Missouri Bar Association
Kansas City, Missouri, September 27, 1963

I am grateful for the opportunity to talk with this distinguished group. Yours is one of the strongest and most vital bar organizations in the country. That you have won the American Bar Association's top Award of Merit twice within the last four years is an honor that speaks for itself—and I am impressed too by several other examples of your leadership in matters of civic concern.

Your scheduling of a discussion on the representation of the indigent accused is only one such example. Everything I have read and heard about your activities suggests courage, high principle, and true engagement with the social realities of our time. You are to be congratulated.

But it is regrettable that the same spirit is not shared by all lawyers and public officials throughout the country. If it were, our nationwide problems in civil rights would be much less severe than they are.

To a far greater extent than most Americans realize, the crisis in civil rights reflects a crisis in the legal profession—in the whole judicial system on which our concept of justice depends.

I'd like to discuss three legal propositions with you. Each of them is part of a time-honored and noble tradition—and each of them, today, is being used to threaten the very foundations of law and order in this country. The first is the proposition that it is proper and just to avail oneself of every legal defense to test either the validity or the applicability of a rule of law. The second is that a court decision binds only those persons who are a party to it. The third is that a court-made rule of law should always be open to re-examination, and is susceptible to being overruled on a subsequent occasion.

All three ideas are basic to our system of justice; none of them needs any explanation or defense to an audience of skilled advocates such as yourselves. But today we have only to pick up a newspaper to see how these honorable principles—used in isolation, invoked in improper contexts, espoused as absolutes and carried to extremes—have placed the sanctity of the law in jeopardy. Separately and in combination, they are being proclaimed by lawyers and public officials as the justification for tactics to obstruct the enforcement of laws and court orders—as the rationale, that is, for withholding justice and equality from the grasp of millions of our fellow Americans. We are all familiar with the catchphrases of that rationale, and with the air of righteous indignation in their utterance. The argument goes something like this:

Brown versus the Board of Education is not the law of the land; it governs only one particular set of facts and is binding only upon the litigants of that case. Only when each separate school district, each state, and each new set of administrative procedures has been tested and judged on its own merits can it be said that a binding decision has been reached.

And furthermore—so the argument goes—a decision like *Brown*, repugnant to certain segments of the population and clearly difficult to enforce, may conceivably be overruled as bad law. To resist it, therefore, is merely to exercise one's constitutional right to seek reversal of a judicial ruling.

When stated that way and surrounded by rhetoric, the argument can be made to have a gloss of respectability. It can even take on the disguise of patriotic, high-minded dissent. Indeed, it is a position publicly espoused today by the governors of two states, by a past president of the American Bar Association, and by a Federal district judge who recently overruled the Brown decision on grounds that its findings of fact were erroneous.

We cannot blame a layman—even a reasonably fair-minded layman—for being confused and misled by this kind of reasoning.

But to lawyers, it smacks of duplicity. When it comes from the mouths of other lawyers, we must recognize it as professionally irresponsible. And when it comes from the mouths of public officials, we must recognize it as nothing more or less than demagoguery.

Let's go over those three legal principles one at a time. Let's examine each of them and look for the danger that lies within it. What do we really mean, as lawyers, when we say that it is proper and constitutional to avail oneself of every legal defense? Surely the Canons of Ethics make clear the impropriety of using dilatory tactics to frustrate the cause of justice.

We have only to imagine that principle being constantly applied across the board, in day-to-day litigation, to see that for all its validity it must be met by a counter-principle—a concept that might be called the principle of good faith.

Every lawyer knows—though his clients may not—that nothing but national chaos would result if all lawyers were to object to every interrogatory, resist every subpoena *duces tecum* and every disposition, seek every possible continuance and postponement, frame unresponsive pleadings, and resist court orders to a point just short of contempt.

We know that tolerances are built into the system. We know what the margins for evasion and dilatory tactics are—and we also know that the system would be hard put to stand up under a concerted effort to exploit them all.

There must obviously be a strong element of good faith, of reciprocity and cooperation, if our court system is to work at all. Take away that good faith, elevate the right to avail oneself of a technicality, into an absolute—and you bring the very machinery of law to a standstill.

What about the second proposition—that a court decision binds only those who are a party to it? Clearly, this too is a principle that conceals as much as it says. Every lawyer knows—though his clients may not—the distinction between the holding of a case and its rationale. We know that although the holding contains a specific disposition of a particular fact situation between the litigants, its reasoning enunciates a rule of law that applies not merely to one case but to all similar cases.

Often there is room for much discretion and honest disagreement as to when cases are alike or unalike. But clearly, in the matter of desegregation, there can be little or no room for argument in good faith as to when one situation is different—in the legal sense—from another in which the law has been laid down. The county is different, the names of officials are different, but the situation—in all legally significant respects—is identical.

There is something less than truth in a lawyer who insists, nine years after the Brown decision and a hundred years after the Emancipation Proclamation, that a law of the land, a guarantee of human dignity and equality, is merely the law of a case.

We come now to the third principle—that a court-made rule of law is always open to re-examination and must be viewed as susceptible to being overruled. No one can prove in strict logic that any given case will never be overruled. But with regard to the *Brown* decision, I think we can all agree that the probability of its permanence is so overwhelming as to counsel the abandonment of anyone's hope for the contrary.

The decision was, after all, a unanimous one. Since 1954 there have been six vacancies in the Supreme Court, which means that by now a total of fifteen justices have endorsed it.

True enough, it was in itself an overruling of *Plessy* v. *Ferguson*, 56 years before. But that reversal had been widely expected through several generations of legal thought. The whole pattern of American and world history pointed to the abolishment of the "separate but equal" concept; and the reform established by the *Brown* decision was all but inevitable.

Moreover, and more importantly, it is clearly a decision that the vast majority of the American public holds to be morally correct. To suggest, at this point in history, that there is any real likelihood of the *Brown* decision's being reversed is irresponsible to the point of absurdity.

No lawyer would advise a private client to contest the validity of a decision as solidly established and as often reiterated as this one; he would not want to victimize his client by raising frivolous questions. Yet, a client is being victimized every time this frivolous question is raised today—and the client is the American public itself.

Right now, all over the Nation, the struggle for Negro equality is expressing itself in marches, demonstrations, and sit-ins. It seems very clear to me that these people are protesting against something more than the privations and humiliations they have endured for so long.

They are protesting the failure of our legal system to be responsive to the legitimate grievances of our citizens. They are protesting because the very procedures supposed to make the law work justly have been perverted into obstructions that keep it from working at all.

Something must be done—and it's a job that can only be done by members of the legal profession.

First, we have got to make our legal system work. We have got to *make* it responsive to legitimate grievances, and to do this we must work to prevent the unscrupulous exploitation of all the obstructive devices available within the system.

Only when our judicial system offers fair and efficient adjudication does it deserve the public confidence; and it seems to me that American lawyers everywhere have a clear obligation to make that confidence justified.

Second, we have a job of education to do. The public must be better informed about the nature of our legal system—and this includes a better understanding of each of the principles and counter-principles I have discussed with you today. Only if we are able to instill that understanding will people with grievances begin to realize that there is a practical and realistic alternative to street demonstrations and sit-ins. But we have to make sure both that there *is* an alternative, and that the nature of that alternative is clearly understood.

If we can accomplish this, I believe we will begin to see a new phase in the movement for civil rights—an increased awareness that sit-ins and demonstrations do not in themselves cure social evils. They serve to awaken the public conscience, and they can form a means of protest when no other means are available, but they will not dictate solutions—they can only alert us to the problems. And in the long quest for solutions, we lawyers have a great deal to offer.

We are a part of an intricate system that has developed over the centuries as man's best hope for resolving disputes and appraising policies—for working out solutions to problems.

If this system of law—of equal justice for all—can be kept viable, and if people of all backgrounds and of all races and creeds can begin to fully understand and fully take advantage of it, then—and only then—will we stand to realize the promise of democracy, both for ourselves and for the world.

Delivered to the 120th Anniversary Dinner of B'nai B'rith Chicago, October 13, 1963

I am delighted to be with you tonight to share in your 120th Birthday Celebration.

This is no ordinary birthday. In addition to being the biblical age of Moses—and therefore an age of special significance—it represents the longest record of continuous service attained by any comparable organization founded in the United States.

But even if it were not so historic an occasion, I would be glad to come here to join in honoring Phil Klutznick.

In his devotion to public service, to the United States, and to causes of human rights, Phil Klutznick has earned our admiration and our gratitude.

He was, of course, president of B'nai B'rith—for he exemplifies the qualities that have made this organization great—and I am glad to say we did not permit him to retire from public service when he left the presidency of this organization.

One of the earliest acts of President Kennedy was to appoint him Ambassador to the United Nations. No sooner did he leave that post than he was asked to head the campaign to build a living memorial to Eleanor Roosevelt.

When this is completed, I know there will be many other tasks for him, because men like him are hard to find.

One hundred and twenty years ago, twelve men who had immigrated to this country came together in New York to dedicate themselves to the assistance of those in need. They saw as their mission the promotion of "the highest interests of humanity."

It has been said that there is no power so great as that of an idea whose time has come. Their ideas and purposes have been nobly fulfilled. I believe they would be proud of the size, the scope and the strength of B'nai B'rith today—and perhaps even more important—of the way their ideas have been developed in "the highest interests of humanity."

It is that concept—the rich legacy of belief in human rights, human dignity and human freedom which we have all inherited but which we sometimes fail to put into practice—that we commemorate and honor tonight.

We believe that freedom has but one message though it speaks in many tongues.

We believe that the denial of religious liberty is an ugly blot on the human conscience wherever and whenever it occurs—whether it restricts the rights of protestants in Communist China, Jews in the Soviet Union, or Catholics in Cuba.

We know that the pangs and pains of hunger and disease distress, without distinction, the child of poverty in Asia and the child of poverty here at home.

All Americans, of every color and creed, are the heirs of those beliefs with the right to share equally in their rewards as well as a responsibility to maintain them for those who will inherit them from us.

The books are still open on this generation's contribution to that legacy. Within our Nation, North and South, equal opportunity for all is still for many citizens no more than an empty phrase.

But although this is a cause for concern, it is not a cause for disillusionment or discouragement. Democracy is never a final achievement. It is by nature an ever changing challenge, a call to untiring effort, to renewed dedication, to new goals to meet the needs of each new generation.

We know full well the faults of our democracy—the handicaps of freedom—the inconvenience of dissent. But I know of no American who would not rather be a servant in the imperfect house of freedom, than be a master of all the empires of tyranny.

What do we mean by freedom? A generation ago, Franklin Roosevelt spoke of a world founded upon four freedoms: Freedom of Speech, Freedom of Worship, Freedom from Want, and Freedom from Fear.

Today, even before these four freedoms are secure, we would add two new freedoms to the galaxy by which our course is charted—freedom to learn and freedom of opportunity.

No doubt we could name other types of freedom that should be added. But in truth, there are not four freedoms, or six freedoms, or any higher number. There is only one.

Freedom is indivisible—and so is its defense. Each gives meaning to the others. The indivisibility of freedom is clear to all.

So long as one American child is denied the full freedom to learn—so long as one American family cannot be free from want—so long as one American citizen does not enjoy the right to speak or read or worship or vote as his conscience directs—then so long will the rights of all Americans be uncertain and unfilled.

There can be no freedom from want without freedom of opportunity; there can be no freedom of opportunity without freedom to learn; there can be no freedom from fear unless each of the other freedoms is attained.

Protecting the rights of minorities is not an act of generosity. For these basic rights cannot be separated in such a way as to apply in whole or in part to less than all of us.

Abraham Lincoln understood this when he wrote: "This is a world of compensation; and he who would be no slave must consent to have no slave. Those who deny freedom to others deserve it not for themselves, and, under a just God, cannot long retain it."

If the President's proposal for Civil Rights Legislation, now be-

scale, and it can only be done through the concerted efforts of private and public organizations within each community.

It was Thornton Wilder who said, "Every good and excellent thing stands moment by moment on the razor-edge of danger and must be fought for."

I would add that it must be fought for by every generation. It is up to us to decide where this generation will stand and how it will prepare its sons and daughters for the future.

I feel confident that you, as individuals and as an organization, will not be content to see things left as they are.

I believe that the traditions of B'nai B'rith—your noble concept of men working together to "promote the highest interests of humanity"—will prove to be as sound and as effectual in the next one hundred and twenty years as they have in the past. I know that you and your organization will give the leadership and that effort will continue to lift the hearts and enlighten the minds of all Americans. For all this I thank you.

Delivered before the Annual Convention
of the Theater Owners of America
New York City, October 28, 1963

I'm very grateful for the opportunity to talk with you this evening.

As theater owners, you have always filled a unique and important role in American life—and lately, with the advent of the national crisis in race relations, your role has become a highly sensitive one.

Along with the owners of restaurants, hotels and retail stores, you have come to be known as "public accommodations," and have found yourselves in the center of a storm of controversy.

In practical terms, the controversy chiefly affects those of you who have theaters in the Southern and Border States; but the civil rights movement is nationwide, and so is something that must concern us all.

Of the many business and professional groups I have met and talked with during these troubled times, none has shown itself to be more responsibly aware of the problem than yours.

You don't have to be told that there is nothing hypothetical about the American Negro's quest for equal opportunity—you know that it is happening, that it is here and now, and that to ignore it is to adopt the self-deluding, head-burying posture of the ostrich.

You know that the time is long past—if indeed it ever existed—when any opposition to civil rights could be argued on moral grounds.

Yet the controversy persists—not so much in moral terms as on grounds of legal technicality.

Does the Federal Government have any right to tell a business-man whom he may or may not serve? That seems to be the main thrust of the argument today.

It's an argument very likely to impede the passage of the Civil Rights Bill now pending in Congress. And it's an argument that cannot instantly be dismissed, if only because it is sincerely held by so many reasonable men.

Assuming that a number of such reasonable men are here in this audience tonight, I'd like to discuss that part of the legislation in some detail. I think it needs to be discussed, because it needs to be understood.

But first I'd like to touch on one aspect of the civil rights movement that has received all too little attention in the Nation's press—the heartening, encouraging fact that voluntary desegregation has become a rapidly increasing trend among theater owners.

Prior to last May, when the President began calling business, labor, civic and religious leaders for conferences in the White House, there were desegregated theaters in 109 cities throughout the Southern and Border States. In the past five months, theaters have desegregated in another 144 cities, bringing the total to 253.

In many cases, theater owners have been able to desegregate their facilities with little or no reaction from the public—which seems to indicate that racial discrimination can sometimes be a product of mere inertia rather than active or militant policy.

And even where community opinion is opposed to integration, theater owners have found they can safely desegregate as long as they do so in unison with their competitors. The individual owner who might be reluctant to take the step alone is encouraged to do so when it comes about as part of a group action.

So far, very few disruptive incidents have taken place as a result of theater desegregation—and for the most part, those that have occurred have been quickly and peacefully resolved.

One theater owner voluntarily desegregated in Cambridge, Maryland—a town world-famous for its racial strife—and there have been no unpleasant repercussions from that act.

Another interesting case in point is that of a middle-sized city in Arkansas, where most but not all of the theaters chose to let down their racial barriers.

A local newspaper trumpeted the story, and for a week or so the theaters were subjected to a costly boycott by white citizens.

But in a matter of days the boycott collapsed, partly as a result of persuasion by civic leaders and representatives of church, welfare and labor groups—and partly because the theaters began to show better movies.

Like all social problems, the racial crisis demands responsible leadership at the community level—throughout the North as well as in the South—and you, as influential and respected men in your own communities, are well qualified to be leaders.

Many of you have already taken on that kind of responsibility, and many others have shown willingness to do so.

There are any number of direct and positive things you can do. You can initiate, help organize and participate in local bi-racial committees, groups devoted to rational discussion as a means of finding peaceful solutions to interracial disputes rather than allowing them to erupt as violence in the streets.

You can concern yourselves publicly with local educational facilities and engage in efforts to combat the problem of school dropouts.

As businessmen, you know that the market for unskilled labor is rapidly shrinking under the advance of automation. You know that youngsters whose education is cut short of a high school diploma are headed for probable unemployment—and since a high percentage of school dropouts today are Negroes, you can see how this dilemma bears directly on the racial problem.

A great need exists, North and South, for adequate vocational and on-the-job training programs to help equip previously unskilled workers with the abilities they need to compete in today's labor market. Here again is an area in which you, as business and civic leaders, can profitably concern yourselves.

You can take the initiative too in helping to put a stop to discriminatory hiring and promotion practices in your business community—you can set the example in your own organization and urge others to follow suit.

All these suggestions, of course, are chiefly applicable in places where the basic structure of official segregation has either broken down or never existed.

In many parts of the South, there remains a considerable feeling of resistance to voluntary change—though quite a few theater owners in those areas have indicated that they would welcome the opportunity to desegregate if the law required it.

Finally, I know that there are pro-segregationists among you— theater owners who question the government's right to regulate the way you conduct your business.

And this leads us back to that persistent question about the public accommodations clause in the Civil Rights Bill. It seems to me that there are three logical answers to that question.

One: There is nothing new or extraordinary in the concept of Federal regulations in private enterprise or private property. Federal health laws govern all businesses that deal in food and drugs for public consumption; Federal safety regulations must be met by all airlines; Federal deposit insurance must be maintained by all banks; zoning laws affect all property owners—and the list of examples could go on and on.

Two: A Federal law prohibiting segregation in places of public accommodation would be no different in principle—and less restrictive—than similar laws that now exist in 31 of the 50 states.

The third, and to me, most logical answer is that a public accommodations business is, by its very definition, a business that accommodates the public. No organization established to serve an exclusive group, such as a private club, would be affected by the proposed law—nor would any business man lose his right to refuse service to a customer, who is, for example, drunk or unruly or improperly dressed.

Both the spirit and the letter of the Civil Rights Bill make its purpose absolutely clear: its purpose is to assure that no man, woman or child in America will be discriminated against because of race, creed or color.

Those of us who are white can only dimly guess at what the pain of racial discrimination must be—what it must be like to be turned away from a public place, or made to use only a segregated portion of that place, for no reason other than the color of one's skin.

Prostitutes, criminals, Communist and Fascist conspirators—these people are free to go to the movies and to choose their own seats, as long as they are white.

How can a Negro father explain this intolerable situation to his children? And how can the children be expected to grow up with any sense of pride in being Americans?

All these things have been said so many times; all these points have been made and clarified so often over a period of so many months, that it's surprising how much misunderstanding still remains about the nature of the proposed civil rights legislation.

On one hand the Administration has been charged with seeking too much power, with trying to usurp and dictate the rights of private enterprise, of going too far—and on the other hand, particularly during the past several weeks, we have been accused of "selling out," of not going far enough.

I suppose this kind of confusion is inevitable in any issue as delicate and as highly emotional as the issue of civil rights. My only hope—and what I trust to be the hope of the vast majority of Americans—is that reason will prevail.

The Administration has believed all along, and still believes, that a strong civil rights bill has every chance of being enacted into a strong and meaningful law—a law that strikes effectively at the injustice of racial bigotry in voting, in public accommodations, in education and in employment.

Indeed, the Administration believes that such a bill *must* be passed, not only for the sake of racial minorities within this country but for the sake of the country itself.

The enactment of a strong Civil Rights Bill will provide American Negroes with legal remedies to many of their grievances, and with an article of faith—a clear indication that their Government is responsive to the settlement of longstanding injustices.

But the law will be only the beginning. In the final analysis, only better education, better employment opportunities, better housing and more enlightened social attitudes will enable the Negroes to attain the full citizenship they have deserved for so long. And only those things will put a stop to the bitter unrest that poses a constant threat of disorder within our society.

The most any law can do is point the way—the rest is up to the people. Civil rights is not an issue that can be solved by governmental edict—it must be dealt with at the community level, within states, within cities, within neighborhoods—wherever a meeting takes place between persons of light and dark skin.

A great deal of hard and conscientious work must be done, all over America, if we are to fulfill our destiny as a just and democratic Nation.

If the disgrace of racial discrimination is to be purged from our land, in our time, it won't be a triumph of government alone. It will be a triumph of civil leadership in every American city and town—leadership of the kind so many of you have already shown—leadership by men responsive to the call for fundamental human justice.

Thank you.

When one recalls with his mind's eye the televised happenings following the assassination of President John F. Kennedy, a picture of the brave widow emerges as clearly as time and the original misty-eyed vision allow. And alongside the bereaved Jackie is the image of Robert Kennedy, always at her side, stoic in subordinating his grief to hers.

The Attorney General did not give another major speech until almost four months later when, on March 17, 1964, he addressed 1,100 members and guests of the Friendly Sons of St. Patrick of Lackawanna County, Pennsylvania, at their 59th Anniversary Dinner. The site was the ballroom of the Hotel Casey in Scranton.

Early that afternoon Mr. Kennedy visited the grave of his brother in the company of Mrs. Jacqueline Kennedy and Hon. Thomas J. Kiernan, Ambassador from Ireland to the United States. At 3 P.M. he left for Scranton.

When the Kennedy family airplane "Caroline" came to a stop at the Scranton-Wilkes-Barre Airport at 4:10 P.M. crowds rushed to see the Attorney General. Many wanted to shake hands with him; others wanted merely to "touch" him. Daniel J. Flood, U. S. Representative from the Wilkes-Barre area, became so concerned for Mr. Kennedy that he shouted to police officers, "Set up a ring around him!" and "Protect him!"

Despite cold rainy weather, crowds followed him, lined the streets, asked him for his autograph, and shook his hand during almost all of his eight hours' stay in the Scranton area. A side trip took him to the Minooka section of Scranton where he spoke at groundbreaking ceremonies where the John F. Kennedy Elementary School will be erected to replace the David Farragut School. He also addressed the Fiftieth Anniversary banquet of the Friendly Sons of Saint Patrick of Greater Pittston at the Mayfair Club in nearby Yatesville. The scene was the same in one respect everywhere Robert Kennedy visited: he was mobbed and cheered by warm and friendly people.

One newsman summed up the reception in this manner: "Though Robert Kennedy was never here before, he was welcomed like a returning hero." Many other observers were quick to comment that the Scranton area had not seen such a reception since 1960, when Senator John F. Kennedy campaigned there for the presidency.

The memory of John F. Kennedy was pervasive. There was spontaneous comparison of the brothers with respect to appearance and manner. Even while the Attorney General was in his room at the Hotel Casey preparing to go downstairs to the St. Patrick's Day affair, a woman appeared at the door with a picture she had taken of his late brother, asking for (and receiving) an autograph.

During the early part of the program, in addition to the toasts usually offered to the President of the United States and the Governor of Pennsylvania, the "Friendly Sons" were led in a special toast— offered by U. S. District Judge William J. Nealon, retiring president of the fraternal organization—to "our beloved late President John F. Kennedy, who while amongst us, in the words of St. Paul, He fought the good fight and he kept the faith."

As might be expected at an Irish festivity, eloquence was not wanting either in quality or quantity. The program of speakers and singers liberally exuded humor, pathos and sheer exuberance. At about 10:25 the principal speaker was introduced by Pennsylvania State Senator Robert P. Casey. Prolonged applause was heard when Mr. Casey climaxed his effusive introduction by saying "There is no place that the name of Kennedy is more loved than here in Northeastern Pennsylvania." And then the State Senator added after the applause died down, "In welcoming you, we are not only extending our hands but we are opening our hearts to you." The ovation thus set off lasted more than a full minute.

The essence of the Attorney General's address was an extended analogy between the rise to freedom of the Irish and the struggle of the American Negro, climaxed by a plea to the audience to help the latter and all struggling peoples. But there was also an added poignancy about the speech: the memory of the late President who had voiced many of the same sentiments.

Robert Kennedy's first words told of how frequently the late

President had spoken with feeling about his own trip to Scranton in 1960. He then quoted Dave Power, John F. Kennedy's close friend, to the effect that the people of Scranton "are our kind of Irish." A grateful applause greeted these remarks.

The prepared speech was read in what was referred to as a "low key" manner—even though humor and other changes of tone were implicit in the language—with the Attorney General using no gestures. But his delivery changed when, toward the end of his talk, he began to read a ballad composed to the memory of Owen Roe O'Neill, "The Liberator" of Ireland.

According to William G. Loftus, staff writer of *The Scranton Times*, "the Attorney General's voice lowered and his reading pace quickened as he read words which could be applied to his brother." The audience hushed perceptibly and the poem ended:

> We're sheep without a shepherd,
> When the snow shuts out the sky—
> Oh! why did you leave us, Owen?
> Why did you die?

Delivered to the Friendly Sons of St. Patrick of Lackawanna County
Scranton, Pennsylvania, March 17, 1964

I am honored and delighted to be here with you tonight. Your dinner has become one of the most famous of the annual celebrations of this hallowed evening.

I'm aware, of course, of the notable number of sons of St. Patrick who live here in Scranton. And as a son of St. Patrick myself, I know how friendly you've always been—to President Kennedy in everything that he did—and to me whenever I've been here.

So I think of these things in addition to the bonds of common kinship that the Irish everywhere feel on St. Patrick's Day. This is the day, you know, when legend has it that three requests were granted to St. Patrick by an angel of the Lord, in order to bring happiness and hope to the Irish.

First, that on this day the weather should always be fair to allow the faithful to attend church. Second, that on every Thursday and Saturday twelve Irish souls should be freed from the pains of Hell. And, third, that no outlander should ever rule over Ireland.

Though I have not received the latest weather report from the Emerald Isle, I am confident that no rain fell there today—officially. Who pays heed to a little Irish mist?

And I have reason to believe that the twelve Irishmen have been regularly released from the nether regions as promised. Judge Nealon just told me he thinks that several of them are here tonight.

We need have no concern over the third promise; in Ireland they are celebrating this day in freedom and liberty.

But you and I know that life was not always this good for the Irish, either back in the old country or here in America.

There was, for example, that black day in February 1847 when it was announced in the House of Commons that 15,000 people a day were dying of starvation in Ireland. And you may recall that Queen Victoria was so moved by this pitiful news that she contributed five pounds to the society for Irish relief.

So the Irish left Ireland. Many of them came here to the United States. They left behind hearts and fields and a nation yearning to be free. It is no wonder that James Joyce described the Atlantic as a bowl of bitter tears, and an earlier poet wrote, "They are going, going, going, and we cannot bid them stay."

This country offered great advantages, even then. But no one familiar with the story of the Irish here would underrate the difficulties they faced after landing in the United States. As the first of the racial minorities, our forefathers were subject to every discrimination found wherever discrimination is known.

But many of them were gifted with a boundless confidence that served them well. One of these was a pugilist from my native Boston. John L. Sullivan won the heavyweight championship of the world not too many years after the flood tide of Irish emigration to this country, and in 1887 he toured the British Isles in triumph.

Some idea of Irish progress can be gathered from his cordial greeting to the Prince of Wales, later Edward VII.

John L. said: "I'm proud to meet you. If you ever come to Boston be sure to look me up; I'll see that you're treated right."

And, referring to the Prince, he later added with Irish generosity: "Anyone can see he's a gentleman. He's the kind of man you'd like to introduce to your family."

Irish progress here has continued. It was some time ago that the late Fred Allen defined the "lace curtain Irish" as those who "have fruit in the house when no one's sick."

But it was less than nine months ago when President Kennedy, in touring Ireland, used to ask the crowds he talked with how many had cousins in America. The usual response was for nearly every hand in the crowd to be raised. It was with great delight that he was able to reply: "I've seen them, and they're doing well."

And, so, it is my great delight to be with you here tonight as we take a few moments to share the rich heritage of the Irish.

It's worth noting, I think, that all the wealth of our legacy stems from a small island in the far Atlantic with a population one quarter the size of the State of Pennsylvania.

The Irish have survived persecution in their own land and discrimination in ours. They have emerged from the shadow of subjugation into the sunlight of personal liberty and national independence. And they have shared the struggles for freedom of more than a score of nations across the globe. Irish soldiers are enroute tonight to help preserve the peace in Cyprus.

Indeed, Ireland's chief export has been neither potatoes nor linen, but exiles and immigrants who have fought with sword and pen for freedom around the earth.

We need but recall the heroic deeds of the "Wild Geese"—the officers and soldiers forced to flee their native Ireland after the battle of the Boyne.

Fighting for the French, they broke the ranks of the English at Fontenoy. Fighting for the Spanish, they turned the tide of battle against the Germans at Melazzo.

And, other Irishmen in other years, going into battle with the Union Army—a green sprig in their hats—bore the brunt of the hopeless assaults of the Confederate heights at Fredericksburg. Twelve hundred soldiers of the Irish Brigade went into action that bitterly cold December day in 1862. Only 280 survived, as President Kennedy noted last summer when he presented the Brigade's battle-torn flag to the Irish people. "Never were men so brave," General Robert E. Lee said of the Irish Brigade.

And of themselves, the Irish soldiers said:

War-battered dogs are we,
Gnawing a naked bone;
Fighters in every land and clime—
For every cause but our own.

Today the Irish enjoy their freedom at a time when millions of people live in deprivation and despair under totalitarian dictatorships stretching eastward from the Wall in Berlin to the troubled borders of South Vietnam.

The free Irishmen marching everywhere today to the tune of "O'Donnell Abu" and "The Wearing of the Green" are a dramatic contrast to the clattering of hobnail boots on darkened streets, the sound that marks the enslaved nations.

So, the first point I'd like to make arises from the traditional Irish concern for freedom—everywhere. I know of few in our land—and I hope none in this room—who would ignore threats to peace and freedom in far off places.

We realize, as John Boyle O'Reilly once wrote, that:

The world is large, when its weary leagues
Two loving hearts divide;
But the world is small, when your enemy
Is loose on the other side.

No problem weighs heavier on the conscience of free men than the fate of millions in iron captivity.

But what is taking place on the other side of the Iron Curtain should not be the only matter of concern to us who are committed to freedom. I would hope that none here would ignore the current struggle of some of our fellow citizens right here in the United States for their measure of freedom. In considering this it may be helpful for us to recall some of the conditions that existed in Ireland from 1691 until well into the nineteenth century against which our fore-fathers fought.

We might remember, for instance, that in the Ireland of 1691 no

Irish Catholic could vote, serve on a jury, enter a university, become a lawyer, work for the government or marry a Protestant. And our pride in the progress of the Irish is chilled by the tragic irony that it has not been progress for everyone.

We know that it has not been progress for humanity. I know it because so much work of the Department of Justice today is devoted to securing these or comparable rights for all Americans in the United States in 1964.

There are Americans who—as the Irish did—still face discrimination in employment—sometimes open, sometimes hidden. There are cities in America today that are torn with strife over whether a Negro should be allowed to drive a garbage truck; and there are walls of silent conspiracy that block the progress of others because of race or creed, without regard to ability.

It is toward concern for these issues—and vigorous participation on the side of freedom—that our Irish heritage must impel us. If we are true to this heritage, we cannot stand aside.

There are two other areas of concern which I feel are of paramount importance and to which the Irish tradition speaks in ringing tones. One is the status of freedom in colonies and second our relationship to the underdeveloped nations of the world.

The greatest enemy of freedom today, of course, is communism, a tyranny that holds its captives in vice-like subjugation on a global scale. For nearly twenty years we and our Allies have striven to halt the Communist advance. But one of the weaknesses in our common front has been the restraint on freedom sponsored by our Allies and accepted by ourselves.

The conduct of our foreign affairs should be consistently based on our recognition of every man's right to be economically and politically free. This is in the American tradition. We were, after all, the victor in our own war for independence. We promulgated the Monroe Doctrine and the "open door" policy with their clear warnings to the colonial powers of Europe.

We gave self-determination to our own dependencies; and for more than a century we opposed colonial exploitation elsewhere. But throughout all this we were still living largely in splendid isolation, removed from a direct control of world destiny.

This was changed by World War II. The frontiers of our national security became the frontiers of the world. We found ourselves obliged to deal with the harsh facts of existence on a global basis.

For the sake of our own security, we found our destiny to be closely linked with that of nations that maintained large colonial empires on which they felt their ultimate security depended. In some of the underdeveloped countries we have found our destiny linked with ruling powers or classes which hold the vast majority of their people in economic or military subjugation.

It is easy for us to believe that the imperialism of the West was infinitely preferable to the tyranny of communism. But the sullen hostility of the African and Asian colonial nations has shown us that not all hold the same view. The bloody struggles for liberty from the sands of Algeria to the steaming jungles of Indonesia and Vietnam proved that others would make the same sacrifices to throw off the yoke of imperialism today that the Irish did more than a half century ago.

And we have a longer way to go in helping the people of some other nations to free themselves from economic domination. This is a part of our national policy not only because it is humane but also because it is essential. Our future may depend on how well this is understood throughout the world—how well it is understood that we still champion the quality of freedom everywhere that Americans enjoy at home.

I like to think—as did President Kennedy—that the emerald thread runs into the cloth we weave today, that these policies in which he believed so strongly and which President Johnson is advancing, are the current flowering of the Irish tradition. They are directed toward freedom for *all* Americans here and for all peoples throughout the world. And I like to think that these policies will survive and continue as the cause of Irish freedom survived the death of "The Liberator," Owen Roe O'Neill.

As you'll recall, O'Neill was one of the great figures of Irish history. It was of the period after his death, when the entire Irish nation was overwhelmed with grief, that the following lines were written:

> Sagest in the council was he,
> Kindest in the Hall;

Sure we never won a battle
        —'Twas Owen won them all
Soft as woman's was your voice, O'Neill:
        Bright was your eye,
Oh! why did you leave us, Owen?
        Why did you die?

Your troubles are all over,
        You're at rest with God on high,
But we're slaves, and we're orphans, Owen!
        —Why did you die?

We're sheep without a shepherd,
        When the snow shuts out the sky—
Oh! why did you leave us, Owen?
        Why did you die?

So, on this St. Patrick's evening let me urge you one final time to
recall the heritage of the Irish. Let us hold out our hands to those
who struggle for freedom today—at home and abroad—as Ireland
struggled for a thousand years.

Let us not leave them to be "sheep without a shepherd when the
snow shuts out the sky." Let us show them that we have not forgotten
the constancy and the faith and the hope—of the Irish.

part viii OPENING TO THE FUTURE

This, the final division of speeches, constitutes a dynamic phase for Robert Kennedy.

In personal terms we see the Attorney General emerge from the shock of his brother's death. The words used to describe him after November 22—"dazed," "depressed," "shocked,"—no longer applied. And while he was more reflective, somewhat slower to speak and to joke than before the tragedy of the assassination, Robert Kennedy was seen more as his own man, no longer as the President's younger brother.

On all sides he was beseiged with questions about what he was going to do after November, for he had already stated that he would retire as Attorney General after the fall presidential election. But he contended that he had "no plans." While it was learned that he had volunteered to serve the Administration in Southeast Asia, he continued to put off those who beseeched him to proclaim his desire to be (a) the Democratic vice-presidential nominee, and (b) the Democratic nominee for U. S. Senator from New York State.

During the historically lengthy civil rights debate in the Senate, he spoke out less on that subject *per se,* while negotiating in private with leaders there to bring about a civil rights bill which would be sufficiently strong to perform its function and yet be acceptable to enough Senators to vote cloture—which was accomplished on June 10 by a vote of 71 to 29—and eventual passage by both Houses of Congress and signed into law by President Lyndon B. Johnson on July 2, 1964.

The Attorney General waited almost a month after his St. Patrick's Day speech in Scranton to give another prepared address. But between April 14 and June 8 he delivered twelve, nine of which are included in this collection. The point of reference for all of these was social change. While civil rights received some attention, most of the emphasis was centered on youth: service by the college graduate and the privileged, help for the delinquent and underprivileged, the President's War on Poverty, and a plea for the youth all over the world who were destined to be future leaders. The final broad area of his attention was the member of the speaker's own profession, the lawyer. This often well-to-do—materially sated and socially satisfied —clerical minion of the law was urged to dislodge himself from his comfortable role and to take an occasional case in defense of the indigent, to attempt to correct the injustices perpetrated by the bail bond system, and to become a genuine force for social justice.

Two of the speeches which follow possess unusual potential. One was delivered on April 16 in New York City at the Herbert H. Lehman Human Relations Award Dinner of the American Jewish Committee Appeal for Human Relations. In this address Mr. Kennedy began to look beyond the passage of the Bill. He asked that the country adopt a new slogan, "Massive Compliance." And he asked that such compliance be made "in the spirit of a nation governed by God, law, and men of understanding."

The other address thought to be possessed of unique potential is the final one in this collection. The date was June 8 and the audience the graduating class at the California Institute of Technology. While an obvious goal of the speech was a plea to have science assume its proper role in our society, the purpose of the talk was much broader. The Attorney General broke new ground in this talk for he spoke of the need for a spirit of openness and courage as a means to a better society. "Our greatest national responsibility," he said, "is to strengthen and enlarge the opening to the future ..."

In a sense, the Cal Tech speech is a résumé of the aspirations Robert Kennedy has for our society, and—projected into the future— for the peoples of the world. For implicit in the "new age of decency, justice and peace" sought in this address are the characteristics of the better society discussed in great detail in the rest of the speeches included in this book.

Delivered at the Herbert H. Lehman
Human Relations Award Dinner of the
American Jewish Committee Appeal for Human Relations
New York City, April 16, 1964

I met this afternoon with members of the American Society of Newspaper Editors in Washington and we got along well, perhaps because some of them realized I used to be a newspaperman myself. I don't think I can lay claim to quite as close a bond at this gathering. None-theless, I am pleased and honored to join with you.

.   .   .   .   .   .

For weeks now, almost every night, the light on top of the dome of the Capitol in Washington has burned late into the evening. Many of the high school students who visit Washington at this time of year know it means that the Senate is still in session. People all over the country know that the debate over the Civil Rights Bill is continuing.

However tedious or extended it may appear superficially, there can be no mistaking the significance of that Great Debate. There are great wrongs in America to be righted and millions who appreciate, daily and first-hand, that civil rights are more of a goal than a reality.

The legislation now before the Senate can do a great deal toward making civil rights a reality. The Civil Rights Bill can help insure equal voting rights. It can help create and extend fair educational and employment opportunities. It can help remove the insult of segregated public accommodations, so irrational that in one com-munity a drug store allowed Negroes to be served, but required them to take Pepsi-Cola instead of Coca-Cola, to stand rather than sit, and to drink from a paper cup rather than a glass.

More generally, the Civil Rights Bill can also demonstrate to all of our citizens that the Congress of the United States, like Presidents Kennedy and Johnson and like the Supreme Court, is committed to the pledge of equality on which this country is founded.

Two centuries ago, Montesquieu wrote: "In the state of nature, indeed, all men are born equal, but they cannot continue in this equality. Society makes them lose it, and they recover it only by the protection of the laws."

The Negro experience in America demonstrates the wisdom of his words and the need for the Civil Rights Bill. But neither this law nor any law can be a solution. The deep social wound of segregation was cut for too long by too many knives of prejudice to be healed by a single poultice.

The Civil Rights Bill, like law in general, can give us an orderly framework for the resolution of discord and dispute among men. Each new outburst of racial frustration in our cities gives evidence of how important that framework can be.

One of the principal aims of the Civil Rights Bill is to elevate this conflict from the streets to the courts. We must recognize that law can only provide orderly ground rules. It cannot play the game.

Law also can offer us a moral precept. To the extent that laws are founded on morality and on logic, they can lead men's hearts and minds. But once again, this aspect of law can have meaning only to the extent that the constituents of law are moral and are rational.

You and I, reflecting on our own heritages in America, know our forebears faced obstacles of prejudice when they came to this country, whether in signs pronouncing "No Irish Need Apply" or in unexplained rejections of applications to medical schools. We know that systematic exclusion of Irish or Jews or Italians or of any ethnic group has ended not only because laws changed, but because men's minds did.

"The problems of our society," President Johnson said last week, "will not automatically disappear with the passage of [the] Bill . . . They will still have to be dealt with by all Americans. The Civil Rights Bill can only chart in law the directions that we must take as individuals."

So I come to you today, as the chief law enforcement officer of the United States, to talk not of Federal enforcement of laws, but of individual obedience to their moral spirit.

Such obedience must exist at many levels, and like all responsibility in a democracy, it must begin with the individual citizen. As John D. Rockefeller, III, observed in a recent speech, "America, we must remember, is no more than the sum of ourselves."

I think it is necessary for us to start by asking ourselves whether we are satisfied with the present ingredients of American social arithmetic. I am thinking of two recent examples in this state.

The first occurred only this week, in Albany. We all read about it: a distraught young man perched on a narrow 12th-floor ledge, ready to jump off, for two hours. Friends sought to coax him to safety. But the crowd below had a different appeal. "Jump, jump, jump," it chanted. One spectator expressed the hope that the youth would jump "on this side. We couldn't see him if he jumped over there."

The other case occurred one night last month. A young woman was stabbed to death over the period of a half hour outside her apartment in Queens. Thirty-eight neighbors looked out at her during that time. None came to her rescue. None even called the police. By way of explanation, one of the witnesses said later, "I didn't want to get involved." No further comment is possible.

Individual conscience and individual responsibility deserve better homage in a land which prizes individualism and whose greatest hero is Abraham Lincoln. Charles Morgan, Jr., the young Birmingham attorney, whose own conduct is an example of the point, tells an illustrative anecdote in his new book, *A Time to Speak.*

> No one knows who will next be called to commit himself or in what way. It might be someone like the tall and lanky soldier in Jackson, Mississippi, the one with the long Southern drawl, who told a white man assaulting Negro Andrew J. Young: "Man, if you wanta fight, fight me! I'm your size and I'm white."

We can reflect as well on the individual responsibility demonstrated by 200,000 Negroes and whites in the March on Washington last summer. There were dire prophecies of angry crowds, of violence and of riot. All of us saw what happened instead. A London newspaper called it "The Gentle Flood."

Individuals can, at another level, help to flesh out the bare framework established by statutes. Consider the example of leadership established by the hundreds of Southern businessmen who have acted to desegregate their establishments in the past year.

Last spring and summer, President Kennedy, then Vice President Johnson and other Administration leaders met with almost 1,500 businessmen, ministers, attorneys and other leaders from all over the country. The purpose of the meeting was to seek voluntary abandonment of discriminatory practices. The response demonstrates that racial attitudes in many parts of the South are not committed to monolithic irrationality.

A recent survey of 566 cities in southern and border states shows that significant progress has taken place in the past few months in the desegregation of such facilities as theaters, restaurants, hotels, motels and lunch counters. There now has been at least some desegregation in nearly 70 per cent of these cities and almost two-thirds of that progress has come since last May.

It is easy for us in the North to patronize the South. It is so very much easier to see the morality of problems in Birmingham when you are sitting in Boston. What these Southern businessmen have done can serve as an example for us in the North in coming to grips with problems that are different only because they are our own.

The desegregation of these public accommodations in the South comes because their owners plainly acknowledge the economic dangers of inaction. But they also have recognized the moral need for action. When viewed in context, their action becomes even more significant.

For half a century, the doctrine of "separate but equal" was perverted by citizens, communities, and local governments into a license not for simple racial segregation, but for racial degradation. For example, although the number of white and Negro students in Mississippi is approximately equal, in a recent year the state spent more than $46,000,000 for white schools and $26,000,000 for Negro schools. And this is the case despite the fact that "separate but equal" has been discredited for a decade.

The lesson is plain. Law is not enough.

How can it be when it requires that Negroes and whites not be served in the same room without a solid, seven-foot partition between them? How can it be when it requires a motel to turn away a weary motorist or a hospital to reject an injured child?

Whatever law is debated, whatever statute is enacted, without public understanding it is mere piety. Neither sober statutes nor individual responsibility alone are enough; men and their laws must march together.

What happens when they do not is evident from the experience of the past ten years. The cost of defiance touches every aspect of community and national life. Five years ago, rural Prince Edward County, Virginia, closed its public schools rather than desegregate them. How can we measure the cost of that defiance?

How did it affect the Negro children whose futures have been permanently crippled because they could not learn to read? How did it affect the white children, sent to makeshift—but segregated—private schools? How did it affect the citizens of the city, who have walked past the vacant public school buildings while children were left to linger in the streets and fields? And how did it affect Virginia, whose leadership helped create this republic?

The point is that the costs of defiance are beyond measure. They touch generations yet unborn. They destroy possibilities for progress in the present. They scar our history.

The lesson of Prince Edward County is the lesson of the entire country. Where were we after the 1954 school decision? Where were the pulpit, the press, the public officials? The answer is that there was a vacuum of leadership—until it was filled, finally, by demagogues with strident slogans of "segregation forever" and "massive resistance."

When a whole generation and a whole region is told by its leaders that a Supreme Court decision is an unconstitutional nullity, how can it be expected that the mortar of public respect will be added to the bricks of law?

Rarely in history are nations presented with a second chance to atone for fundamental failures. I wonder, however, if that isn't exactly the opportunity America has today.

When the Civil Rights Bill passes this year, ten years after the Brown decision, we can have a new leadership, of the kind Southern businessmen and public officials, newspapers and clergymen have already demonstrated. And we can have a new slogan—not "massive resistance" in the manner of an anarchy, but "massive compliance," in the spirit of a nation governed by God, law, and men of understanding.

The Prince Edward County school case is still in the courts and public schools are still closed. But Negro children are being educated, in a free private school system which resulted from the efforts of President Kennedy, private foundations, and leaders and citizens of Virginia.

Not long ago, one of the teachers in the free school system was asked how her students responded. It reminded her, she said, of her childhood on the farm. When you set a chicken on the ground after holding it in your hands, it sits, motionless. Only after it is sure of its freedom does it dash away. Her students were like that for the first month, she said—not moving, insecure in their freedom. When it sank in, they leaped ahead in their desire and their capacity to learn.

The freedom of those students and the spirit of the establishment of their school can be the freedom and the spirit of our time. We cannot solve our problems with a law or in an instant, but we can begin to weld laws and men together in an effort to provide fulfillment of the pledge America makes to all men.

Benjamin Muse, a Virginia writer, says in his new book about integration in the past decade: "The unrest will end sometime because it is inevitable that in America, justice and humanity in time will prevail."

Let us join today not only in his sentiment but in his certainty. Let us join in the faith in man and law President Kennedy expressed last June when he said:

> I ask you to look into your hearts—not in search of charity, for the Negro neither wants nor needs condescension—but for the one plain, proud and priceless quality that unites us all as Americans; a sense of justice. In this year of the Emancipation Centennial, justice requires us to insure the blessings of liberty for all Americans and their posterity—not merely for reasons of economic efficiency, world diplomacy and domestic tranquility—but, above all, because it is right.

Thank you.

Delivered to a Joint Meeting of the Kanawha County Parent-Teachers Council and Members of Action for Appalachian Youth, Inc. Civic Center, Charleston, West Virginia, April 29, 1964

Coming back to West Virginia is like coming back to an old home. My trip through Kanawha County today brought back memories that, after four years, are still fresh.

Standing in this very room in September of 1960, Senator John F. Kennedy declared that he was the only candidate for President who did not need a guide to get from Charleston to Beckley, and who knew that you spell Mullens, West Virginia, M-u-l-l-e-n-s.

All of us who walked your roads and met your people in the spring of 1960 learned something about the meaning of courage and determination. Senator Kennedy came to love this state and its people. He called it the state that refused to die: towns that wouldn't give up and proud men who could not find jobs but kept on looking.

After the West Virginia primary made possible my brother's nomination, he took the story of West Virginia to the nation.

He pledged that if he were elected, the American government would do more for West Virginia, and for every state where decent, able men are smothered by social and economic forces beyond their control. I believe that pledge was kept.

In the past three years we have seen the birth of new progress in West Virginia. The Federal Government has begun to meet its responsibilities to this state. A new partnership has been formed, aided by such legislation as the Manpower Development and Training Act, the Area Redevelopment Act, and the Juvenile Delinquency Act.

In fiscal 1963, the Department of Health, Education and Welfare contributed $237 million for programs in child care, education, health and social security. The area Redevelopment Administration invested $33 million in the future of West Virginia.

The Housing and Home Finance Agency put $28 million into better housing for your people, and the Labor Department spent $6 million on job training for West Virginians.

And West Virginia will benefit from another great national program when Congress approves President Johnson's War on Poverty.

Of all these important undertakings, I have been most involved in the juvenile delinquency program. As chairman of the President's Committee on Juvenile Delinquency, I have helped implement the Juvenile Delinquency Act of 1961, and I have become increasingly concerned about the complexity of the problems facing our youth, particularly the children of our urban and rural slums.

I know these problems are of vital concern to you, the members of Action for Appalachian Youth, and the Kanawha County Council of Parents and Teachers, and I would like to look back tonight on some of the things we have learned in the past three years.

We started with the belief that delinquency cannot be understood or dealt with by shock at its results, but rather with rational evaluation of its causes. And we began with the belief that we could not look to any single cause, because there are many: slum housing, youth unemployment, racial discrimination, inadequate schooling, broken homes—all the handicaps that combine to strip young people of any hope for their own futures in society.

As President Johnson observed in his message on Poverty to Congress:

> Worst of all, poverty means hopelessness for the young. The young man and woman who grows up without a decent education in a broken home in a hostile and squalid environment, in ill health or in the face of racial injustice; that young man or woman is often trapped in the life of poverty. . . . He faces a mounting sense of despair which drains initiative and ambition and energy.

Our goal was to support a limited number of local demonstration projects which would show how hope could be restored, how delinquency can be fought effectively by being fought on many fronts —through simultaneous, cooperative efforts in job training, health, education, rehabilitation, recreation and social services.

No city was ready at that time to start such a program. So our immediate goal was to help willing communities develop the plan and marshal the resources necessary for action. As a result, we made preliminary grants to sixteen cities, including Charleston, to draw up the plans for broad community youth programs. In short, we set out to help these communities learn how to begin.

This job of planning is hard work. There is no glory in it. But without planning, despite the best intentions, we continue with haphazard, fragmented efforts that waste good intentions, good work, money and, worst of all, the lives of our young people.

Thus, this planning period is the test of a community's resolve. Action for Appalachian Youth has been among the most successful projects, and no one deserves more credit for this than Judge William J. Thompson, whose dedication to the cause of youth is unexcelled throughout the Nation.

Today, all but a few of the sixteen cities have come back to us with their action proposals. From them we have found five standards by which to measure the effectiveness of juvenile delinquency efforts.

The first standard, plainly, is the quality of the programs with which we set out. Our efforts should treat causes, not symptoms. They should be based on fact, not speculation. They should reach the poor who are the victims of the problem, not the middle-class.

Most important, the individual programs, whether in education, job training, recreation, probation, social work, or other fields, must work together.

The second requirement is capable professional leadership. The need is for men whose vision is not confined to one field of specialization, but who can see and act against total problems. This means men who see what must be done, can communicate these plans to the lay community, and can direct a staff to get the job done. Such professional talent, responsible to the community leadership, is imperative if good ideas are to become reality for the community.

The third need is for full cooperation between local institutions and social agencies. City, county, state, and private welfare agencies, the school system, the courts, the police, civic groups, churches—all these have a vital role to play.

Clearly, this is an ideal. While these different groups share in a resolve to help youth, they also represent particular, sometimes differing interests and approaches. What one finds in the real world are friction, rivalry and misunderstanding.

Thus, a major function of the planning effort is to create an effective working relationship among these agencies, joined in the understanding that maximum results depend on maximum cooperation. Such cooperation is not simply desirable. It is essential. Our youth problems are too serious to permit us the luxury of fragmentation, discord and delay.

The fourth need is to involve the leaders of the target population in the program. We must plan with these people, not for them. We must seek out the leaders of the slum community or of the hollow and get their ideas and assistance.

In one city, a massive community improvement program has been snubbed by the very people it was meant to help. The program had the best of intentions. It had the involvement and support of public officials in the area. But the problem remained, and the reason was simple: the program was imposed from the outside.

We need to remember—and nowhere is this more true than in West Virginia—that to be without money is not to be without pride.

All of these factors are important, but the fifth factor is the most important of all: the commitment of the top level leadership of the community. I refer here to elected officials, and also to the high officials of business, labor and education. I am not talking about lip-service, but about a real commitment of time and money and influence.

No city can deal effectively with its major social problems without this high-level commitment. The most sensible plan and the most extensive efforts of hundreds of dedicated teachers, social workers and policemen will be thwarted unless they get money and moral support from those who make far-reaching community decisions.

We have seen one city flounder because its mayor is not committed. In another city, rivalry between the city and county governments has crippled the program. Education and jobs are basic to preventing the problem, yet we have heard high school superintendents and corporation executives say they are not involved in the delinquency problem.

But in most communities, public officials have assumed their responsibilities and we have seen progress. Certainly we have seen this in Charleston, with the firm commitment of Judge Thompson, Senators Randolph and Byrd, Congressman Slack, Governor Barron, Mayor Shanklin and many, many others I see here tonight.

Indeed, we have seen all five basic elements of a successful program develop in Action for Appalachian Youth. Your project has completed the groundwork. Now it is in the action phase and is beginning to pick up speed.

Two of your major programs, neighborhood development and youth employment, are funded and in action. AAY is beginning to tap the reservoir of human resources available in Kanawha County. AAY's workers are carrying the concept of self-help into the city slums and rural hollows. Close ties have been established with community and state agencies. The working relationship between AAY and the Kanawha County School Board is of particular importance. The Community School Program being planned by your school board, to keep schools open evenings and weekends to serve as community centers, is a creative beginning.

And, more important than even a specific program, is the foundation you have built for future community action. You know where you are and you know where you are going. The AAY program will face challenges as it moves ahead and it will need the support of every citizen. But you have given every indication that you will succeed.

You have the community support to carry out a youth program today—or an anti-poverty program tomorrow. The problems are easy to see and are identical. The solutions are obscure and enormously difficult.

But you in Charleston, working with AAY, have demonstrated that they are not impossible. Given the ingredients of resolute community action, working in partnership with Federal assistance and stimulation, we can succeed.

Norman Podhoretz, the editor and writer, recently wrote: "In the past few years poverty has penetrated into the consciousness of middle class America for the first time since the Depression."

To our credit as a Nation, he is right. Today millions of Americans are concerned about dropouts, automation, migrant workers and pockets of poverty. I don't think people talked much about these things before the spring of 1960.

I think the turning point came when Senator Kennedy travelled up and down this state and felt the plight of many of its people. As a candidate, he turned the eyes of the Nation on West Virginia. As President, he did everything in his power, as President Johnson is doing, to help the poor in this state and every state.

We can launch an all-out attack on poverty now because the American public understands the issues and the need for action. This war can be won if we, as citizens of West Virginia, or Washington, or America, give it our fullest support. Nothing is beyond the capacity of this Nation when its people speak with a united voice.

President Kennedy expected a great deal from the people of West Virginia and he would be proud to know that a program like Action for Appalachian Youth has become a model for efforts to solve the problems of young people throughout the country.

And there can be no more important effort. Theodore Roosevelt wrote in 1910, "The object of government is the welfare of the people. The material progress and prosperity of a nation are desirable chiefly in so far as they lead to the moral and material welfare of all good citizens."

That is our goal today, as it has been throughout our history. All of you who invest your hours, your energy, and your interest in the young people of Kanawha County contribute to that goal. You have my warmest wishes in your work.

Delivered at the University of Chicago Law School
Chicago, Illinois, May 1, 1964

Law Day is a day which is set aside for all of us to reaffirm our faith in a Government of law.

We lawyers can celebrate it in two ways: by speeches which praise the law—and, by implication, ourselves; or by using it as an occasion to examine the problems which face our society and whose resolution should challenge us as lawyers.

Tonight I wish to do the latter.

We meet here today at a great law school in the heart of a great metropolitan center. In the area surrounding this school there live thousands and tens of thousands of people who are daily coping with —or failing to cope with—the problems which beset an urban and industrial society.

In this area are problems of crime and delinquency, of education and overcrowded housing, and all the other problems which accompany poverty.

This in not a unique area. These are not unique problems. They are the problems of an urban and industrial society.

And because law does not exist in a vacuum, they are the problems which law faces today in the United States.

I think the solution to these problems should be a challenge to all of us—and particularly to young people who are now embarking upon professional careers.

I think we must be deeply concerned over whether, as a profession dedicated to the rule of law, we are meeting—or even seeing —the challenge which the peculiar character of our urban society is making daily. We concentrate too much on the traditional part of the law—on lawsuits, courts, and formal legal learning—too little upon the fundamental changes in our society which may, in the last analysis, do much more to determine the fate of law and of the rule of law.

No single set of experiences has brought this point home to me more forcibily than the contacts we have had with juvenile delinquency.

The Justice Department's traditional concern is with law enforcement. But in coping with an ever mounting number of young offenders, law enforcement is a small part of the total picture.

In formulating our program on juvenile delinquency it quickly became clear to us that the emphasis could not be upon law violations and law violators. But upon the causes of violation.

To put it differently, youth offenses are not the illness to be dealt with. They are merely symptoms of an illness that goes far deeper in our society.

To arrive at this conclusion one need not be a sociologist, or a social worker or a planner. One simply needs to walk the slums of Washington, or New York, or Chicago or in the communities of Appalachia and talk with the young people.

For many of these young people law violation is not the isolated outburst of a social misfit. It is part of a way of life where all conventional routes to success are blocked and where law abidingness has lost all meaning and appeal.

You cannot look into their eyes or look up and down the asphalt jungle or the desolate hollows in which they live without sensing the despair, the frustration, the futility and the alienation they feel. One is strongly impelled to do something, to make some gesture that says: "People do care; don't give up."

Surely the answer to this problem is not simply to provide more and better juvenile courts, more and better juvenile institutions, or more and better lawyers to prosecute or defend young people, who then return to the same desolation which caused their difficulty in the first place.

What is needed are programs which deal directly with the causes of delinquency. These are programs to impart skills, to instill motivation, to create opportunity. These are programs which urge young people to stay in school.

These are summer job programs for high school students. These are programs to provide decent recreational facilities. These are, in short, programs which indicate that people do care, that there is hope, and that all young people do count in this society.

We know something about that helplessness. The inability of a poor, uneducated person to defend himself, unaided by counsel in a court of criminal justice, is both symbolic and symptomatic of his larger helplessness.

But we, as a profession, have backed away from dealing with that larger helplessness. We have secured the acquittal of an indigent person but only to abandon him to eviction notices, wage attachments, repossession of goods and termination of welfare benefits.

To the poor man, "legal" has become a synonym simply for technicalities and obstruction, not for that which is to be respected or looked up to. The poor man looks upon the law as an enemy, not as a friend. For him the law is always taking something away.

It is time to recognize that lawyers have a very special role to play in dealing with this helplessness. And it is time we filled it. It is long overdue.

Some of the necessary jobs are not very different from what lawyers have been doing all along for Government, for business, for those who can pay and pay well. They involve essentially the same skills. The problems are a little more difficult. The fees are less. The rewards are greater.

First, we have to make law less complex and more workable. Lawyers have been paid, and paid well, to make law difficult. It is about time we brought our intellectual resources to bear on eliminating some of those intricacies. A wealthy client can pay counsel to unravel—or to create—a complex tangle of questions concerning custody matters for instance. It makes no kind of sense to have to go through similarly complex legal mazes to determine whether Mrs. Jones should have been denied social security or aid to dependent children benefits. To put a price tag on justice is to deny it!

Second, we have to begin asserting rights which the poor have always had in theory, but which they have never been able to assert on their own behalf. Unasserted, unknown, unavailable rights are no rights at all!

Lawyers must bear the responsibility for permitting the growth and continuance of two systems of law—one for the rich, one for the poor. Without a lawyer of what use is the administrative review procedure set up under various welfare programs? Without a lawyer of what use is the right to a partial refund for the payments made on a repossessed car?

What is the price tag on equal justice under law? Has simple justice a price which we as a profession must exact? Is that what we have come to? It is certainly the way the underprivileged, the poor, the helpless regard us.

Helplessness does not stem from the absence of theoretical rights. It can stem from an inability to assert real rights. The tenants of slums, and public housing projects, the purchasers from disreputable finance companies, the minority group member who is discriminated against—all these may have legal rights which—if we are candid—remain in the limbo of the law.

Third, we need to practice preventive law on behalf of the poor. Just as the corporate lawyer tries to steer company policy away from the antitrust, fraud, or securities laws, so too, the individual can be counselled about leases, purchases and the variety of common arrangements whereby he can be victimized and exploited.

Fourth, we need to begin to develop new kinds of legal rights in situations that are not now perceived as involving legal issues.

We live in a society that has a vast bureaucracy charged with many responsibilities. When those responsibilities are not properly discharged, it is the poor and the helpless who are most likely to be hurt and to have no remedy whatsoever.

We need to define those responsibilities and convert them into legal obligations. We need to create new remedies to deal with the multitude of daily injuries that persons suffer in this complex society, simply because it is complex.

I am not talking about persons who injure others out of selfish or evil motives. I am talking about the injuries which result simply from administrative convenience, injuries which may be done inadvertently by those endeavoring to help—teachers and social workers and urban planners. These are not unusual tasks. Lawyers do them all the time in every major field of law.

It is time we used those traditional skills—our precision, our ability to probe for facts, our understanding of technicalities, our adversary skills, our negotiating skills—on behalf of the poor.

Only when we have done all these things, and more, when we

have created in fact a system of equal justice for all—a system which recognizes in fact the dignity of all men—will our profession have lived up to its responsibilities.

That job is not going to be done by simply writing a check for $100—or $1,000—to the Legal Aid Society. These are jobs that will take the combined, sustained commitment of our intellectual and ethical energies, a pledge to donate not once or twice but continuously the resources of our profession and our legal system.

For example, every law firm could assign one attorney on a rotating basis for a period of time to work on problems in the community. I would ask each law firm to do so.

Our professional mandate goes far beyond protecting the presumption of innocence throughout a criminal trial.

Our obligation extends to championing a large presumption—the presumption of individual sanctity and worth which must attend all—rich and poor alike—if the rule of law is to prevail in reality as it does in Law Day speeches.

These are obligations of the legal profession. But here at this university they are peculiarly yours. That is so because—whether you welcome it or not—graduating from a great school puts an obligation squarely upon you.

Last October, President Kennedy—visiting Amherst College—said:

> There is inherited wealth in this country and also inherited poverty. And unless the graduates of this college, and other colleges like it, who are given a running start in life—unless they are willing to put back into our society those talents, the broad sympathy, the understanding, the compassion—unless they are willing to put those qualities back into the service of the great republic, then obviously the presuppositions upon which our democracy are based are bound to be fallible.

All of us have this obligation. We can and we must meet it not only as attorneys, but as individual citizens. Active individual participation is the strength of our society. It is what has kept our system from stagnating. It is what we require now—as much as in any time in our history—to make law both the guardian and the agent of freedom.

Delivered at the Commemoration of the
125th year of the Founding of
Central High School
Philadelphia, Pennsylvania, May 6, 1964

I will tell you, I have to catch a plane back to Washington at 9:45, but I am not going to get on it without taking Bernie Siegel with me. I am just going to have him keep saying that every morning as I get up. I hope they made a tape of it. On gloomy days I can play it. I appreciate it very much.

I appreciate your Central High making me an honorary graduate. If Bernie was speaking of my life, I would speak on behalf of my mother and father, who were worried about me getting through one high, let alone two, so I thank him.

People keep bringing up the time when my brother was looking around for the best lawyer in the United States to make Attorney General and happened to light on me, and when he asked what was wrong with giving me a little experience before I went out and practiced law. I thought I had really straightened all of that out when I went to speak at Pennsylvania Law School this afternoon, where I traced a little bit of my career.

You know, you can hear all that just so long, and if you are a sensitive soul it begins to affect you. I went through it and I explained this to them three hours ago. I would have thought it had gotten through to Bernie Siegel and the rest of you that I got out of law school and went to work in the Department of Justice as a regular attorney in 1951. It is not as if I had had no experience when I worked there. I worked very hard. I took my work home at night. I was diligent, industrious, and then ten years later I became Attorney General.

But I appreciate very much the kind remarks that Bernie Siegel made about me and about my brother. I am delighted to be here with you this evening, and I am greatly honored to be recipient of the first Farnwell Distinguished Service Award.

For 125 years your school has maintained the tradition of excellence. That is one of the beacon lights of the public school system here in the United States. The tradition is a great credit to all of you, to your insistence on the highest standards, and to your continuing interest in young people. You have developed that kind of graduate in Central High School, a great legacy of education. Your city and our Nation are the richer for it. So I am proud to be able to share a small part of that with all of you tonight.

In some ways we are very fortunate in the United States. We have attained a political stability needed for such traditions to flourish. Here men of vision and high purpose can create lasting educational values which will endure for generations to come. But in many nations of today's world such orderly development is not possible.

Under conditions of turbulence, social and political change, the young are often directly involved not in learning history in the classroom, but in making history themselves. These young people are vitally important to all of us. It is this importance that I would like to discuss briefly with you tonight.

President Kennedy was intensely interested in young people, the young people of the world. He sought them out at every opportunity, and I believe was really able to communicate with them better than almost any other world leader. He enjoyed their company, but even beyond that, he felt that what they thought and what they did would powerfully influence the world of today as well as five, ten, fifteen, or twenty-five years from now.

This role in our future life cannot be seriously questioned. In the unsettled atmosphere of the world today, the young have significant advantages in influencing affairs, as they are even now proving in country after country. This is particularly true of the developing nations, where there is great impatience and great pressure to race through centuries to the present.

Perhaps the first aspect of the importance of young people is that there are so many of them. In every Latin American country, for example, a majority of the citizens are under the age of twenty-five. In Brazil, 64 per cent of the population is under twenty-five. In Venezuela, the figure is 72 per cent. In India, where the population of 450 million is more than double the population of the United States and Canada combined, six out of every ten people are under the age of twenty-five.

There are comparable figures for most of the other developing nations, and higher figures in some of them. I know, of course, that these figures include children, the very young. But they also include the university students in all of these countries, and students in the world today are a dynamic force, with an importance out of all proportion to their numbers. With education, they become the thinkers, the doers, and the leaders.

You will recall the Hungarian uprising of 1956. Students organized it and led it and, of course, this movement was ultimately repressed with Russian tanks. But before the Freedom Fighters died and fell on the bloodstained cobblestone streets of Budapest, the world knew them. They had rocked the structure of international communism to its very foundations. It would never be the same again.

Students and young workers rioted in Warsaw that summer with less bloodshed, but with more practical results.

Then came Latin America. Many here reacted in shocked disbelief when the Vice President was jeered and stoned by students in Peru, and the windows of his car smashed by students in Venezuela.

Then not long after, student riots in Japan forced President Eisenhower to cancel his visit to that Nation and forced the resignation of Premier Kishi.

Two years later 100,000 youthful rioters swarmed through the streets of Seoul and more than 100 persons lost their lives, but the government of Syngman Rhee was toppled.

The Mendaris government of Turkey fell after violent demonstrations of students and Army cadets.

And the students, as you know, played a key role in the overthrow of the Diem Government in South Vietnam.

Nearly four months ago the Panamanian and American students' actions led to riots in Panama, where more than a score of people lost their lives, and the relationships between our two countries were broken.

These are but a few examples, just in the last ten years, of the impact of youth on the world scene. But young people have a special importance today for still another reason. A number of them, particularly in Africa, are leading their nations. Others are in a position of significant political power. The classroom in many areas is only a few short years away from the Presidential Palace. Just let me name and tell you about just a few of them.

This Kenneth Kaunda, for example. He is thirty-nine years old and head of the Rhodesian Nationalist Movement since he was thirty-two. In a few months, when Northern Rhodesia becomes an independent country, he will be their first Premier.

Oskar Kambona, Foreign Minister of Tanganyika, is only thirty-two. Jonas Savimbi, Angolan exile leader, is only thirty. Sekou Toure, President of Guinea, was only that same age when he became President, when Guinea became independent.

Tom Mboya, the Minister of Justice of Kenya, has been in the front rank of his country's leadership for a number of years, and he is still in his thirties, as Justin Bomboko and Mobutu of the Congo are.

The list could go on and on, and it is not limited to Africa. Rufino Heckonova, Minister of Finance of the Philippines, is only thirty-three.

All we have to do is look a little to the south of us and see Fidel Castro, who took over when he was thirty-two. Nasser became President at the age of thirty-six, and General Khanh, Prime Minister of Vietnam now, is only thirty-six.

When we go back to our own history, through our own Revolution, we find that the ages were much the same. Thomas Jefferson was only thirty-three when he wrote the Declaration of Independence, and Alexander Hamilton but thirty when he wrote the Federalist Papers. Madison was only thirty-six when he wrote the rest of them.

But I mention these young leaders of today only as one important aspect of the youth of the world, for current history suggests that the trend to youth will continue, and that the leaders of the developing nations throughout the world for the next few decades will come from the young intellectuals, from the young students, from the young labor leaders, and from the young politicians of today. These are the ones with whom we should all have an important and primary concern.

This is what I suggest to you as thinking American citizens, as those who are interested in youth here in the United States, to those who are interested in education. We must be concerned with these young people, with who they are and where they live, with what they are thinking and what they are saying, and with what we are saying to them.

I raise this point for two reasons. First, I think that we often tend to overlook the real significance of young people, and to look toward the established order, the status quo, and to those who run it. Seniority is sometimes impressive for its own sake.

Secondly, I think that it is always difficult to look past what we have in the present and to guess for the future. That is what is required when we turn to those who are in the so-called "outs" today. The military have been criticized for training for the last war instead of for the next. But many of us do that in our thinking every day. It requires a conscientious effort to think ahead, an intensive effort to be concerned with the problems of the young in other nations.

But the young throughout the world will not wait for our concern. They are going ahead with their own revolution, not waiting for us. They are going ahead in their own way and in their own time. In many countries today they are in open revolt against oppression and against poverty, against the grinding condition of systems which have not allowed progress. They are in revolt against the established order, against the status quo.

History is on their side, and in one way or another they will achieve a large measure of success in their endeavors, whatever the cost. In so many instances, their revolution is an easy decision for them, for they feel they have nothing to lose. What they think and what they do has a direct effect on all of us here in the United States. Across the globe they are a force of whirlwind proportions, and the world of tomorrow will bear the imprint of their ideals and their goals. For this reason, we must be concerned about them.

Where do we stand? Someone will share their aspirations and their leadership—if not us, another system—in what may be a tragic price for them and for all of us. There is, I believe, an even stronger reason for our concern. In essence, these young people throughout the world are engaged in a phase of the same battle that we have fought since the days of the Founding Fathers. In America, we no longer have to carry on the battle with arms and with blood. We have had our Revolution. For us, the field of battle has shifted, because we have formed a government capable of adjusting to change. It is within the orderly processes of that government that we fight today, and fight we must to provide a future for our young people, the young Negroes in the cities, and the young whites caught up in the valleys of despair in Appalachia, who are beginning to doubt what future there is for them under this system.

We must not lose sight of the fact that we have a common cause and purpose with the young revolutionist of the world. We must remember that, as President Kennedy said, we are the heirs of the first revolution. It was here in Philadelphia, as a matter of fact, just a little over 100 years ago, that Abraham Lincoln described the single great principle of the Declaration of Independence as "something in that Declaration giving liberty not alone to the people of this country, but hope for the world for all future time."

I feel that we cannot too often remind ourselves of that great tradition as it applies in the world of today. It is this tradition which establishes our identity with the young in the developing nations and enables us to talk directly to them across oceans and continents, and through the barriers of time, culture, and language; for we are engaged in an epic struggle for the hearts and the minds of men.

To recognize that this struggle is perilous is to also recognize that it is exciting. If the odds seem long, as Edith Hamilton said of Aeschylus, "to the heroic, desperate odds fling a challenge." Men were not made for safe havens.

But it isn't the long odds that impress me. I view the real odds as strongly in our favor. We overlook our great advantages, but we do not make the most of them. We are not always as tough, articulate, and as aggressive as we might be in the war of ideas. We sometimes do not recognize our revolutionary tradition with the candor and the pride that it deserves.

But I feel we can approach the young people of the world with strength and with confidence. We have made a representative government work, and maintained freedom at the same time. We have no apologies to make for what we have done here in the United States. We are big enough to admit our errors and strong enough to be tolerant of ideas and diversity.

I think the advantage is irrepressible. No other system can match it in our conquest for inquiring young minds. We are a young Nation, and we have in addition the strength, the spirit, the vigor to lead the world by our example. What we need is the discernment to identify true values and goals, however difficult that may be.

It was Emerson who said, "God offers to everyone his choice between truth and repose. Take what you please. You cannot have both." I think that is what the real test for all of us is today: whether we are going to move forward or whether we are going to be satisfied; to apply what you have applied in Central High, to put forward the same values, the same effort, around the world; to realize that the young of this country are important, but the young who are going to be the future leaders of other countries are important also.

In this effort, the efforts of all of us are required. None of us can stand by. So I would hope that you will join with me in believing that we cannot afford to sleep. The only thing that we can afford is energy and effort.

I thank you.

Delivered before Young Israel of Pelham Parkway New York City, May 20, 1964

It is ten years, almost to the day, since the Supreme Court of the United States asked the historic question, "Does segregation of children in public schools solely on the basis of race . . . deprive the children of the minority group of equal educational opportunities?"

The Court's answer was simple, but resounding: "We believe that it does."

The nation has traveled a long difficult road since then. Little Rock; Clinton, Tennessee; New Orleans; Oxford, Mississippi; Tuscaloosa and Birmingham, Alabama—all testify to the length and difficulty of the road.

But there also have been quieter successes. A number of other communities, Atlanta, Chattanooga, and Dallas, for example, have met the wrenching change of desegregating schools with good faith and with order. And, to their great credit some of the communities first troubled by disorder are now making progress with responsibility and calm.

Yet, the bulk of the problem remains. Less than 2 per cent of the Negro children in the South are in schools with white children. More than 1,800 of the 2,256 bi-racial school districts in the South remain totally segregated.

These figures reflect the depth of the problem. It will require new social attitudes and new laws to solve. The pending civil rights bill alone cannot provide the solution, for there is no single solution. But it is an essential step and it will be of great assistance.

In the meantime, those of us in other parts of the country have our own kind of school discrimination to face up to and in many ways it is a more difficult problem in Boston or Chicago or New York than it is in the South.

"It does no good," President Kennedy said a year ago in California, "to say that segregation in education is the business of another state. It is the business of our country. These young, uneducated boys and girls know no state boundaries. . . . They are your citizens as well as citizens of this country."

But even after we acknowledge the breadth of both the problem, and the responsibility, we run the risk of laying too much stress on only the first word in the phrase "desegregated education." By so doing, we obscure the importance of the quality of education.

Desegregation of schools does not automatically transform them into better schools. It is only a step. The larger goal is to see that the education of our youth is not merely desegregated, but that it is excellent. And the place to start is in schools which for too long have been separate, or unequal, or inadequate.

There is little need to proclaim the necessity of education to an audience whose ancestors have been teaching that necessity to the world for fifty centuries. But it *is* relevant to observe how painfully the lack of education can affect the life of an American citizen today.

There are already more than 4,000,000 Americans seeking employment and unable to find it. As our society becomes more complex, their search becomes harder. A recent business survey disclosed that many companies now will not hire persons even for assembly line jobs unless they have high school diplomas. The companies are willing to pay more, but they want better workers.

The rate of unemployment among those who have graduated from college is 1.4 per cent. The rate among those who did not finish high school is *six times higher*—8.1 per cent.

At present, automation is eliminating more than 4,000 jobs a day —precisely the kind of jobs which unskilled or semi-skilled people can fill. Approximately 10 per cent of the work force today is employed in unskilled jobs. By 1970, the figure will be down to 5 per cent.

In short, a more direct relationship between education and employment exists in modern America than ever before. A very real cycle of ignorance and poverty is at work throughout our country.

Not long ago, I visited a rural hollow of despair in West Virginia where nearly all of the men were unemployed. Many of the children had never known their fathers to have a job. Many had never known either of their parents to have been to high school. It was discouraging to learn—but it could not be surprising—that the school dropout rate among these children is 95 per cent.

Similar observations could be made about city children here and across the country, where second and third generations are undereducated, unemployed and on relief. A recent nationwide study showed that more than half of the men between thirty-five and forty-four who did not finish high school were sons of men who did not finish grade school.

The lesson of these facts, rural and urban, is clear: We must do a better job of educating our youth, particularly those with built-in handicaps of race, or poverty, or both. As Secretary Wirtz has observed, "There probably won't be full employment until we make education our number one industry."

When I say we must do particularly well for the socially handicapped, I do not call for favoritism or preference. To educate the undereducated more does not mean we need educate our other children less. But it does mean we recognize that the American pledge of equal opportunity is meaningless without equal preparation.

There is no question that we have the skills and the resources to do so. The Federal Government is seeking to stimulate action on behalf of socially handicapped youth throughout the country.

The poverty legislation proposed by President Johnson includes a $150,000,000 work-training program for teenage students and an extensive experiment in remedial reading to help young people master the skill which is so fundamental to all other learning.

The President's Committee on Juvenile Delinquency and Youth Crime already is helping establish demonstration projects to illustrate what can be done by local authorities, in a number of cities.

Here in New York, on the lower east side and in Harlem, programs are now underway to rescue boys and girls from the discouraging cycle of poverty and lack of education.

We—federal, state and city officials—have found that much *can* be done for children who must rely on their communities for the stimulation and education that cannot come from their homes.

We have found that much more *must* be done for these children —like those in Harlem who, when they reach the eighth grade, are two and a half years behind the city average in reading ability.

Neither the problems nor our capacity for solving them are limited to urban, metropolitan areas. In Prince Edward County, Virginia, 1,700 Negro children are attending school for the first time since public schools were closed there in 1959 to avoid desegregation. They are attending a free school system established last fall through the efforts of President Kennedy and state and local leaders.

I wish you could have been with me when we visited Prince Edward County not long ago and heard the Negro children, who had been deprived of education for four years, sing "America, the Beautiful." For schoolchildren to sing patriotic songs elsewhere would be unremarkable. But what should be understood is that when the free schools opened in Prince Edward last September, only one child could even recognize the National Anthem. And he identified it as "the baseball song."

The latest test scores taken at the free schools demonstrate that their students have gained literacy skills in the past year at *twice* the national average. In one year of excellent education, most of the students will make up for two of the four years they lost. A few have even surpassed the level they would have reached in public school.

Whatever the success of such individual projects, however, it should be plain that the Federal Government's role can only be to help. Its efforts can only be demonstrations. For the sample solutions to have meaning, citizens everywhere must understand the common problem. They must initiate and support efforts in their own communities—and they must participate in such efforts themselves.

Every week in Minneapolis, for example, the Council of Jewish Women takes a hundred underprivileged school children on field trips, or helps them to put on plays, or to build toy telephone networks, or other activities related to their school studies.

Every week in New York, Public Education Association volunteers spend three hours, or more, with 11,000 public school students who need help in reading, or learning English, or other subjects. One teacher observed that in a period of months, these children have gained years of reading skill.

These examples show us what it is possible to do. They show us that we do not need to abandon our children to the sullen world of the hollow or the slum. They show us that education can and must be the vehicle out of hopelessness.

When our forebears—yours and mine—came to America, they came because this country promised them something. It promised them an opportunity, nourished by education, not merely to grind for a bare living, but to strive for a good life.

Now the question is whether the America of today still offers that opportunity to its citizens. Now the question is, are we going to give these children of the hollow and the slum the education and the support they must have to make that opportunity mean something?

Our failure to provide adequate answers to those questions will not be a mere failure of conscience or charity. It will be a failure within our society. We develop the kind of citizens we deserve. If a large number of our children grow up into frustration and poverty, we must expect to pay the price.

As Thomas Jefferson observed, 150 years ago, "If a nation expects to be ignorant and free, in a state of civilization, it expects what never was and never will be."

Education can provide us with the means. It can be the means to a job and a share in our unparalleled wealth. It can be a means to the solution of some of our most pressing social problems—of race, of poverty, or crime.

But let us recognize that education also should be a means to more than vocational skills or physical comfort. The desegregation of education, the quality of education—these can have ultimate meaning only as they can help to elevate the spirit of man.

Lord Tweedsmuir once wrote that civilization is "something more than the cushioned life made possible by science." Civilization must provide, he wrote, for "a soul to develop, a mind which could rejoice in the things of the mind, an impulse towards spiritual perfection."

It is this spirit which has motivated the Jewish people through centuries of physical duress. It is this spirit which has made America not merely a political experiment, but an enduring dream. With energy and optimism, let us work today to release that spirit for every

on a street corner in Harlem. They can be found—differing only in number—in every city and hamlet in these United States.

Do they have rights without substance? Do they have opportunity that has been stalled—promise that has been delayed?

In the same fashion that some of us have public accommodation laws and fair employment practices legislation, all of us have public education statutes. But how meaningful and how uniform are these—not on the law books, but in practice? How uniform is the quality of classroom teaching, the quality of the teacher, and the quality of the books in one part of the city as opposed to another—in a suburb as opposed to a slum.

Recently, on a visit to Harlem, I was told that between the third and sixth grade in this troubled community's schools the average I.Q. of students drops ten points and that 94 per cent are one-to-two years behind in their reading ability.

The law is not enough. The right defined by law is not enough whether it concerns education or civil rights. Within weeks we shall have a civil rights bill. It will be the law of the land and it will call for compliance, which is merely a submission to the process of law.

And we all know how painful and how hard our struggle has been in the last decade for just compliance with the law. Again, we will have to ask ourselves, is just compliance enough? Again, we must ask ourselves: How willing and how meaningful will we make that compliance?

This is not a question that must *only* be answered by the South. Recent events in northern cities have demonstrated amply that significant compliance—compliance backed by intent, heart and mind—is a problem there as well. For compliance *anywhere* does not begin at the end of a nightstick; nor is it easily achieved.

The mere presence of machinery—for civil rights or idle youth and their impoverished parents—does not insure service. The fact that the structure exists has not insured its full use—and particularly its use to best advantage.

Recently in the Capital—in the City of Washington—this lag of structure behind use was dramatically illustrated. We have many Government and private agencies dedicated to relieving some of our severe social problems.

More than a thousand families who live in what is gently called a "deteriorating neighborhood" were surveyed to learn how many had contact with our private and public social agencies. These were some of the findings:

Fewer than 5 per cent of the families were involved with the Boy Scouts.

Fewer than 3 per cent of the families were reached by the Boys Clubs.

Fewer than 3 per cent had contact with the Salvation Army.

And one highly publicized settlement house reached three-tenths of one per cent of the families.

The U. S. Employment Service reached about 11 per cent; the PTA and other school groups, 9 per cent, and only about 14 per cent had any contact at all with churches.

Now the church, the Employment Service and the settlement house all were there. But again, this was not enough to reach the troubled youths and their parents in this neighborhood.

Today we have the new war on poverty and a host of expanded Government services—all intent on bridging the gap between structure and use. While these will be debated and hammered into legislation on the Federal level, they will be organized and carried out by and in the communities.

To organize our communities we need not bodies, but brains. We need not simply able bodies, but the best brains.

The hardest task is to appoint and incorporate in our work a group of men and women with the power and willingness to look at our community difficulties, dissect them, criticize areas of shortcoming—and make meaningful suggestions.

Sometimes, too, it is hard to accept that sort of recommendation. For sometimes it carries with it announced or implied criticism of programs that have failed us in the past. Change means that someone's professional feathers will be ruffled, that a glass-topped desk might be moved to another office or abandoned, that pet programs might die.

Progress is the nice word we like to use. But change is its motivator. And change has its enemies.

The willingness to confront that change will determine how much we shall really do for our youth and how truly meaningful our efforts will be.

The test will be not how elaborate we make our proposals for new programs and new funds, but how well these programs affect the inadequacies of old, how willing we are to change the old.

Each of us as office holders has a very precious piece of that irreplaceable commodity that ticks away at our backs—the commodity called time. We hold it and expend it for constituencies. Are we prepared to expend it by seizing the initiative now? Are we prepared to invest however many months or years remain in our respective offices to forge meaningful compliance?

I wish I could stand here this afternoon and tell you that we who are part of the Federal Government can provide the answers, that we have provided very many answers.

Many of you have suggested in easy to understand language that we haven't; that we, too, must look at the old; that we, too, must achieve the meaningful working relationships among our own agencies that we desire others to achieve. And much of the criticism has been right.

I'm sure that in this room there is no shortage of examples.

As a matter of fact your very able chairman could tell of the day when Federal officials were sitting in his office discussing with him how to organize both city and Federal resources in a concerted attack on community problems. A newspaper reporter interrupted the meeting to inform the mayor that the city had just received a Federal grant —a grant unknown to the mayor and, for that matter, unknown to the Federal officials sitting in that room.

We plead guilty as charged. I must ask you, though, to provide an organized community approach that will help us to line up our own forces. But however well we put our own house in order, the bulk of the burden will still fall on you.

The right to eat in a restaurant may be given Americans beneath the marble dome of Congress, but the food will be served up in your town. A large part of a school dropout program may be financed out of a Federal office building, but the youngster will be chosen and helped by you.

Wherever dropout programs have worked, or job training has been successful, or educational approaches have been revised—in all of these places we have found full political commitment. We have seen the political and business leadership of the community combine to back up the social worker, the youth leader, the teacher who all have cried out about these problems for so long. And they have worked. We have proved again and again that important changes can be made in the deprived areas, that compliance to our social obligations can be meaningful.

Teachers have been trained to serve in the slums. And they have served well. Residents of impoverished areas can be called upon to help each other. And they have helped greatly. College youth can be recruited to teach their less affluent neighbors. And they have taught enthusiastically.

We have shown that I.Q.'s in the slums can rise rather than fall, that training programs provide jobs for the idle, and that new educational approaches provide hope for the previously hopeless.

In the last few weeks, I was in Prince Edward County in Virginia to accept 9,964 pennies donated by children for the John F. Kennedy Library. For four years there were no schools at all in Prince Edward County. Youngsters who were ten and twelve years old formerly couldn't read the cover of a first grade book. They read now. They do arithmetic now. They have meaningful education now.

Our task is to spread these achievements from the isolated to the general, from the test cases to all cases. The question facing us is: Can we combine all of these isolated successes within a single community? Can we combine the established city leadership with the new leaders of the impoverished in an organized attack that will benefit both?

I firmly believe that your talents and your willpower dictate a unanimous answer of yes.

If we do this together, then that child born last year, that Negro child, that Appalachian child—and all children like them, will disappoint the oddsmakers and the handicappers. And together we shall collect the winnings for having cheated failure and having glorified opportunity.

Delivered at the Dedication of the
John F. Kennedy Interfaith Chapel, West Georgia College
Carrollton, Georgia, May 26, 1964

I come today to express the pride and the deeply felt appreciation of the Kennedy family for the honor you pay to President Kennedy by naming your chapel after him, and to join with you in expressing thanks to Our Lady of Perpetual Help Catholic Church for its creative generosity.

I thank you for I know that what you are doing here, at this growing and enlightened institution which has done so much for its community, would be a source of great satisfaction to President Kennedy. And I thank you for the many kindnesses Georgia extended to him, beginning in November 1960.

His candidacy and election exemplify tolerance. This chapel is an expression of the same spirit of tolerance. And that is a spirit which is as old as Georgia.

The charitable groups in England which sponsored settlement of the colony of Georgia saw it as a haven for the persecuted and the poor. Contributions poured in from all classes of people. The clergy, for example, gave thousands of books. One of the notable titles was *A Friendly Admonition to the Drinkers of Gin, Brandy and Other Spirituous Liquors*, a volume whose message, I am certain, is still being taken to heart.

Your first settlers were warmly received by the other colonies. South Carolina sent horses, cattle, hogs, rice, and 2,000 pounds in cash. Thomas Penn sent 100 pounds in cash. In my home state, however, the opponents of foreign aid prevailed; the Governor of Massachusetts sent his best wishes.

Georgia flourished nonetheless. Its promise for religious refugees was so great that before the colony was six years old, it had as varied a population as any, with Swiss, Salzburgers, Moravians, Germans, Jews, Piedmontese, Scotch Highlanders, Welsh, and English.

Yet not even in the New World, not even in Georgia, did all the early settlers find freedom of faith. Catholics, for example, were not admitted to Georgia for seventy years. In other colonies, they were harassed, Quakers were jailed and Protestant sects were hounded.

It was in the South, in Virginia, that resentment against these practices flowered into religious freedom. With Madison and Jefferson in the vanguard, the Virginia Bill of Religious Liberty was enacted, to be followed by the First Amendment, separating church and state.

Official intolerance thus ended. Religions were free to preach, to grow, and to multiply. If a group of Boston people thought the world was going to end in the mid-nineteenth century, they were free to congregate in a theater, clad in robes, ready to perish together.

If Mormons or Christian Scientists—or followers of sects with more limited appeal, like that of the mystic Madame Blavatsky, have sought to express their faith in new ways, they have been free to do so. If Catholics have chosen to attend mass early Sunday and Jews to observe the Sabbath at sundown Friday, there has been none to forbid them.

And yet, as has been demonstrated repeatedly during our history, legal separation of church and state is not enough. It ended official intolerance; it could not end private intolerance.

And there have been those, throughout our history—and particularly in times of crisis—who have preached intolerance, who have sought to escape reality and responsibility with a slogan or a scapegoat. Religious groups have been the first targets but they have not been the only ones.

There are those who suspect their neighbors because they pray to a different God—or because they pray to none at all. And there are those who bellow that a former President of the United States is a tool of the Communist conspiracy.

There are those who preach that desegregation of the schools will destroy our society. And there are others who believe that calamity will occur because of the way we may treat our drinking water.

There is freedom in this country to be extreme, to propose the most reactionary or the most utopian solutions to all the problems of the country or even the world. There is freedom here to believe and act with passion, whether for the cause of religion, or party, or personal welfare.

"If there be any among us," Jefferson said, "who would wish to dissolve this Union or to change its Republican form, let them stand undisturbed as monuments of the safety with which error of opinion may be tolerated where reason is left free to combat it."

What is objectionable, what is dangerous about extremists is not that they are extreme, but that they are intolerant. The evil is not what they say about their cause, but what they say about their opponents.

The intolerant man will not rely on persuasion, or on the worth of the idea. He would deny to others the very freedom of opinion or of dissent which he so stridently demands for himself. He cannot trust democracy.

Frustrated by rejection, he condemns the motives, the morals, or the patriotism of all who disagree. Whether he is inflamed by politics, or religion—or drinking water, he still spreads selfish slogans and false fears.

America's answer to the intolerant man is diversity—the very diversity which our heritage of religious freedom has inspired.

The largest Scandinavian nation in the world is the United States. The largest Irish nation in the world is the United States. The second largest German nation in the world is the United States. And like statements could be made about other American ethnic groups.

Many voices, many views all have combined into an American consensus, and it has been a consensus of good sense. "In the multitude of counselors, there is safety," says the Bible, and so it is with American democracy. Tolerance is an expression of trust in that consensus and each new enlargement of tolerance is an enlargement of democracy.

President Kennedy's election was such an enlargement. It expanded religious freedom to include the highest office in the land. President Kennedy's Administration was such an enlargement. It advanced the day when the bars of intolerance against all minority groups will be lifted, not only for the Presidency, but for all aspects of our national life.

And this chapel is a warmly fitting tribute to President Kennedy not only because it bears his name but because it, too, expresses and advances the spirit of tolerance among religions and among men."

It was for this spirit that President Kennedy spoke, acted, lived, and led. "Let us go forth," he said, in the closing words of his Inaugural Address, "to lead the land we love, asking His blessing and His help, but knowing that here on earth, God's work must truly be our own."

Delivered to the Academy of Trial Lawyers
of Allegheny County
Pittsburgh, Pennsylvania, June 1, 1964

I am happy to be here with you this evening because I have always had great respect for trial lawyers as leaders of the legal profession.

I am aware, as is every student of American history, of the sterling leadership that the trial bar has contributed to our Nation and to the crucial issues of every period. The courtrooms have been our great training grounds for leadership from the days of John Adams to the present.

As trial lawyers you have an insight not necessarily shared by all members of the legal profession. You see how the law works in actual practice. You see what the law *is* as well as what it is supposed to be, and for that reason you have a better understanding of the problem I'd like to discuss with you tonight.

I refer to the problem of the bail system as it exists in the United States today—a classic example of law having an entirely different effect from its apparent purpose.

You may recall that the institution of bail originated in medieval England. Our Bill of Rights, in the Eighth Amendment, prohibits excessive bail; and the right to bail is guaranteed in the Judiciary Act of 1789 and in the constitutions or statutes of all but seven states. The decisions of most appellate courts somehow give the impression that our system of bail preserves one of the most valuable rights of freedom. That is what the law appears to be.

But you know from your experience in the courts that it just doesn't work that way. Through most of the United States today the bail system is a cruel and illogical institution which perpetuates injustice in the name of the law.

In actual practice, control is frequently in the hands of bondsmen rather than the courts. The system is subject to widespread abuse. It involves the wholesale restriction of freedom, impairment of the defendant's chances at trial and millions in needless detention costs at all levels of government.

I know that your Academy has a record of demonstrated concern for improving the quest for justice in your courts. I offer this then as a challenge to you as leaders of the legal profession and as American citizens.

Our bail system today needs thorough study, the most searching re-examination and drastic revision. This work has really just begun; men of judgment and purpose are needed to carry it forward in every community. Let's take a look at some of the facts.

As you know, the bail system determines whether someone accused in a criminal proceeding is released or jailed before trial. Usually, the *amount* of bail is set by a judge or a committing magistrate. Then if the defendant is able to post bond in the bail amount or pay a bondsman to post it for him he is released. If not, he is detained in jail.

The theory of the bail system—the *only* justification recognized for it by the courts—is that a bail bond is necessary to insure the appearance of the defendant at trial.

In actual practice, the bail system measures human freedom by financial ability. In the words of a recent report:

> Those who go free on bail are released not because they are innocent but because they can buy their liberty. The balance are detained not because they are guilty but because they are poor. Though the accused be harmless, and has a home, family and job which make it likely that—if released—he would show up for trial, he may still be held. Conversely, the habitual offender who may be dangerous to the safety of the community may gain his release.

As citizens in an age of reason, this may be offensive to us. As members of a profession concerned with the protection of human rights we may be shocked. But a close examination of the bail system reveals that it is shot through with other illogical and inconsistent features.

It is one of the basic premises of the bail system, for example, that the higher the bail, the greater the likelihood that the defendant will appear in court. But since almost all bail requirements are met by a commercial bail transaction, it is the bondsman rather than the defendant who bears the risk in most cases.

The defendant's stake in appearing is limited to the collateral— if any—which the bondsman may have required him to put up in order to get the bond. If the bondsman does not require collateral, the defendant ordinarily has *no* financial stake in complying with the terms of the bond. And this is a matter which the court does not decide or even know in most instances.

Whenever there is a commercial bail transaction, of course, it is the bondsman who assumes the paramount role in determining the defendant's freedom. The bondsman is an independent businessman who is free to reject a prospective client for any reason without regard to the consequence to the defendant.

As Judge Skelly Wright said in a recent opinion: "Professional bondsmen hold the keys to the jail in their pockets. . . . The court and the commissioner are relegated to the relatively unimportant chore of fixing the amount of bail."

There are many examples of how the bondsman's right to reject any application may conflict with the interests of a defendant. Bail in a "nominal" amount may be too small for a bondsman to bother with. As a business judgment, the bondsman may prefer professional criminals who know the rules over amateur offenders who may panic. The professional criminal rarely has the difficulty of making bail that many poor people experience.

Here in Pittsburgh you might be familiar with the recent charges that jail officials have received a cut on bond premiums. It may not be great consolation to you to know that similar charges have been made in most major cities.

There are other abuses of the bail system every bit as flagrant as this petty graft. Far too often bail is used to give defendants "a taste of jail" or to coerce them in some other way. Too often simple mistakes have resulted in gross unfairness.

Because of the importance of time and money in the practice of your profession, I know that you will have a keen appreciation of what the bail system actually costs us. Just a few of the figures will illustrate.

Last year alone Federal prisoners spent 600,000 man days in jails awaiting trial at a cost of $2 million to the Federal Government. In the city of New York in 1962, nearly 60,000 prisoners spent an average of 30 days each in pretrial detention. At $6.25 per man per day that cost the city more than $10,000,000 for that one year.

There are comparable figures for every large city. A substantial part of their facilities and budget are devoted to the detention in jails of prisoners who are presumably innocent and awaiting trial. And beyond that their welfare budgets are paid to the families of wage earners that they have thus imprisoned.

But the cost in human resources, the tragic loss in the lives of many individuals is far greater. The man who goes to jail for failure to make bond is treated in almost every jurisdiction just like the convicted criminal serving a sentence. His home may be disrupted, his family humiliated and his chance of making a living permanently taken away.

Recently in Los Angeles a man accused of a minor crime waited 207 days in jail because he did not have the money to get out. At his trial a jury found him not guilty.

Here in Pennsylvania a defendant accused of driving without a license and unable to raise a $300 bond spend 54 days in jail awaiting trial. The maximum penalty for the offense with which he was charged was five days.

In Glen Cove, N. Y., Daniel Walker was arrested on suspicion of robbery of a delicatessen. He couldn't raise the $10,000 bail or the bondsman's fee. He spent 55 days in jail. His wife had to move in with her parents, his car was repossessed, his credit destroyed. Later, he was found to be the victim of mistaken identity. When freed, it took him four months to find another job.

And remaining in jail may have substantial effect on any defendant's ability to make a proper defense. He is severely restricted in the contribution he can make to the pretrial investigation and in conferences with his attorney. The experience in jail may affect his demeanor and attitude in the courtroom and as a witness.

If he is convicted, the defendant who has lost his job and been removed from his family will have much less chance for probation than one who has kept his job, earned money and maintained his family ties.

All available data indicated that the defendant held in jail until his trial is severely disadvantaged when compared with the defendant who is released. The jailed defendant is far more likely to be convicted and far less likely to receive probation if he is convicted.

In a Philadelphia study only 52 per cent of bailed defendants were convicted compared with 82 per cent of those jailed. Among the convicted, only 22 per cent of the bailed defendants got prison sentences compared with 59 per cent—almost three times the rate—from the group that had been jailed. In the District of Columbia another study of those convicted revealed that 25 per cent of those who had been on bail were released on probation against only 6 per cent of those who had been kept in jail.

Now you might well ask yourselves, if the bail system is as bad as I've said it is, why hasn't someone done something about it. And that is not an easy question to answer.

It is not because the defects haven't been known. In 1927, nearly 40 years ago, Arthur Lawton Beeley published a thorough study of the bail system in the city of Chicago which parallels most of our findings of the present day. But from then until ten years ago, when the University of Pennsylvania Law School did a study of bail in Philadelphia, very little was done.

I suppose there has been a failure to recognize the problem for what it is. You may have heard the story of the man who was obsessed with the idea that he was a corpse. His family and friends finally sent him to a psychiatrist and for more than two hours he explained to the psychiatrist how he knew he was actually a corpse. Finally the psychiatrist asked: "Will you acknowledge that a corpse cannot bleed?" and the man said yes, that he did know that was so. Then the psychiatrist leaned over and pricked the man's finger with a pin and a drop of blood appeared. The man looked down at his finger and whistled softly to himself. "Well I'll be darned," he said "a corpse can too bleed."

Beginning with the Philadelphia bail study ten years ago, however, some significant progress has been made. It was followed by the extensive Manhattan Bail Project in New York and a bail study conducted by the Junior Bar Section in Washington, D. C.

The current efforts to remedy the defects of the bail system came together last week at the National Conference on Bail and Criminal Justice, a three-day conference in Washington, D. C. Jointly sponsored by the Department of Justice and the Vera Foundation, the conference was attended by scores of judges, defense attorneys and law enforcement officials from throughout the Nation.

Chief Justice Warren addressed its opening session. The meetings were devoted to exploring practical methods to avoid the unnecessary detention of thousands of accused persons each year while still protecting society from those who are really dangerous.

Some of the proposed alternatives to bail are still in the idea stage; others have been tried for long periods with remarkably satisfactory results. I would like to tell you about one of the most notable experiments: the Vera Foundation's Manhattan Bail Project.

This project was begun in the fall of 1961 with a grant of $115,000 from the Ford Foundation. It was staffed by law students from New York University. The staff interviewed felony defendants paying particularly close attention to those factors which would make the defendant a good parole risk.

Currently it has been found that 65 per cent of the defendants interviewed can be recommended for release on their own recognizance before trial. The project has been so successful to date that 70 per cent of its recommendations are accepted by the court and almost 80 per cent are agreed to by the District Attorney's office.

Of the 2,195 defendants paroled in this way through April 8, 1964, only 15 failed to show up in court. This is a rate of 7/10 of 1 per cent, well below the no-show rate for those out on bail and impressive enough to make the project an unqualified success. The point was proved.

In the Department of Justice we are making a wholesale re-evaluation of bail practices. We began a little over a year ago by instructing all U. S. Attorneys to recommend the release of defendants on their own recognizance in every practicable case.

With this step we have tripled—from 6 per cent to 18 per cent—the rate of release of defendants without bail. In four judicial districts more than 65 per cent of the defendants are so released. And we have found that the percentage of those who failed to appear has remained just about the same—2½ per cent—as those required to post bail.

We are also undertaking an experimental study of other approaches. I hope within the next year we can expand in the U. S. Attorneys' offices the experimental use of a summons in lieu of arrest, a procedure now the subject of an extensive study in New York City.

In the work already done on revision of the bail system there have been invaluable contributions by many individuals and groups. The press has been vitally important. Bar associations and law schools have played key roles.

This leads me to the specific challenge I would propose for you. The progress made to date has no more than scratched the surface. In this as in so many other problems, the essential effort must be made at the community level, and by that I mean the organization of a community bail project.

There are now nearly twenty such local projects throughout the country—they have quadrupled since one year ago. But before the problem is licked there must be hundreds, and large metropolitan areas like Pittsburgh are of prime importance.

We have talked about the problem, and in closing I would suggest three steps that a bail project for this metropolitan area might take initially:

First, collect the facts. There is a whole mythology of bail and misconceptions are widely held. Knowing how it actually works in your community is the essential starting point to correction.

Second, let the public know. There are many who have no occasion to think of the bail system, let alone its abuses. But this is a matter of legitimate public concern, and public knowledge can provide broad public support for efforts at reform.

Third, start now. From the experience already gained much can be done now without legislation. The same procedures now employed in New York and in parts of the Federal system can be used to effect the safe release of hundreds now unnecessarily detained in your jails.

There is great work to be done in the cause of securing better justice in our courts. In the field of bail reform particularly the rewards are indeed rich for those who take the lead at this time. So much can be accomplished.

I am hopeful that with your leadership, and that of others like you throughout the Nation we can move ahead without delay. Until we have improved the administration of justice, until our laws bear evenly on all, rich and poor alike, we cannot be satisfied that we have achieved the American dream.

Thank you.

Delivered at California Institute of Technology
Pasadena, California, June 8, 1964

Many of you, I know, are approaching the end of your schooling. The time of graduation—and liberation—is upon you. This is a time when you must expect to endure a good many profound remarks about your past and your future, your obligations and your challenges. I hesitate to afflict you further—and am consoled only by the fact that I went through a comparable ordeal when I finished college a few years back and I can recall not one word of what was said. This gives me, I might add, a pleasant sense of irresponsibility today.

Yet I suppose that the end of the academic year is one of those watersheds of life where a backward and then a forward look become almost mandatory. Students, after all, stand on the brink of the future. And you men of the California Institute of Technology stand there in a very special sense; not only because you are young, but because you are trained in the methods and ideals of modern science. If you believe, as I do, that our greatest national responsibility is to strengthen and enlarge the opening to the future, then science must obviously play a central role in this effort.

No two Americans thought more profoundly about the future of our country than Thomas Jefferson and John Adams. A century and a half ago Jefferson wrote Adams, "If science produces no better fruits than tyranny, murder, rapine and destitution of national morality, I would rather wish our country to be honest, ignorant and estimable, as our neighboring savages are."

Fortunately very few scientists turn out to be Dr. Strangeloves. Nonetheless, the advance of scientific knowledge now confronts our planet with the possibility of a disaster far greater than anything Jefferson and Adams could have imagined.

No one can be sure what sort of a future science will give us. The reason for that is plain. It is because science depends on what men do with it. And men, as this grim century has reminded us, are capable of unreason and destruction fully as much as they are capable of reason and creation.

Science began as one of the noblest expressions of man's reason. It will continue to serve humanity so long as it never forgets that human beings remain the heart of its purpose.

Many years ago Albert Einstein addressed the students of this Institute. "It is not enough," he said, "that you should understand about applied science in order that your work may increase man's blessings." And he added, *"concern for man himself and his fate must always form the chief interest of all technical endeavors, concern for the great unsolved problems of the organization of labor and the distribution of goods*—in order that the creations of our mind shall be a blessing and not a curse to mankind. Never forget this in the midst of your diagrams and equations,"* he went on to say.

And thus I come to talk to you not as scientists, but as citizens— as some of the best-educated, most rational and most creative citizens of our country. Accordingly, you have a larger responsibility to apply the fruits of your education, your reason and your creativity to the future of society, as well as the future of science.

There can be no greater concern for each of us as citizens, than how wisely and how honorably our Nation discharges its responsibilities of preserving peace and promoting freedom. And the first obligation, if we are to preserve an opening to the future, is to make sure that there will be a future at all. For the first time in the long history of man, the obliteration of human life has become a technical possibility.

The leaders of the world face no greater task than that of avoiding nuclear war. While preserving the cause of freedom we must seek abolition of war through programs of general and complete disarmament. The Test-Ban Treaty of 1963 represents a significant beginning in this immense undertaking.

We cannot pretend that such beginnings signal a millenium or an armistice in the cold war. They are modest steps. But they are steps *forward*, steps toward the ultimate goal of effective and reliable international controls over the destructive power of nations. Until such a goal can be achieved, however, we have no other choice than to insure that we can defend our country and help other peoples who are willing to work for their own independence.

With the irony of a paradoxical world, the surest guarantee of peace at present is the power for war. The United States has that power. It comes from our programs of strength and deterrence— programs to which this institute has made such substantial contributions for so many years. Without this strength, we could not have achieved the truly momentous victory of the 1962 Cuban missile crisis. Without this strength we cannot reasonably expect to achieve other objectives, even at the conference table, in our constant pursuit of peace.

This is not really a controversial point. We are agreed that American nuclear superiority is essential to unanimous nuclear restraint. But as we all know so well, the actual fighting since World War II has not involved nuclear weapons or even conventional warfare. It was in 1937 that Mao Tse-Tung wrote: "The guerrilla campaigns being waged in China today are a page in history that has no precedent. Their influence will be confined not solely to China in her present anti-Japanese struggle, but will be world-wide."

That prophecy has proved accurate. We have seen it in Malaya and Greece, the Philippines, and Cuba. We have seen the streets of Caracas become the front line of this era, and Communist guerrillas are fighting today over all of South Vietnam and Laos and at the outskirts of Bukavu in the Congo. The struggle has been broadened today to include violence and terrorist activities that could not even be described as guerrilla warfare. And this really has vastly increased the importance of local police forces and those who preserve an internal defense.

We might well wonder what would have happened in the closing weeks of Venezuela's national election campaign last December if heroic local police had not regained the upper hand there. And the fate of entire nations hung in the balance during those first turbulent months after independence in the Congo and in Panama and in the mines in Bolivia. These experiences point up the absolute necessity of our maintaining balanced strength. I believe they show that while we seek peaceful settlement of disputes, we need far greater strength in the field of unconventional warfare and the control of violence.

We have made a beginning. We have achieved some notable successes, but we have not mastered the art. More importantly, perhaps, in a practical sense, we have not perfected the technique of training foreign nationals to defend themselves against Communist terrorism and guerrilla penetration.

Having an adequate defense against terrorism is only part of the answer, however. To the extent that guerrilla warfare and terrorism arise from the conditions of a desperate people, we know that they cannot be put down by force alone. The people themselves must have some hope for the future. There must be a realistic basis for faith in some alternative to communism.

It is for that reason that the United States must continue to expand its efforts to reach the peoples of other nations—particularly young people in the rapidly developing southern continents. Governments may come and go, but in the long run, the future will be determined by the needs and aspirations of these young people.

Over the years, an understanding of what America really stands for is going to count far more than missiles, aircraft carriers and supersonic bombers. The big changes of the future will result from this understanding—or lack of it.

We have made some progress in reaching the peoples of other countries. The aid and information programs, the Peace Corps, Presidential trips abroad, are all ways of getting beyond mere government-to-government contact. But the critical moves—the moves that will determine our success—are the kinds of political choices this country makes in picking its friends abroad—and its enemies.

Far too often, for narrow tactical reasons, this country has associated itself with tyrannical and unpopular regimes that had no following and no future. Over the past twenty years, we have paid dearly because of support given to colonial rulers, cruel dictators, or ruling cliques void of social purpose. This was one of President Kennedy's gravest concerns. It would be one of his proudest achievements if history records his administration as an era of political friendships made for the United States.

He valued most highly the cooperation established with the India of Nehru, the rallying democratic leaders in Latin America to the Alliance for Progress, the support won from all the New African States for the American position on the Congo.

It is these examples and others like them now being advanced by President Johnson which will go a long way to determine our future. By achieving harmony with broadly based governments concerned with their own peoples, we do more than make our way easier for a year or two. We create for this country the opening to the future that is so essential.

Ultimately, communism must be defeated by progressive political programs which wipe out the poverty, misery, and discontent on which it thrives. For that reason, progressive political programs are the best way to erode the Communist presence in Latin America, to turn back the Communist thrust into Southeast Asia, and to insure the stability of the new African nations and preserve stability in the world.

But however wise our efforts may be in unconventional diplomacy, however sensible our diversity of weapons, and however great our military power, there is another obstacle to enlarging our opening to the future and preserving freedom. That is what some of our own citizens believe the shape of the future to be.

To say that the future will be different from the present is, to scientists, hopelessly self-evident. I observe regretfully that in politics, however, it can be heresy. It can be denounced as radicalism, or branded as subversion. There are people in every time and every land who want to stop history in its tracks. They fear the future, mistrust the present, and invoke the security of a comfortable past which, in fact, never existed. It hardly seems necessary to point out in California—of all States—that change, although it involves risks, is the law of life.

Nevertheless, there are those, frustrated by a difficult future, who grab out for the security of the non-existent past. Frustrated by change, they condemn the wisdom, the motives, and even the patriotism of those who seek to contend with the realities of the future.

The danger of such views is not that they will take control of the American Government. In time, the consensus of good sense which characterizes our political system will digest and discard frozen views and impossible programs. But there is a *short-term* danger from such voices. If they cause enough confusion, stir enough irrational fear, and attract enough political allies, they can restrict and inhibit a President's freedom to take maximum advantage of the openings which the future may present.

The answer to these voices cannot be reason, for they speak irrationally. The answer cannot come merely from government, no matter how conscientious or judicious. The answer must come from within the American democracy. It must come from an informed national consensus which can recognize futile fervor and simple solutions for what they are—and reject them quickly.

And such a consensus must begin with the leaders of society. As people associated with one of the great educational institutions of the world, you are such leaders. While your specialized concern is a world of scientific creativity, you must also contribute to our Nation's political creativity. You have a responsibility to lead and enrich the American consensus. You have a responsibility to fight against the debasements of political discussion and diplomatic alternatives by slanders and slogans.

A century ago, Lincoln observed that the dogmas of the quiet past were inadequate to the stormy present. "As our case is new," he said, "so we must think anew and act anew. We must disenthrall ourselves."

Once again, our case is new—and nothing is more urgent than the obligation to disenthrall ourselves from the dogmas of the quiet past. Let us not suppose that we can freeze the United States—or the world—into the mold of today, or of a generation ago.

President Kennedy, in the speech he was going to deliver in Dallas last November 22, wrote that while dissident voices will always be heard in our country, other kinds of voices are being heard in the land today—"voices preaching doctrines," he would have said, "wholly unrelated to reality, wholly unsuited to the sixties, doctrines which apparently assume that words will suffice without weapons, that vituperation is as good as victory and that peace is a sign of weakness. We cannot expect that everyone, to use the phrase of a decade ago, will talk sense to the American people. But we can hope that fewer people will listen to that kind of nonsense."

President Kennedy felt we deserved better—that as a people and as a country, we had the strength, courage and fortitude to face the future. He believed, as he told Congress in January 1962, that "while no nation has ever faced such a challenge, no nation has ever been so ready to seize the burden and the glory of freedom."

It is that faith which must sustain us as we face these difficult times. It is that faith, enlarged by you and by each succeeding class of this great university, which will enable us to meet our responsibilities, be worthy of our strength, and propel the whole world forward toward a new age of decency, justice, and peace.

IN RETROSPECT: AN APPRAISAL

The office of Attorney General is often referred to as that of the chief Federal law enforcement officer. Simply stated, this is essentially his function. Established by the Judiciary Act of 1789, the office of Attorney General was principally that of presenting the Government's case before the Supreme Court and serving as legal advisor to the president. For many years a position requiring only a fraction of one man's time, the office expanded until recognized by Congress in 1870 as the Department of Justice. Most holders of the position were, in the original language of the Act of 1789, "meet persons learned in the law," and interested primarily in technical legal matters. Some were lawyers of note who were also cronies of the presidents and/or political stalwarts.

In his tenure as Attorney General, Robert Kennedy appears to have extended the concept of the position. In the area of Civil Rights he has been not only the chief Federal officer, he has been the leading spokesman. Moreover, Mr. Kennedy—in over two score public speeches—broadened his scope of interest to include not only areas directly relating to law enforcement, but those affecting matters of welfare, employment, education and foreign affairs. And, finally, it is clear that the Attorney General not only helped to compose proposed legislation, but played a major part in the formulation of the Administration's policy on civil rights.

The fact that his brother was President and preferred that Robert undertake so broad a role enabled the Attorney General to speak and act with far more power than any of his predecessors. So close were the brothers in the eyes of the public that both praise and blame in the area of civil rights were often directed toward "the Kennedys."

Yet this relationship was not so close in the minds of civil rights advocates that one brother was identified absolutely with the other. This was particularly true in the first half of 1963 when there was a clamor for the President, himself, to speak publicly and at length on his own views in this area. With this notable exception, the Attorney General was acknowledged to speak and act with the highest possible authority. In the light of the increasing importance of the issue—until it became this country's most critical domestic problem—Robert Kennedy's apparent power was unprecedented for the office he held and perhaps even for any Administration officer other than the President. Thus, the authority he represented, as he crisscrossed the Nation to give the speeches included in this volume, demanded the attention of those interested in knowing the Administration's posture in the vital area of civil rights.

Perhaps the most obvious observation one can make about these speeches is that they represent a virtual one-man public information program which reached all parts of the country: North, South, East and West. As a result, many thousands of citizens were informed of the nature and extent of the Government's position at the time in the civil rights struggle. When mass media are considered, the number of persons reached by these messages is very impressive.

A careful reading of the texts leads one to another conclusion. The Attorney General's approach to the civil rights problem was neither narrow nor simple. Writing for *Harper's Magazine* in August 1963, Joseph Kraft wisely observed that "shallow, black-and-white portraits" of Robert Kennedy say more about the artist than the subject. It is true that the most important element in Robert Kennedy's concept of the problem was not complex: All men are equal and should be treated as such—the law of the land spelled out this truism in many particulars. But beyond this, he saw the need for a multi-faceted attack on this very complex problem.

The anomaly of the denial of a citizen's basic rights in a democracy, and its adverse affect on international affairs, was given a thorough airing. This was true, too, of the syndrome of social inequities which can now be seen as having been a precursor of the "War on Poverty": unemployment, poverty, substandard housing, and inadequate education. Thus, the most apparent points of contention—denial of the right to vote and discrimination in travel, eating, and overnight accommodations—were treated both directly and, as effects of conditions inimical to the enjoyment of the freedoms and opportunities offered to all citizens by the Constitution, indirectly.

The ultimate objective of such a varied attack was to help the Negro, but also all American citizens suffering the indignities of prejudice and deprivation.

In a larger sense, Robert Kennedy spoke of a future in which man would be assured of his basic rights, liberties and opportunities. Such a world would be brought about by setting the example in this country, but then extending our influence by encouraging the present and future leaders of other nations to make human dignity their principal concern. This topic was developed in his speech of June 8, 1964.

Civil rights advocates did not always demonstrate an appreciation of the efficacy of this broad approach. Often there was an impatience to have the Administration press for specific and explicit civil rights legislation; that is, bills designed to eradicate certain and limited inequities. This was not given first priority by President Kennedy during the early part of his Administration. At that time there was no effective sentiment for such legislation; therefore to have pushed such bills during that early period would have resulted in impeding his legislative program—most of which would be of significant aid to a large segment of the Negro population.

Events seem to have sustained President Kennedy's strategy. Congress did pass bills designed to improve the economy, including those affecting the following matters: redevelopment of areas having chronic unemployment, extension of Social Security benefits, housing, agriculture, increase of the minimum wage, retraining of the unemployed, family rehabilitation, trade expansion, higher education, and personal and corporate tax reductions. In addition, the Internal Revenue Service liberalized tax allowances for the depreciation of industrial plants and equipment, thus freeing additional monies for capital investment.

When the comprehensive Civil Rights Bill was signed on July 2, 1964, by President Lyndon B. Johnson, following a Senate debate of almost three months, the economy was dramatically stronger than in January 1961. All economic indexes had turned upward and most economists agreed that the country was enjoying an unprecedented period of prosperity. Some even dared to use the word "boom" to describe the economy. While Negroes and other minorities shared some of this bounty, their share was decidedly not proportionate to their numbers.

Department of Labor statistics for June 1964 showed that the proportion of the unemployed among the non-white labor force was not only double that of the unemployed of the white labor force but that the non-white employee was unemployed for a longer period, and, when ultimately hired, earned less than his white counterpart. Referring to the "minority group poor" on April 25, 1964, Special Assistant to the Secretary of Labor Arthur A. Chapin said that those involved are the "last hired, first fired, never rehired." He explained: "Automation and technological changes each day remove thousands of skilled and semiskilled jobs from the job market; thus competition is increased among those least able to compete in the labor market for the remaining few jobs."

Therefore, the economic fortunes of the Negroes depend primarily upon a nationwide burgeoning economy. For until that time when education, training, and retraining put the Negro employee on a par with his white fellow citizen, it follows that the greater the total demand for workers, the greater the number of jobs there will be for the Negro to fill.

In the face of such frustrating prospects, the leaders of the various responsible Negro organizations cannot be blamed for the enthusiasm they exhibited in demanding legislative and other reforms. As would be expected, tension often existed between the Negro leaders and Administration officials. In addition, other interested individuals found themselves at loggerheads with spokesmen for the Government's approach.

The contrasting attitudes of James Baldwin and Robert Kennedy during their meeting of May 25, 1963, served to highlight and symbolize the widening gulf between the impatient civil rights advocates and the Administration.

The month of June saw a considerable change, for President Kennedy was then able to give public demonstration of his position. On June 11 Administration representatives, led by U. S. Deputy Attorney General Nicholas deB. Katzenbach, saw to it that Negro students Vivian Malone and James Hood were registered at the University of Alabama in spite of the boasts of Governor George C.

Wallace. And that evening in a national television address, the President spoke emotionally of his regard for the Negro in this "moral crisis." Then, on June 19 he sent a message to Congress in which he requested the most comprehensive package of civil rights laws since Reconstruction days, almost a century earlier.

In spite of these moves, criticism of the President was to continue through the summer and into the fall from extremists on both sides of the civil rights controversy. This personal attack stopped only when the President was assassinated.

Civil rights in the early nineteen sixties was by far this country's most inflammatory domestic issue. Any person taking a stand instantly had ready-made, excitable enemies and proponents. Even the person who refused to indicate a commitment found himself being exhorted one way or the other.

The Negro magazine *Sepia,* in its August 1964 issue, likened civil rights to "an octopus whose tentacles have touched every citizen in America—an octopus who could squeeze the very lifeblood from our democracy."

Robert Kennedy, by pursuing the Government's role in the conflict, was never without opponents—and friends—and sometimes the same persons alternated in their attitude toward him, depending upon his most recent words and deeds. Indeed, the leaders of the various Negro groups—the ostensible beneficiaries of the Attorney General's efforts—presented a study in apparent ambivalence and fickleness as they continued to attack—and applaud—Mr. Kennedy's words and actions. Much of this was responsible criticism, though sometimes exaggerated by zeal. But some was obviously erratic, irresponsible and unconstitutional, such as demands that the Federal Government take over the administration of the State of Mississippi, and that Federal marshals and agents of the Federal Bureau of Investigation take the initiative in police matters in Southern states. Allegations asserting that the Department of Justice was slow to act in crises were often made without knowledge of the facts; for the Justice Department tried to play a preventive role long before a crisis resulted. John Doar, First Assistant in the Civil Rights Division, was normally on the scene very early in such cases.

Among the pro-segregationist critics of the Attorney General, the rabid extremists can be dismissed for their irrelevance and absurdity.

But perhaps the most tragic figures of the civil rights struggle are the Southern leaders who had distinguished themselves in the service of the country but now chose the more traveled road. It is incredible to contemplate the most illustrious of them, U. S. Senator Richard B. Russell of Georgia, who chose not to lead his people toward noble ends, but instead remained a follower of the most backward of his constituents and fellow Senators.

Senator Russell's speech of July 15, 1964, at Berry College, Rome, Georgia, gives singular insight into his pattern of thought on this matter. Addressing the annual meeting of the Coosa Valley Area Planning and Development Commission, the Senator dealt at length —quite naturally—with the economy of the Coosa Valley and of Georgia as a whole. He cited his accomplishments in procuring Federal assistance and aid that resulted in locating "almost a score of major research facilities in Georgia"; securing funds to erect a ten million dollar Agricultural Utilization Laboratory in Athens, Georgia; the continued maintenance of "15 major military establishments in the State that bring about three-quarters of a billion dollars annually to our economy"; attracting defense industries including the Marietta aircraft plant employing 17,500 persons; awarding of two important grants to Georgia Tech from the National Space Agency; developing a U. S. Department of Agriculture project in the Coosa Valley; and planning of a $2.5 million Southeastern Regional Laboratory of the Public Health Service to be established in Athens.

But when, in his closing remarks, Senator Russell spoke disparagingly of the Civil Rights Act of 1964, he stated that "the people of this Nation will turn back the trend toward statism."

In all fairness it should be pointed out that in the conclusion of this address Mr. Russell did urge compliance of the Act "for as long as it is there," and said that he deplored violence.

It was in the context of heated controversy—from the student riots at the University of Georgia to the testing of the Civil Rights Act of 1964—that Robert Kennedy's speeches were composed and delivered.

Such a milieu was an open invitation to the demagogue. But to his credit, the Attorney General never used the devices and techniques of the demagogue. His approach was serious, his tone calm, his manner reasoned, his language moderate.

Typically, his audiences were friendly and enthusiastic. Normally he was met by cheering and applause; autograph seekers blocked his path before and after the speeches. While such an atmosphere might well invite excessess—sarcasm, boasts, threats, invective, exaggerated praising or blaming, name-calling—Robert Kennedy did not yield to temptation, nor is there any indication that the thought ever crossed his mind. To the contrary, not only did his language lack emotionalism but his delivery was generally matter of fact. His voice did not vary greatly in volume or inflection, and his gestures were limited to occasional thrusts of his right hand.

On the dais Robert Kennedy has been no spellbinder. Enthusiastic applause greets him as he is introduced and his initial remarks, usually composed of self-effacing humor, provoke quiet laughter. His references to the immediate occasion, the sponsoring occasion or prominent individuals present are most often good-natured and complimentary. His prepared speech is then read with occasional glances at the audience and neither his text nor delivery is calculated to evoke huzzahs. Rather, they encourage a polite and thoughtful listening to this tuxedoed and earnest young man with a message. With the end of the talks, which usually last from fifteen to twenty minutes, there comes more spirited applause.

The speeches—with few exceptions—could be described as "quite good, but unexceptional" if delivered by any other person of equal governmental rank. Plainly, the unique quality of a Robert Kennedy speech is in the person of the speaker and what he symbolizes as a "Kennedy." The excitement attendant upon his arrival and departure is stimulated by few in our society, making his appearance a guarantee of success for the occasion and a dramatic event. That he is no orator in this age of the conversational style appears to disappoint few in his audience. Still, his inability or reluctance to inspire or excite his listeners by his speaking has been evident. Even when his address has been written in a particularly interesting style, Robert Kennedy has not indulged himself in his delivery; rather, there has been a reticence suggesting obligation rather than zeal, a task to be performed rather than an opportunity to be exploited.

Alistair Cooke recently likened a prepared speech with a kind of "Sunday-go-to-meeting-suit." And the question naturally arises as to how Robert Kennedy's demeanor at such functions as those referred to in this book compares with his manner in other situations. While the scope of this work is necessarily limited, the writer feels impelled to observe that during the more than three years covered, there were no significant differences in the behavior of the man as a public figure. The characteristics noted in his speeches were the same whether he served as a congressional witness, gave countless interviews to the press, or performed other functions of his position. Except for occasional spirited remarks in repartee, his manner varied only slightly.

The writer is inclined to agree with Allan Nevins (*The Strategy of Peace*, Harper & Brothers, 1960) that "speaking for good old Buncombe County in Congress" is no longer good enough. Mass media, especially television, make speaking one way and acting another a very difficult—and hazardous—deception for the public figure.

All of the speeches in this collection have apparent goals. Understanding seems to have been an objective of some; thus the liberal use of examples, statistics, names, dates, places. And often the understanding hoped for was designed to be a step toward action. In a great many instances the Attorney General was quite outspoken about what he wanted the members of his audiences to do. Frequently this involved personal participation in the process of desegregation. Sometimes—as before audiences composed of lawyers —his listeners were urged none too subtly to insure the right of indigents to adequate counsel, or to take steps to remove inequities in the bail bond system, or to take a more active role in social and political matters.

It was this determined and persistent insistence on candor which gave a particular significance to the content of the speeches taken as a whole. Risking antagonism where innocuous addresses would have sufficed, the Attorney General discussed problems forthrightly before the audiences most involved: problems of the South were discussed before southerners; legal problems before lawyers; public accommodation problems before theater owners; Negro responsibility before Negroes; discrimination in labor unions before labor leaders; fair and balanced coverage of current happenings before newspaper editors and publishers. Perhaps it is superfluous to mention that this trait is not exactly typical of American politicians and bureaucrats.

In order to try to reach the essence of the problems it was often necessary to touch sensitive areas. Mr. Kennedy, therefore, found himself grappling with age-old obstacles to progress—apathy, avarice, bigotry, ignorance, myopia, pride—in pursuit of the freedom of man. In toto, the speeches represent an affirmation of the sanctity of the individual, unfettered by man-made limitations which inhibit rather than aid his proper fulfillment as a person. As this thesis was applied to our most critical domestic issue, and to our foreign policy as well, Robert Kennedy emerges as a man very much of his times possessed of the acuity to discern the problems and to determine upon courses of action calculated to ameliorate them.

Six of the speeches differ sufficiently from the others to attract special notice. The most significant historically, as well as the most effectively organized and worded address was that given in Athens, Georgia, on the 6th of May 1961. The most excessive style is that used in the speech given before the meeting of the Fund for the Republic on January 22, 1963. The language of the text, while dealing with material of worth, appears contrary to the personality of the speaker, as well as to the sophistication of the audience, in its amateurish over-dramatization and not quite successful attempts at the light touch. The Trinity College speech of June 2, 1963, was written in a very attractive style by the late James M. McInerney, a close friend of the Attorney General.* The Attorney General and his administrative assistant, John Nolan, joined efforts to compose the most poignant of the addresses, that of St. Patrick's Day, 1964. And, finally, the speech showing the greatest breadth and promise was given June 8, 1964, and called for an "opening to the future."

One does not read many of Robert Kennedy's addresses before observing that he has a penchant for the apt quotation. And it is through this device that he most obviously attempts to adapt to different audiences. The Henry Grady quotation at the conclusion of the Athens speech of May 6, 1961, is a case in point. Legal audiences will hear quotations from Supreme Court Justices, usually Chief

---

* Mr. McInerney, who had a private law practice at the time and who had been an Assistant U. S. Attorney General during President Harry S. Truman's Administration, was killed in an automobile accident on October 8, 1963.

Justices; Jewish groups will be treated to Brandeis; all may on occasion hear the words of the apparent sources of many of his ideas—Jefferson, Lincoln, de Toqueville, Theodore Roosevelt, Wilson, John F. Kennedy. It is revealing to observe how very frequently Robert Kennedy referred to his brother, the President, for inspiration and authority.

A final note might be added; one more significant with respect to content than style. In roughly the first half of these addresses, the Attorney General voiced unbridled and almost pollyannaish optimism. After the late summer of 1962 this was toned down considerably; yet even after that, one notes that the youthful Attorney General still exudes a consistent self-confidence. He does not say "We shall prevail"; the audience is simply left to draw that inference.

Opinions as to Robert Kennedy's effectiveness in his role as a leader in the civil rights issue could not be more varied. Hodding Carter, liberal Mississippi journalist, believes him to be "a conscientious, courageous, and eminently able public servant"; but, not unexpectedly, Governor George C. Wallace of Alabama unequivocally states: "Mr. Kennedy is not qualified to be Attorney General of the United States and I have absolutely no fear that history will sustain my position."

Senator Kenneth B. Keating, Republican of New York, wrote in a letter to the writer October 3, 1963, that "the Department of Justice waited much longer than was justified in backing meaningful civil rights legislation." Conversely his colleague, Senator Strom Thurmond, Democrat of South Carolina, believes that Robert Kennedy "pushed too hard and too fast on the so-called 'civil rights' front."

Ironically, the Negro leaders who were asked during the early Fall of 1963 for comments on Robert Kennedy's stewardship of the Department of Justice in connection with the civil rights issue—the Rev. Martin Luther King, Jr., James Farmer, James Baldwin, Whitney Young, Roy Wilkins—did not comply.

Of those whose analyses encompassed the complexity of the issues involved, the comment of Harry Ashmore, former editor of the *Little Rock Gazette* and now chairman of the Board of Editors of the *Encyclopaedia Britannica*, merits close attention. On September 23, 1963, he concluded a letter to me with the following observation: "On balance I would say his record is good—by far the best of any responsible Federal official, outside the Supreme Court, since the troubles began."

History will have to assess the influence of Attorney General Robert F. Kennedy on the civil rights struggle. Plainly we are too close to make lasting judgments. But time will not change one critical fact. The forces on behalf of equality for the Negro could plan their moves after the Athens speech of May 6, 1961, in the knowledge that the power of the United States Government would be sympathetic to their legal attempts to redress their grievances. And they knew full well that the chief of the U. S. Department of Justice—with the complete confidence of the President of the United States, first John F. Kennedy and then Lyndon B. Johnson—was an uncompromising advocate of the civil rights the Negro is entitled to as a citizen of this country. Robert Kennedy's words and deeds made that clear. Seen in that light, the Freedom Rides, the Meredith case, the sit-ins, the picketing, the Wallace confrontation, the March on Washington were all in a sense operating under the protection of the Government of the United States. The magnitude of this fact can never really be known. But when the dignity and well-being of almost eighteen million people are immediately affected—and indirectly another hundred and seventy million—the total effect is of epic proportions.